THE SOURCES
OF
KEYBOARD MUSIC IN
ENGLAND.

THE SOURCES

OF

KEYBOARD MUSIC IN

ENGLAND

BY

CHARLES VAN DEN BORREN
Professor at the Université Nouvelle of Brussels.

TRANSLATED FROM THE FRENCH BY
JAMES E. MATTHEW

GREENWOOD PRESS, PUBLISHERS
WESTPORT, CONNECTICUT

Originally published in 1914
by Novello and Company, Ltd., London
and The H.W. Gray Co., New York

Reprinted from an original copy in the collections
of the Brooklyn Public Library

First Greenwood Reprinting 1970

Library of Congress Catalogue Card Number 78-106714

SBN 8371-3444-7

Printed in the United States of America

PREFACE.

———

DURING the years 1910-11 and 1911-12 the writer delivered at the Université Nouvelle of Brussels a course of lectures on the sources of Keyboard Music in England. It has occurred to him that this material formed the foundation for the production of a book containing the substance of these lectures.

Keyboard music owes much to England. At the time when in the other countries of Europe it still dragged in the wake of vocal and organ music, in the British Isles it acquired an individuality and a technique of its own which place it on a very high level as a factor in evolution. Moreover, there has come down to us from the period of these sources—which extend from about 1550 to 1630—a considerable quantity of material, the æsthetic value of which cannot be gainsaid.

The principal collection from which a fairly complete idea of this music can be formed, the *Fitzwilliam Virginal Book,* has now been made accessible by the edition in modern notation produced in 1899 by Messrs. Fuller Maitland and

Barclay Squire. The greater part of the following study is based on the analysis of this precious document. There are some others[1] which circumstances have allowed the author to become acquainted with in a manner only partial or at second hand. For this reason the work now given to the public has no pretentions to be definitive. Its only merit is to offer for the first time a general view of the subject, together with a thorough analysis of its various aspects. The writer has endeavoured above all things to be clear and systematic, and to co-ordinate the subject at all times with the general lines of the history of music in Europe. Never losing sight of the claims of erudition, it has been his object not to neglect the attractions either of general inferences or of purely æsthetic considerations : of set purpose he has avoided the examination of certain questions of a too technical nature and of insufficient actual importance, such as notation, fingering, and the collation of the different manuscripts of keyboard music. In this manner he hopes that he has succeeded in performing a duty which by its character of general interest answers at once to the demands of modern musicology, and to the wishes of artists and enlightened amateurs to penetrate the secrets of a subject of exceptional interest.

Published originally in French in 1912, the present work has been translated into English on

[1] They are set forth in chap. i.

the initiative of Messrs. Novello & Co., Ltd. The author has availed himself of this opportunity to make certain improvements, and to add to its completeness by means of new material which he has since been able to collect.[2]

CH. VAN DEN BORREN.

UCCLE-BRUSSELS,
October, 1913.

---

[2] The principal works in which the sources of Keyboard Music in England are treated of are the following :—

Hawkins (*A General History of the Science and Practice of Music*, 1776), vol. iii., pp. 287, 288.
> [A modern edition of this work has been published by Novello & Co., Ltd.]

Burney (*A General History of Music*, 1776-89), vol. iii., chap. i.

Ambros (*Geschichte der Musik*, 2nd edition), vol. iii., pp. 468, 470 ff.

W. Nagel (*Geschichte der Musik in England*, 2 vols., Trübner, Strassburg, 1894-97), vol. i., chap. vii., pp. 120, 121 ; vol. ii., chap. iv., pp. 76 ff, and chap. vii., pp. 149 ff.

Oscar Bie (*Das Klavier und seine Meister*, Bruckmann, Munich, 1898), chap. i.
> [There is an English translation of this work, *A History of the Pianoforte and Pianoforte-Players*, by E. E. Kellett and Dr. Naylor, London, 1899.]

Seiffert (*Geschichte der Klaviermusik*, Breitkopf & Härtel, Leipzig, 1899), Book I., chap. v.

J. A. Fuller Maitland and W. Barclay Squire (Introduction to the modern edition of the *Fitzwilliam Virginal Book*, Breitkopf & Härtel, Leipzig, 1899).

Sir C. H. H. Parry (*Oxford History of Music*, Clarendon Press, Oxford, 1902), vol. iii., pp. 83-98.

E. W. Naylor, Mus.D. (*An Elizabethan Virginal Book*, Dent, London, 1905). This work is entirely confined to a critical analysis of the *Fitzw. V. B.*

E. Walker, Mus.D. (*A History of Music in England*. Clarendon Press, Oxford, 1907), pp. 66-68, 105 ff.

H. Riemann (*Handbuch der Musikgeschichte*, Breitkopf & Härtel, Leipzig, 1912), vol. ii., part i., chap. xxiii., § 82.

W. Niemann (*Das Klavierbuch*, Kahnt Nachfolger, Leipzig, 3rd edition, 1913), p. 6 ff.

TABLE OF CONTENTS.

TABLE OF CONTENTS

INTRODUCTION.

I.—THE INSTRUMENT.

ACCORDING to the most recent hypotheses, there is a strong probability that the most ancient type of stringed instrument provided with a keyboard —the clavichord—had England for its cradle. Carl Krebs dates its approximate origin as far back as the beginning of the 13th century,[1] while, in a more recent work, Goehlinger suggests the first half of the 12th century.[2]

In whatever way this obscure point is settled, we have very vague information as to the development which stringed instruments provided with a keyboard underwent in England from their remote origin until the beginning of the 16th century,

[1] *Die besaiteten Klavierinstrumente bis zum Anfang des 17. Jahrhunderts*, by Carl Krebs ; *Vierteljahrschrift für Musikwissenschaft*, 1892, Heft I. See pp. 94-96.

[2] *Geschichte des Klavichords*, by Fr. A. Goehlinger (E. Birkhäuser, Bâle, 1910). According to the author, the *monacorde* spoken of in the *Roman de Brut*, written by Wace in 1157, was nothing but a primitive clavichord. The *Roman de Brut* is in "langue d'oïl," but Wace was an Anglo-Norman troubadour attached to the Court of King Henry II. of England (1154-89) and the work recounts "the annals, real or imaginary, of the British Isle"—a further presumption in favour of the probability of the English origin of the clavichord.

whether belonging to the type of "clavichord," in which the strings were struck, or to that of "clavecin," in which the strings were plucked.

From the beginning of the 16th century we see spreading in England with great rapidity the habit of playing on an instrument bearing the name of Virginal,[3] which is none other than an instrument with strings and a keyboard. This fashion continued to spread until the end of the 16th century, and attained to an extraordinary efflorescence during the first thirty years of the 17th century.

Numerous are the evidences which prove in what favour the virginal was held in the 16th and 17th centuries.

Mme. Farrenc (1804-75) relates in the *Préliminaires* (p. 3) prefacing her great collection, *Le Trésor des Pianistes* (1861-72) that Elizabeth of York, wife of King Henry VII. (1485-1509), played on the virginal, and that on the occasion of an entertainment given in 1502 at Westminster Hall, twelve young girls showed their skill as performers on the clavichord, the clavecin, &c.

Willibald Nagel[4] and Otto Kinkeldey[5] also give us interesting references, from which we learn to what an extent music was esteemed at the Court of England at the beginning of the 16th century, and in what honour the virginal was held. Thanks to the letters of the Venetian Ambassador to London, Giustiniani, and of the Secretary of

[3] It seems fairly well established that the virginal took its name from the fact that it was the favourite instrument of young girls.

[4] *Annalen der englischen Hofmusik von der Zeit Heinrichs VIII. bis zum Tode Karls I.*, by Will. Nagel (Breitkopf & Härtel, Leipzig, 1894. See pp. 3 and 4).

[5] *Orgel und Klavier in der Musik des 16. Jahrhunderts*, by O. Kinkeldey (Breitkopf & Härtel, 1910, p. 149).

the Embassy, Sagudino, who was himself an organist and player on the virginal; thanks also to another Italian settled in England, Sanuto, we can form a pretty accurate opinion of the musical atmosphere which then reigned in England. Sanuto tells us, among other things, in his *diarii* of 1506, that at the time of Henry VII. the ladies of the Tudor family delighted in playing the virginal. One of these ladies was Catherine of Aragon, who became afterwards the first wife of King Henry VIII. (1509-47.)

We know that this monarch himself delighted in playing the virginal[6]. He had in his service a professional virginal player, John Heywood, whose name appears for the first time in 1520 in the Royal Accounts,[7] and who still remained attached to the English Court under the successors of Henry VIII.—Edward VI. (1547-53), and Mary Tudor (1553-58).

Mary Tudor and Queen Elizabeth (1558-1603) both played the virginal, and had in their service several skilled performers, as did James I., who succeeded Elizabeth and reigned from 1603 to 1625.[8]

We have ample information as to the part played by the virginal at the English Court from the

---

[6] See Grove, *Dictionary of Music and Musicians* (art. *Virginal*). Moreover, Henry VIII. possessed an important collection of musical instruments, among which were a great number of virginals (Nagel, *Annalen*, p. 6).

[7] See Nagel, *Annalen*, p. 15 ff. The same author mentions in his *Geschichte der Musik in England* (vol. ii., pp. 77, 78, Trübner, Strasburg, 1894-97), a manuscript (Add. MS. 4900, British Museum) containing among a considerable series of arrangements of secular and religious songs for single voice, with accompaniment for the luth, a song of no great merit by Heywood, *What harte can think.*

[8] See Grove, *Dictionary* (art. *Virginal*).

4   INTRODUCTION

Royal Accounts, from which important fragments have been published during the last few years.[9]

In conclusion, Shakespeare himself, who lived during the most brilliant period of the flourishing of the repertory of keyboard music in England, alludes to the virginal in his works. Dr. Naylor has published in the *Musical Antiquary* of April, 1910, an article on "Music and Shakespeare,"[10] in which he proves that there are to be found in the works of the great dramatist about five hundred passages referring to music or to matters having reference to music. Among others, he analyses the Sonnet cxxviii., where Shakespeare speaks of the virginal, from which it appears that the poet had a perfect acquaintance with the interior mechanism of the instrument.[11]

[9] See Nagel, *Annalen*, pp. 16, 17, 19, 23, 24, 32, 33, 38, 43. See also *The King's Musick*, by the Rev. Henry Cart de Lafontaine (Novello & Co., London, 1909), p. 11 ff. and *The King's Musicians from the Audit Office Declared Accounts*, in the *Musical Antiquary*, October 1911 ff; again in the same periodical, January, 1910, pp. 125 and 126, a special account relating to the reign of Elizabeth ; also in April, 1913, p. 178 ff., accounts relating to the reign of Henry VIII. The items of these accounts refer either to salaries paid to players on the virginal (there were three of them from the year 1552 ; see Nagel, *Annalen*, p. 23), or else to the prices paid by the Sovereign for the purchase of virginals ; for instance, Henry VIII. bought five virginals from William Lewes in 1530 and 1531. See Nagel, *Annalen*, pp. 17, 18.

[10] Dr. Naylor has also published a book on *Shakespeare and Music* (Dent & Co., London, 1896).

[11] Shakespeare. Sonnet cxxviii. :—

> How oft, when thou, my music, music play'st
> Upon that blessed wood whose motion sounds
> With thy sweet fingers, when thou gently sway'st
> The wiry concord that mine ear confounds,
> Do I envy those jacks, that nimble leap
> To kiss the tender inward of thy hand,
> Whilst my poor lips, which should that harvest reap,
> At the wood's boldness by thee blushing stand !
> To be so tickled, they would change their state
> And situation with those dancing chips,
> O'er whom thy fingers walk with gentle gait,
> Making dead wood more bless'd than living lips.
> Since saucy jacks so happy are in this,
> Give them thy fingers, me thy lips to kiss.

But the virginal did not remain confined to aristocratic circles only. It rapidly became a popular instrument. Chappell[12] relates that in the 16th and 17th centuries there were generally to be found sundry instruments of music, among which was a virginal, in the shops of the barbers, and that the latter passed their time in playing on these instruments while waiting for their clients. Towards the middle of the 17th century the virginal had spread with such profusion that at the time of the Great Fire of London, in 1666, there were to be seen a pair of virginals in at least one out of three of the small craft with which the Thames was crowded, loaded with articles of furniture saved from the fire.[13]

What precisely was the virginal? The first description which has been given us dates from the year 1511, and is to be found in the *Musica getutscht* of Virdung.[14] According to the woodcuts which this author has left us, the virginal and the clavichord present very nearly the same external appearance —that of a small rectangular chest without feet; but the mechanism of the virginal depends on the plucking of the strings by means of the quill part of the feather of the crow, whilst that of the clavichord consists of the striking of the strings by a tongue of brass.[15]

[12] *Popular music of the olden time* (Cremer, Beale & Chappell, London, 1855-57, pp. 101 and 104).
[13] *Popular music of the olden time*, p. 486. [See Pepys's *Diary*, September 2, 1666.]
[14] See Grove, *Dictionary* (artt. *Virdung* and *Virginal*).
[15] At the beginning of the 16th century we still find the word "clavichord" in use under the form "cleyvecordes," or "clavycordes," to describe certain instruments belonging to the King of England (see extracts from the accounts of the private expenses of Henry VII. (years 1502 and 1504), in Chappell, *Popular Music*, p. 49). An inventory of goods belonging to Henry VIII. (Harl. 1419, f₀. 202) mentions *two pairs of clavicordes* (see *A Catalogue of the Manuscript Music in the British Museum*, by A. Hughes-Hughes, vol. iii., London, 1909, p. 359).

B

According to Messrs. Fuller Maitland and Barclay Squire[16] the virginal in use at the end of the 16th and beginning of the 17th centuries was an instrument with plucked strings resembling the harpsichord. The vibrations produced by plucking the strings lasted almost as long as those obtainable on the pianoforte. But an absolute *legato* could not be produced; on the other hand, rapid figuration produced a remarkable effect of brilliancy and fulness, as did the rapid repetition of the same note.

We will not consider here the compass of the keyboard; for the investigation of this question we refer the reader to the special note to be found at the end of the volume. We equally avoid at present any question of " temperament "; we shall have in fact the opportunity of returning to this subject further on in all its practical bearings, in the analysis of the compositions belonging to the repertory of virginal music.

To sum up, the term "virginal " served in England to designate all the varieties of keyboard instruments with plucked strings from the end of the 15th to the end of the 17th century. With the beginning of the 18th century its meaning became gradually narrowed, and soon was only applied to little instruments of rectangular shape, as opposed to instruments *à queue*—*i.e.*, that of the modern grand pianoforte—which received the name of harpsichord. From that time the terms " spinet " and " virginal " became entirely synonymous.[17]

---

[16] See the introduction to their edition of the *Fitzwilliam Virginal Book* (Breitkopf & Härtel, Leipzig, 1899).

[17] See on this point Krebs, *Die besaiteten Klavierinstrumente*, p. 114.

II.—KEYBOARD MUSIC IN ENGLAND FROM THE 14TH CENTURY TO THE MIDDLE OF THE 16TH CENTURY.

We may assume that the actual history of keyboard music in England can scarcely be said to begin earlier than the second half of the 16th century. For the latter period we possess, in fact, a considerable number of available documents, which together are of sufficient importance to enable us to form certain general deductions. On the other hand, for the period which precedes it, the only information we possess is too fragmentary to enable us to arrive at anything but conjectural conclusions. The object of the present chapter is to put on record the results of these researches so far as they bear upon those distant sources, and to endeavour as far as possible to systematize from them the slender materials which these investigations have brought to light.

Johannes Wolf records the existence of English organ music dating from the first half of the 14th century. Although designed for an instrument differing from the clavier, we will nevertheless speak of it here, since at that epoch the repertory of the organ and that of the clavier were completely indistinguishable, and because, moreover, the organ compositions in question show details of figuration specially instrumental in character, in which it is possible to trace in the germ certain of those phases which distinguish the virginal music of the most flourishing period.

Wolf has brought forward the result of his researches in his *Beiträge zur Geschichte der Musik des 14. Jahrhunderts*, which appeared in the *Kirchenmusikalisches Jahrbüch* of 1899, and in a chapter of his *Geschichte der Mensural-Notation von 1250-1460.*[1]

The compositions to which he has drawn attention are to be found in a manuscript in the British Museum (Add. MS. 28550), and are reproduced in facsimile in vol. i. of *Early English Harmony from the 10th to the 15th century*, by Mr. H. E. Wooldridge (London, 1897).

These compositions are six in number, the first and the last being unfortunately incomplete. They are written in two parts; nevertheless, in certain places, such as cadences and ritornelles, they admit three parts. Their compass extends from—

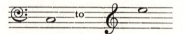

Certain chromatic notes, F sharp, C sharp, G sharp, B flat, and E flat occur. The first three pieces are purely instrumental; the last three consist of vocal compositions in tablature, and provided with *colorature*. The purely instrumental pieces have the character of preludes. They consist of a succession of chords, the upper part of which is figured. There is no actual melodic development, but it is possible to distinguish certain attempts at rhythm. The figuration, which Wolf terms "variation," is accomplished in two ways—in the first place, by means of little figures

[1] Part I., p. 357 ff. (Breitkopf & Härtel, 1904).

obtained by the use of adjoining notes; for example :—

is figured in the following manner :—

Secondly, the spreading of intervals or of chords; for example :—

The consonances which we meet most frequently in these preludes are octaves, fifths, and sixths, which is moreover in conformity with the musical custom of the period. Parallel octaves and fifths are very numerous ; the third prelude consists almost entirely of a succession of fifths. Among dissonances we meet in many places with augmented fourths and fifths ; for example :—

We notice also among the unusual harmonic elements the unprepared entry of the ninth on the accented note, this dissonance resolving itself on the octave :—

As to chords of three notes, they most frequently leave out the third, consisting only of the tonic, octave and fifth.   Example :—

From the point of view of formal structure, each of these compositions consists of a series of four or five episodes characterized as *puncti*, which sometimes are more or less joined together by ritornelles (*returns*), at others have no connection whatever. Each *punctus*[2] splits into periods of three or four measures which only exceptionally have any appearance of symmetry. And moreover the general plan of the pieces in no respect makes for symmetry.

In performance these pieces produce the impression of a very primitive instrumental art, but exhibiting certain tentative efforts which carried further would be capable of producing in course of time less barbarous results, especially on the ground of figuration and variation.

The last three pieces of the manuscript examined by Wolf are transcriptions in tablature of vocal compositions, or motets. Two of the motets contained in the English manuscript are borrowed from the celebrated French collection of the early part of the 14th century, *Le Roman de Fauvel* (National Library of Paris, fonds français, No. 146).

There is to be noticed in these transcriptions, as well as in the preludes, an anxiety to break up the long notes by giving colour to them by means

---

[2] For the meaning of the word "punctus," see Joh. Wolf, *Geschichte der Mensuralnotation*, vol. i., p. 363, and Pierre Aubry, *Estampies et danses royales* (*Mercure Musical* of September 15, 1906).

We find survivals of the term in the German and English instrumental pieces of the 15th and 16th centuries. Thus the expression *Fundamentalis punctus* occurs in the *Buxheimer Orgelbuch* (MS. 3725 of the Royal Library at Munich), reproduced in modern notation by Eitner in the *Beilagen zu den Monatsheften für Musikgeschichte* to signify a short piece (exercise) by Conrad Paumann (about 1450). *Thomas Mulliner's Book* (MS. 30513 of the British Museum), dating from the middle of the 16th century, contains four pieces (one by Tallis, one by Shephard, and two by anonymous musicians) entitled, *A poynte, A pointe, A poyncte*. One of these, that by Shephard, is reproduced in Hawkins (*General History*, &c., vol. ii., p. 932). It is a short prelude or exercise in four parts, in an imitative style, with a theme subjected to four entries in *stretti*, with accompaniment in free counterpoint.

of adjacent notes, and thus to obtain a clearer rhythm. For example—

becomes—

In places where the vocal original consists of a single voice, the tablature pretty often adds a second part, which is arranged as skilfully as possible to agree with the re-entry of the second voice in the original.

At two places in the first motet (*Adesto*) the copier has left out several bars of the original, doubtless in order to avoid passages unsuited for instrumental effects; he also manages here and there to make changes in his model, with a view to obtaining better consonances. The second motet (*Tribum*) transposes the original a tone higher than that appropriated to it in *Le Roman de Fauvel*. For this no reason is apparent. Wolf observes that this is the most ancient example known of the transposition of a polyphonic composition. The third motet (*Flos vernalis*) is incomplete : in the fragment which remains is to be found an example of the use of a seventh without preparation.[3]

Unfortunately we are as badly provided as possible with the means of investigating the transition stages between this primitive music of the 14th century and the virginal music of the second half of the 16th. At the time when Wolf analysed the compositions in the Add. MS. 28550—that is, fifteen years ago—a gaping void existed in the domain of English keyboard music between these distant productions and the most ancient piece of virginal music the date of which was known—the first plainsong, *Felix namque* of Tallis (1562), which is to be found in the *Fitzwilliam Virginal Book.* The existence of this gap was the more to be regretted inasmuch as the instrumental technique of this " figured " plainsong seems to be very advanced for the period, and to be free from any Continental influence; from which one might come to the conclusion that it is in England itself that we must seek for the origin of this technique.

At the present time the position is somewhat improved, and we begin to get a glimpse of the possibility of reconstructing some of the links in the development which took place in the music of the organ and the clavier from the 14th century up

[3] If the hypothesis of Kinkeldey (*op. cit.*, p. 100 ff.) is admitted, according to which the compositions of the 14th century contained in the celebrated *Codex Squarcialupi* were organ pieces, we must come to the conclusion that there existed in Italy an important repertory for the organ at the identical period in which the pieces in Add. MS. 28550 appeared in England. But up to the present time the truth of this hypothesis has not been acknowledged. See on this head *Das kolorierte Orgelmadrigal des Trecento*, by A. Schering, in the quarterly *Sammelbände* of the International Musical Society, XIII., i., p. 172, and more especially the arguments to the contrary of Johannes Wolf, in an article by Springer, which appeared in the monthly *Zeitschrift* of the same Society, XIII., viii., p. 265, *Der Anteil der Instrumentalmusik an der Literatur des 14-16. Jahrhunderts.*

to the middle of the 16th. Nevertheless the investigations which have been made in this direction have carried us no further than to clear up the condition of things which existed during the first half of the 16th century. The gap still remains for the whole of the period comprised between the commencement of the 14th century and the dawn of the 16th—that is to say, for nearly two centuries. No available document belonging to that period has been discovered up to the present time, so that it is impossible for us to form an opinion as to what may have been the state of music for the organ and clavier in England during the course of these two centuries.

This absence of evidence is not due to the fact that England may have experienced at that period some sort of eclipse or decline from a musical point of view. On the contrary, the period in question is, for the British Isles, one of the most brilliant in their musical history. We know the prominent part played by the English in the 15th century in the formation of polyphonic art in Western Europe, and the work of Dunstable (died in 1453) proves to how great a degree this participation was active and fruitful. On this period we are moreover well provided with evidence by a whole series of works, vocal or vocal-instrumental, which has been preserved to us, the mysteries of which modern musicology enables us little by little to penetrate by means of recent reprints and learned commentaries.[4]

[4] See particularly the seventh year of the *Denkmäler der Tonkunst in Oesterreich*, in which are published in modern notation compositions of Dunstable, taken from the codices at Trent (Artaria, Vienna). See also Riemann, *Handbuch der Musikgeschichte*, II., 1st part, chap. xviii. and xix. (Breitkopf & Härtel, 1907).

Apart from this, music was loved and protected by the royalty of that time, quite as much as it was later on by the Sovereigns of the 16th century. Henry VI., who reigned from 1429 to 1460, was himself an excellent musician, versed in the art of polyphonic writing, if one may judge from those of his compositions which have come down to us.[5]

Finally, there is one point worthy of notice : it is that a large number of the English polyphonists of the end of the 15th century were organists.[6] This is a fact peculiar to England, the parallel to which it would be difficult to find on the Continent. It shows that the organ was an instrument in common use, and widely cultivated by preference in Britain during the second half of the 15th century.[7] We may fairly suppose that this was a real tradition, the rise of which it would not be rash to date as far back as the beginning of the 14th century, that is to say, at the period in which were composed the works forming part of Add. MS. 28550. Besides, even well before the extreme end of the 15th century, we find in England organists of reputation, such as Henry Abyndon, born about 1418 and died in 1497, who as early as 1452[8] was renowned both as a singer and an organist, and

---

[5] See Grattan Flood, *The English Chapel under Henry V. and Henry VI.* (Quarterly *Sammelbände* of the International Musical Society, X., iv., p. 563).

[6] See Riemann, *Handb. der Musikg.* II., i., p. 296.

[7] We may remark that the same conditions continued during the whole of the 16th century. Riemann, *Handb. der Musikg.*, pp. 296 and 338.

[8] That is to say, in the very period when Conrad Paumann wrote his *Fundamentum organisandi* (1452), in which numerous examples of the organistic art of the 15th century in Germany have been preserved.

characterized in one of his two epitaphs as *optimus orgaquenista*.[9]

If we think over this state of things, it will not be surprising that the first half of the 16th century presents us with examples of organ music which exhibit a comparatively advanced acquaintance with the resources of the instrument. We can easily convince ourselves of this by the examination of certain pieces in the manuscript *Thomas Mulliner's Book*, which have been rendered accessible in modern editions. This collection, which is to be found in the British Museum, under No. 30313, takes its name from the fact that it originally belonged to Thomas Mulliner, Master of the Choristers at St. Paul's Cathedral, London, towards the middle of the 16th century. It is supposed that a part of the manuscript was written by Mulliner's own hand. Its precise date cannot be established, but it is scarcely rash to suggest that its compilation may be dated approximately about 1550.[10] Mr. Hughes-Hughes gives in vol. iii., p. 77, of his *Catalogue of the Manuscript Music in the*

[9] See a short study by Dr. Grattan Flood on Abyndon in the *Musical Times* of June 1, 1911, p. 377, and the *Entries relating to music in the English Patent Rolls of the 15th century*, published by the same author in the *Musical Antiquary* of July, 1913 (p. 225 ff.), in which we find the name of Abyndon mentioned on several occasions between 1446 and 1484. Further, we find in the *Patent Rolls* the names of two other English organists of the 15th century, John Ferlegh or Ferley (in 1427) and John Bank (in 1445).

[10] In support of this claim we may bring forward the fact that Mulliner, of the details of whose life very little is known, seems to have disappeared at about this time from the musical horizon in England (see on this point *Master Sebastian of Paul's*, by Dr. Grattan Flood, in the *Musical Antiquary*, April, 1912, p. 140). On the other hand, there is no reason to believe that any one of the compositions collected in *Mulliner's Book* is later in date than 1550-60). Sir Hubert Parry (*Oxford History of Music*, vol. iii., p. 83 (Clarendon Press, Oxford, 1902)), thinks that *Mulliner's Book* dates from at least as early as 1565. Mr. Hughes-Hughes puts it still further back, and dates it from the end of the reign of Henry VIII. (1509-47).

British Museum, a detailed list of the pieces contained in *Mulliner's Book*, to the number of 117.[11]

[11] The 117 pieces in *Mulliner's Book* are divided between the following authors: John Redford (22 pieces), Thomas Tallis (18), William Blitheman (14), John Shephard (5), Richard Alwood (5), Robert Johnson, sen. (3), F. (or J.) T. (3), Richard Farrant (2), Newman (2), William Shelbye (2), Richard Edwards (2), Nicholas Carleton (1), John Taverner (1), Tye (1), Munday (1), Heathe (1), and 34 anonymous.

The majority of these pieces consist of sacred vocal compositions, arranged for the organ under the form of figured plainsong. A small minority is composed of secular vocal pieces, also arranged for a keyboard instrument. Can we, or should we, attribute a part of these arrangements to Mulliner himself?

Among the pieces bearing a title denoting a particular *genre* we must first of all mention the *Meanes*, and *Plainsongs with a meane*. They are of the number of twelve, and have for authors Redford (11) and Blitheman (1). Then follow *Poyntes* (to the number of 4), *Voluntaryes* (2 in all), and the *In nomine* (4 in all).

A fansye and *A pavyon* (pavane) of Newman represent the share of secular music not of vocal origin. Lastly, the MS. contains a pretty large number of pieces without title.

The antiquity of *Mulliner's Book* being acknowledged, the detailed study of it becomes of the greatest importance for a knowledge of keyboard music in England during the first half of the 16th century. Up to the present time we have only very cursory details of its contents. According to Nagel (*Gesch. der Mus. in England*, vol. ii., pp. 84, 85, and 152), the compositions in *Mulliner's Book* have a more or less general relationship with the *ricercare;* but we find in them, nevertheless, certain peculiarities—passages in thirds divided between the two hands, complicated rhythmical combinations, &c.—which give them, taken together, a transitional character between the ancient style and the new style peculiar to the virginalists. Dr. Walker (*A History of Music in England*, p. 50 ff.) gives us some information as to the contents of *Mulliner's Book*. According to him, the pieces of Redford and Shephard are the least interesting. Those by W. Blitheman already more or less foreshadow the virtuoso fireworks of his pupil, Bull. The rhythmical complications contrived by the latter are already surpassed in pieces such as the *Fantasia-Miserere* (No. 40 of the MS.) by Shelbye.

Mr. John E. West speaks very briefly of *Mulliner's Book* in his study (*Old English Organ Music*) in the *Sammelbände* of the International Musical Society, XII., ii., p. 213, and in an article on the same subject published in the *Proceedings of the Musical Association*, session 1910-11 (Novello). According to him, a certain number of the pieces in the MS. of Thomas Mulliner consist of parts of accompaniment, figured, on a given plainsong.

The pieces from *Mulliner's Book* which have been reproduced in modern notation are the following : *Voluntary* by Alwood (in Hawkins's *History*, and in the anthology, *Old English Organ Music*, edited by Mr. John E. West (Novello)), *A poynte* by Shephard and a *Meane* by Blitheman (Hawkins), *Gloria tibi trinitas* by Blitheman (in Rimbault, *The Pianoforte*), *Glorificamus* by Redford (in the anthology of Mr. West).

We have only been able to form a first-hand opinion of the contents of *Mulliner's Book* from a *Voluntary* by Richard Alwood[12] and a *Glorificamus* by Redford,[13] published by Mr. John E. West in his collection, *Old English Organ Music* (Novello), part 24, and from the *Meane* of Blitheman, reproduced by Hawkins in his *General History*.[14]

The *Voluntary*[15] of Alwood may be compared to a *ricercare* in which several subjects or fragments of subjects are treated in a style of imitation, austere but scarcely strict as regards the regularity of their entry. There is one point rather curious for the period: the third subject, which the musician has discarded for a long time, reappears five times at the conclusion of the composition. One of the subjects seems designed as a countersubject to another. From the point of view of expression this piece has both charm and suavity; it has a foretaste of the sweetness of William Byrd's style.

The *Glorificamus* of Redford possesses a character more definitely archaic than the

[12] Alwood is a musician completely unknown. All the information we have about him is that he was a priest.

[13] John Redford was organist and almoner of the Cathedral of St. Paul from 1491-1547. These dates are accepted with all reserve by Dr. Grattan Flood in his article already cited on *Master Sebastian of Paul's*. It is with the same reservations that Dr. Flood accepts the tradition according to which Thomas Mulliner was the successor of Redford at St. Paul's from 1547-51. Mr. John E. West (article cited) makes the assumption that the duties of organist by Redford at St. Paul's started in 1530 only. According to Grove, *Dictionary* (art. *Redford*), Christ Church, Oxford, possesses a MS. which contains *Fancies* and a *Voluntary* by Redford.

[14] We pass over in silence the insignificant *Poynte* by Shephard, reproduced by Hawkins, of which we have already spoken (p. 17, Note 11).

[15] The English call *Voluntaries* (see Grove, *Dictionary*, art. *Voluntary*), organ pieces which are played before, during, and after divine service. The word probably comes from the fact that the piece forming no official part of the liturgy, it was at the discretion of the organist to play it or not to play it. We still find voluntaries well into the 19th century.

Voluntary of Alwood. It consists of the figuration, by means of accompanying counterpoints, of a sacred plainsong given out in long notes in the alto part. The counterpoint parts include a certain number of subjects which borrow their details from each other, and give opportunity for certain imitations. The archaic character of the piece arises in part from the fact that one of these accompanying counterpoints closes at one place with a form of cadence which was in current use in the 14th and 15th centuries, but which had almost entirely disappeared in the 16th. It consisted in the interposition between the leading note and the final tonic of a minor third below the latter :—

A few words as to the *Meane* in three parts by Blitheman, reproduced by Hawkins. The title *Meane*[16] arises probably from the fact that the intermediate part, either alto or tenor, to which in ancient times they gave the name of *meane*, is obbligato—that is to say, it is the most important of the three. It is therefore very probable that this part announces and develops at its full length some sacred or secular subject already existing. The subjects forming counterpoints with the principal melody are pretty numerous and are not always very well defined; the imitations are not strict, and the free counterpoints are devoid of figuration, often making among themselves

---

[16] See Grove, *Dictionary* (art. *Meane*).

successions of sixths, with which the English organists of the 16th century were very much taken. The general feeling of the piece gives the impression of a sort of *ricercare*.

Modest as they were in their extent and in their absence of all straining after effect and originality, the *Voluntary* of Alwood, the *Glorificamus* of Redford, and the *Meane* of Blitheman are none the less precious evidences of the advancement of organ music in England at a period when, on the Continent, they had not yet succeeded in freeing this kind of music from the yoke of vocal polyphony.[17] Doubtless these compositions, like the *ricercari* of Cavazzoni or the figured chorales of the German organists of the first half of the 16th century, have still undeniable affinities with the contemporary motet. But there are already apparent exceptional qualities of adaptation of the vocal style to the capabilities of the instrument, and an easy gait which contrasts with the heaviness of the greater part of the Continental productions. Perhaps the Spaniard Cabezon alone can be put in the same category with Redford, Blitheman, and Alwood for the happy adaptation of the conduct of the voices to the uniformity of tone of the keyboard of the organ.[18]

[17] It must be understood that the German *preludes* or *preambles* of the 15th century and the beginning of the 16th century, as well as the French of the first half of the 16th century, in which the origins of the free style of the *toccata* are to be met with, must be excepted.

[18] There is a strong probability that more than one among the works of Cabezon which have come down to us are virtually contemporary with the *Glorificamus* of Redford. Very specially to be noted is a *tiento* from the *Libro di Cifra* of 1557 (No. iii., p. 37, of vol. viii. of the *Hispaniæ Schola musica sacra* of Pedrell), in which the Spanish master has made use of the form of cadence of the 15th century which we have pointed out as an archaic element in the piece by Redford.

Still, whatever may be their æsthetic value, these organ pieces teach us but little if we take up the point of view of the evolution of instrumental figuration. The latter, properly speaking, plays no part in these three little compositions. And if one sets aside the accepted fact that there existed in England during the first half of the 16th century an organ literature worthy of our full attention,[19] we find ourselves again in presence of a blank as to the immediate source of that varied or figured style for the virginal which we discover in process of such brilliant development from about the year 1560.

This blank, however, is not absolute. In fact, in an article of the *Sammelbände* of the International Musical Society, XIII., i., p. 133 (*English influence in the evolution of Music*), Johannes Wolf draws fresh attention to certain virginal music of the beginning of the 16th century (about 1510), the importance of which the historians of music have not sufficiently insisted upon, and in which the principle of the variation has already acquired a high degree of perfection. The master to whom we owe this music is Hughe Ashton or Aston,

---

[19] Schering (*Das Kolorierte Orgelmadrigal des Trecento; Sammelbände* of the International Musical Society, XIII., i, p. 185, Note 3), points out the existence at the British Museum of a series of manuscripts (Nos. 15233, 29996, and Roy. app. 56), in addition to *Mulliner's Book*, which also contain English organ compositions dating from the first half of the 16th century.

According to the *Catalogue of the MS. Music in the British Museum* (vol. iii. p. 79 ff), the Addl. MS. 15233 (middle of the 16th century) contains six fantasies (figured plainsongs) for the organ by Master [John] Redford ; the MS. 29996, partly dating from the 16th century, contains certain organ pieces by Redford, Tallis (?), Thomas Preston, R. Parsons, Byrd, and anonymous authors ; the MS. Roy. app. 56 (16th century) contains, *passim*, nineteen anonymous organ pieces.

Nagel (*Gesch. der Mus. in Engl.*, vol. ii., p. 152) gives a few details of the latter. They consist in the instrumental treatment of a *cantus planus* placed sometimes in the *superius*, at others in a middle part, and surrounded by the composer with contrapurtal parts. The effect produced is pedantic and dry.

C

an organist and composer of sacred music of the time of Henry VIII. (1509-47).[20] We come across his name again in 1591, in *My Ladye Nevells Booke*, a celebrated manuscript of pieces for the virginal, which consists of compositions by Byrd alone; No. 35 of this collection is entitled *Hugh Astons Grownde*, from which one may form the conclusion that the theme on which it is founded is by Ashton. Wolf has been kind enough to forward us a copy of a composition by that musician, by the analysis of which we have been enabled to form an accurate opinion of the progress made in the technique of virginal playing at the commencement of the 16th century. This piece, extracted from the Royal manuscripts, App. 58, of the British Museum, is entitled *A Hornepype*.[21]

---

[20] See Grove, *Dictionary* (artt. *Aston, Musica antiqua* and *Musical libraries*). The library of the Music School at Oxford possesses a *Te Deum* for five voices, and a motet for six voices, by Ashton. We find also fragments of vocal compositions by Ashton in the Add. MS. 34191 in the British Museum (No. 5, a tenor or bass part of a motet, *Gaude Virgo*, by Hugh Asheton), and in the MS. Harl. 7578 (Brit. Mus.) the alto part of an *Ave, Domyna* for three voices by H(ugh) Astone (see *A Catalogue of MS. Music in the Brit. Mus.*).

[21] Nagel had already given some particulars concerning this manuscript in his *Gesch. der Mus. in Engl.* (1894-97, vol. ii., p. 80). According to him, this document contains, among others, three compositions for the virginal, of which the *Hornepype* alone (of which Herr Wolf has given us a copy) bears the name of Ashton. But it is very probable that the two others, *Lady Carey's Dompe* and *The short mesure off my Lady Wynkfyldes Rownde*, also have this master for author. Nagel looks on *Lady Carey's Dompe* as the most interesting of the three. He gives certain details as to their structure, and affirms that at least the first two are based on the variation form. The three pieces have been published in the *Musica antiqua* (1812) of Stafford Smith, a work which it has become almost impossible to meet with.

Dr. Walker (*History of Mus. in Engl.*, p. 32) is of opinion that there is no apparent reason for attributing to Ashton the virginal pieces of MS. 58 other than the *Hornepype*. He adds: " *My Lady Carey's Dompe*, though shorter and less elaborate than the *Hornepype*, is much more musical and expressive, and is in its slight way a really charming little piece." *My Lady Carey's Dompe* is also reproduced in Wooldridge, *Old English Popular Music*.

This is a word to be met with frequently in English music up to the dawn of the 19th century. According to Grove's *Dictionary*[22] it signifies "an English dance, probably called after an obsolete instrument," which appears to have had a popular character, and was similar to the bagpipe. We find a *Horne pipe* by Byrd in *Forster's Virginal Book* (No. 8). Purcell furnishes us with several examples of *hornpipe*, more particularly at the ends of Acts II. and III. of *King Arthur*. Handel also favoured this type of dance; we come across it, among other places, in the finale of his *Concerto grosso*, Op. 6, No. 7. In Handel's period the hornpipe was written in $\frac{3}{2}$ time.[23]

Ashton's *Hornepype* is a piece of some length, and without regularity of structure. At first sight it seems to be formed on a somewhat varied harmonic bass. But a more attentive perusal shows that apart from some passing-notes it rests entirely on the alternative pedals of F, tonic, and of C, dominant. This bass is nothing but the old popular drone, borrowed from instruments of the bagpipe type, which gives a rural air to the compositions in which it is used. We shall more than once again come across this

According to the *Catalogue of the Manuscript Music in the British Museum*, vol. iii., p. 103, the Royal MS. Appendix 58 contains, *passim*, other compositions for the virginal than the three pieces to which Nagel and Dr. Walker allude. Here is the complete list: 1, 2, *La bell fyne*, and a little piece without title; 3, 4, 5, the three pieces mentioned by Nagel; 6, *The emperorse pavyn*; 7, *Galliard*; 8, *King Harry the VIIIth pavyn*; 9, *the crocke* (?); 10, *The Kyng's marke* (?); 11, *Galliard*.
It is much to be desired, considering the great interest which these pieces possess from the point of view of the evolution of keyboard music, that they should be brought out together in a reprint in modern notation.

[22] 1st edition (art. *Hornpipe*).

[23] Chappell, *op. cit.*, gives examples of hornpipes forming part of popular music (see pp. 544 and 740).

drone among the virginal writers of the end of the 16th century, notably in the writings of Byrd, the pastoral musician *par excellence*.

Upon this bass of a persistent nature, Ashton constructed various counterpoints, the essential peculiarity of which is that they do not adapt themselves to the laws of the vocal style in accordance with which the musical texture demands the parallel and rigorous development of a fixed number of parts. In the *Hornepype* of Ashton, for example, we find four parts in the eighth bar, then at the beginning of the ninth two parts, and in the second half three parts, while these entries and disappearances have no similarity with those which appear in contemporary vocal compositions. It is well known that the time in which Ashton wrote is actually that of the severest style of vocal imitation. But our *Hornepype* offers us no real example of strict imitation. The apparent imitations which we there come across resemble rather sequences, in that they never make for *stretti*, and that they consist in the repetition, on various degrees of the musical scale, of the same thematic fragment rather than actual re-entry of this fragment. At times this repetition is textually exact so far as the intervals are concerned, at others it is not actually so, and we then have to look on it as what may be called a " quasi-sequence." In a few cases, among others in the beginning of the composition, it presents itself in the shape of certain modifications, ornamental or otherwise, which may be likened to variations. Further on, with several repeats, it is maintained with such obstinacy that the hand whose duty it is to execute the passage of which it is formed, passes in a few moments over an extent of the keyboard which is quite exceptional :—

Examples of this purely instrumental peculiarity are easily multiplied. Let us point out one more, the absolutely exceptional character of which demands a special mention :—

We note in this passage a succession of instrumental figures which are truly surprising for the period, especially when we consider the enormous skips which the right hand must make to execute the last of them.

We shall not see these abrupt skips reappearing till the beginning of the 17th century, with the virginalist G. Farnaby, who often makes use of this practice.[24]

Along with these sequential repetitions we find, and that very frequently, repetitions having rather the character of repeats which aim in no respect at any melodic design, but at an ensemble of the voices of certain fragments of the composition, which all consist of two bars. The repeat is never quite textual; it appears with slight variations, the character of which is only exceptionally that of pure ornament: most frequently one or two of the parts are transposed to the octave below or to the octave above, in such a way as to vary the effects of timbre or to produce the effect of echo.[25]

Successions of thirds or sixths, so beloved of the English primitives, and derived from their predilection for the *gymel* and the faux-bourdon, are to be

[24] In the *Tabulaturen etlicher lobgesang und lidlein uff die orgeln uñ lauten* (1512) of Arnolt Schlick the elder, a German contemporary with Ashton, we meet with passages—unusual, however—where the full extent of the keyboard is exploited in the same way in a purely instrumental, as opposed to vocal, manner. Thus, in the *Salve regina* for the organ (see a reprint in modern notation in the *Monatshefte für Musikgeschichte* for 1869) :—

It is evident that Ashton's technique was much more advanced and more daring than that of Schlick.

[25] An almost analogous tendency is to be noticed in a *Fantasy* in the German organ tablature of Kleber somewhat later in date (about 1520). The organ pieces of Kleber have been reproduced by Eitner as supplement to his edition of the *Buxheimer Orgelbuch* (*Beilagen zu den Monatsheften für Musikgeschichte*, 1888).

found in the *Hornepype* of Ashton, but they are far
from having any preponderance.

The virginalistic figuration of the composition
comprises few actual ornaments. Those which we
do meet in it consist most frequently of graceful
forms of cadence—in any case used rather sparingly
—reminding us of Paumann and the French
musicians in the collections of Attaignant in 1530.
The most advanced figure which the composition
of Ashton presents is the spreading of chords; it
is to be found as yet only under the primitive form
of the separated fifth, which we shall find adopted
later by Byrd, and submitted by him to a peculiar
rhythmical treatment. Here is one of the most
curious aspects of this figure :—

In spite of its length, Ashton's composition
charms us by the picturesqueness of its pastoral
character. Its melodic inflections, many of which
are founded on the use of the natural scale of
sounds produced by an instrument of the pipe form,
are full of grace and freshness. Do we not find
in it, with a slightly different rhythm, the principal
motive of the *finale* of the Pastoral Symphony of
Beethoven :—

Doubtless a piece like the *Hornepype* of Ashton is
far from resolving the question of what intervened
between the rudiments of English instrumental

music of the 14th century, which we have analysed above, and the figured plainsong of Tallis of 1562. But it establishes very completely the fact that the virginalists of the second half of the 16th century had very remarkable predecessors during the first half of the century ; and this is a result all the more valuable in that we can find nothing at that period in Western Europe which can stand comparison with this composition from the point of view of the novelty of instrumental technique.[26]

[26] There can be no doubt that further researches will bring about the discovery of new virginal documents dating from the first half of the 16th century, and will thus result in the confirmation of the existence of a technical tradition specially English. It is above all things to be hoped that the virginal pieces of the John Heywood to whom we have alluded above will be recovered, as well as those of other virginal players such as Antony Chaunter and Robert Bowman, who were attached to the English Court under Mary Tudor (1553-58). (Nagel, *Annalen*, p. 24.)

KEYBOARD MUSIC IN ENGLAND FROM THE SECOND HALF OF THE 16TH CENTURY TO THE FIRST THIRD OF THE 17TH CENTURY.

CHAPTER I.

THE SOURCES.

A.—PRINCIPAL SOURCES, MANUSCRIPT AND PRINTED, DATING FROM THE 16TH AND 17TH CENTURIES.

IF sources fail us almost completely for the period which preceded the second half of the 16th century, in compensation we possess a wealth of material for the period ranging from 1560 to about 1630.

To Seiffert belongs the merit of being the first to form a list of the principal manuscripts of music for the virginal bearing upon that period.[1] The *Dictionary* of Grove also contains, in the article *Virginal Music, Collections of,* a succinct analysis of the four most famous collections, followed by an enumeration of all the compositions which they include.

We propose to make a fresh inventory of these various sources, adding certain new data to those already current.[2]

---

[1] See *Gesch. der Klaviermusik,* p. 54 ff.

[2] We shall not refer again to MS. 30513 (*Mulliner's Book*) which Seiffert quotes under No. 7, since it belongs to an earlier period than that which we are studying at present. For the same reason we pass by the MS. Roy. App. 58 in which Ashton's *Hornepype* is to be found, and MSS. 15233, 29996 and Roy. App. 56, of which we have spoken in a previous note (see p. 21).

1. The most important document which we possess is the *Fitzwilliam Virginal Book*. For a long time it was wrongly called *Queen Elizabeth's Virginal Book*. As a matter of fact this manuscript had no connection whatever with Queen Elizabeth, who died in 1603, several years before the collection was formed. Messrs. Fuller Maitland and Barclay Squire have published it in modern notation (1899), and devote many pages of their Introduction to its description, and to comments upon its main features.

The title of *Fitzwilliam Virginal Book* arises from the fact that the manuscript belonged at the end of the 18th century to Lord Fitzwilliam. It is to be found at the present time at Cambridge, in the Fitzwilliam Museum, the foundation of which (1816) is due to the munificence of that nobleman.[3]

It derives its importance from the fact that it contains about three hundred compositions by the most celebrated masters of the 16th century and the opening of the 17th, as well as a great number of masters of the second rank, and a few foreign musicians, such as the Dutch Sweelinck (four works), and the Italians Giovanni Pichi (one work) and Galeazzo (one work). Among the most illustrious English names we come across those of Tallis, Byrd, Morley, Philips, Bull, Giles Farnaby, and Orlando Gibbons. Thirteen compositions of the *Fitzwilliam Virginal Book* are dated; the most ancient, the first *Felix namque* of Tallis, bears the date of 1562; the most recent, a scholastic piece by Sweelinck (*ut, re, mi, fa, sol, la, a 4 voci*) that of 1612. But there is a multiplicity of reasons for believing

---

[3] See Grove, *Dictionary* (art. *Fitzwilliam Collection*).

that among the works without date in the manuscript there are some of which the production is later than 1612. We shall see in a moment why it is difficult to admit that the *Fitzwilliam Virginal Book* contains works written after 1619. On the other hand there is no detail allowing us to assert that it contains compositions the conjectural date of which could be earlier than 1562.

The origin of the *Fitzwilliam Virginal Book* is a problem which as yet has received no absolute solution. Messrs. Fuller Maitland and Barclay Squire have attempted to penetrate the mystery of this origin, and have arrived at conclusions which have a good deal of seductiveness on account of the romantic atmosphere with which they surround the birth of the celebrated manuscript. On examining it with care, they noticed that the proper name Tregian occurred in several places, either in full, or under an abridged form.[4] Now this name is that of a rich and powerful Cornish family, which was violently persecuted by the English authorities during the second half of the 16th century on account of its Catholic opinions. The head of this family at that time was Francis Tregian, who was persecuted, arrested, subjected to a host of annoyances, and passed a number of years of his life in prison. He had a great number of children, the eldest of whom, also called Francis Tregian, was, as seems well established, convicted of rebellion against the English Government about 1608-9, which resulted in his arrest and imprisonment ; there he remained until his death, which occurred about 1619. It appears from official

---

[4] See the enumeration of these passages in the Introduction to the modern edition of the *Fitzw. V. B.*, p. vi.

documents that at the time of his decease he had contracted a debt of more than two hundred pounds sterling to his jailer, for the supply of meat, drink, and lodging. His rooms contained hundreds of books about which his sister and his jailer disputed, the one as heiress, the other as creditor.

It will be noticed that the *Fitzwilliam Virginal Book* contains a large number of compositions the presence of which shows most obviously that the manuscript was compiled either by or for someone who was in intimate relation with the English Catholic refugees on the Continent. There will be found in particular (which is not the case in other English collections of virginal music) a great number of compositions by Peter Philips, who, after a series of persecutions brought about by his Catholic convictions, emigrated probably about 1591[5] to the Netherlands for the remainder of his life.

The *Fitzwilliam Virginal Book* contains also compositions by Sweelinck, the great organist at Amsterdam, and it is the only one among these manuscripts of English origin which does so. Lastly, we find a considerable number of the compositions of John Bull, who lived in the Netherlands from 1613 till his death in 1628.

These various particulars, and moreover the fact that the manuscript was written from end to end by one and the same hand, during a comparatively short period, have led Messrs. Fuller Maitland and Barclay Squire to admit that there is a great probability that the *Fitzwilliam Virginal Book* was

[5] Does not the fact that of the twelve dated compositions of the *Fitzw. V. B.* eight are by Philips, suggest that the compiler or the first owner of the manuscript had a special acquaintance with that master, and was in constant personal relations with him?

written by Francis Tregian the son, to pass the time during his imprisonment, from 1609 to 1619. Unfortunately, since we possess no authentic autograph of his, enabling a comparison to be made with the handwriting of the manuscript, there exists up to the present time a series of presumptions only in favour of this hypothesis, but no certain and absolute proof. In opposition to the ingenious suggestion of Messrs. Fuller Maitland and Barclay Squire, an objection has been brought forward which seems to destroy its value. No. 138 of the *Fitzwilliam Virginal Book* bears the title of *Dr. Bull's Juell;* now, a manuscript of Netherlands origin,[6] of which we shall have to speak later, contains a piece by Bull bearing the same title in Dutch : *Het Juweel van Doctor Jan Bull,* and dated December 12th, 1621 (*quod fecit anno 1621, 12 Dec.*). Now, if Francis Tregian died in 1619, and if identity exists between *Dr. Bull's Juell* and *Het Juweel van Dr. Jan Bull,* it is certain that the noble prisoner could not have included in his collection a piece written in 1621.

But on closer examination it will be perceived that No. 138 of the *Fitzwilliam Virginal Book* is a version altogether different from the melody which Bull made use of in writing his *Juweel* of 1621. There is, therefore, nothing to prevent that version being more ancient than the last, and consequently dated before the death of Tregian. Moreover, the same Dutch manuscript in the British Museum contains, under the title *Courante Juweel,* an undated version of the *Juell* inserted in the *Fitzwilliam Virginal Book.* Under these conditions the objection raised against the hypothesis of

[6] MS. 23623 of the British Museum.

Messrs. Fuller Maitland and Barclay Squire falls to the ground.

2. After the *Fitzwilliam Virginal Book* we come across first of all the manuscript known under the title of *My Ladye Nevells Booke*, which belongs to the Marquis of Abergavenny. It is dated September 11, 1591, and contains the compositions of William Byrd only. These amount to forty-two, of which about a dozen are also to be found in the *Fitzwilliam Virginal Book*.[7]

3. Then comes *William Forster's Virginal Book*, which is in the possession of the English Royal Family. At the beginning of the manuscript is to be found a *Table of the lessons* written in the same hand as the rest of the collection, signed *W. Forster* and dated January 31, 1624. This collection contains seventy-eight compositions by Byrd, Morley, John Ward, Englitt, and Bull. About fifteen of the pieces by Byrd and Bull occur again in the *Fitzwilliam Virginal Book*.

4. The fourth important manuscript is *Benjamin Cosyn's Virginal Book*, which also is the property of the English Royal Family.[8] The original owner was Benjamin Cosyn, a composer who lived about the year 1620,[9] a great number of whose compositions are collected in the manuscript. According to Mr. Barclay Squire there is strong probability that the greater part of them are wrongly attributed to him, and that they are actually written by Bull

----

[7] *Nevell's Booke* is to be found at Eridge Park, Tunbridge, in the library of the Marquis of Abergavenny. [Communicated by Mr. Barclay Squire.]

[8] *Cosyn's Book*, as well as *Forster's Book*, have been deposited by the English Royal Family in the British Museum. | Together with a large collection of other musical treasures from Buckingham Palace.—TR.]

[9] According to the most recent researches Cosyn was organist at Dulwich College from 1622 to 1624, and the first organist of the Charterhouse from 1626 to 1643. Dr. Cummings possesses some MS. voluntaries by him.

or other musicians.[10] *Cosyn's Book* contains ninety-eight works by Cosyn, Gibbons, Bull, Tallis, Byrd, Bevin, Strogers, and Thomas Weelks.   Some of these pieces are to be found also in the *Fitzwilliam Virginal Book*. *Cosyn's Book* is not dated.   It must in any case be later than 1605, for the reason that Gibbons is entitled *Bachellor of music* (in No. 55), and it is not till 1606 that this musician received this degree at the University of Cambridge.   Moreover Gibbons became Bachelor, and at the same time Doctor, of the University of Oxford in May, 1622. We may fairly conclude from the absence of this last title in *Cosyn's Book* that this collection was formed before the month of May, 1622.   Lastly, the large number of compositions of Gibbons contained in the manuscript are such as to make us believe that it dates from a tolerably late period of the master's existence, and consequently nearer to 1622 than to 1606.   In short, we may look on *Cosyn's Book* as very nearly contemporary with the *Fitzwilliam Virginal Book*.[11]   We must notice that it contains also (as No. 44) a *Doctor Bulle's Jewell*.   Unfortunately we cannot deduce from this fact any argument either for or against the completion of the *Fitzwilliam Virginal Book* before 1620, on account of the absence of any particulars establishing a precise date for the formation of the manuscript of Cosyn.[12]

[10] See Grove, *Dictionary* (art. *Virginal Music, Collections of*). In the *Oxford History of Music* (vol. iii., p. 89) Sir Hubert Parry says that if Cosyn is really the author of the pieces attributed to him, he must have been a great admirer and imitator of Bull ; he reproduces two passages extracted from these pieces which consist of daring spreading of chords in the style of Bull.

[11] In fixing about 1600 as the date of *Cosyn's Book*, Dr. Naylor (*An Elizabethan Virginal Book*, p. 1 (Dent & Co., London, 1905)) seems to us to attribute too ancient an origin to this manuscript.

[12] Grove, *Dictionary* (art. *Virginal Music, Collections of*), gives the detailed contents of the *Fitzwilliam* (291 pieces), of *Nevell's* (37 pieces), *Forster's* (78 pieces) and of *Cosyn's Book* (98 pieces).

D

5. The following manuscript belongs to the British Museum, where it bears the No. 23623; it is dated 1628, and is of Netherlandish origin. A complete description is to be found in the *Catalogue of the manuscript music in the British Museum*, vol. iii., p. 82. It contains seventy pieces, all by Bull, except one, the *Toccata di Roma* by Hieronimo Ferabosco.[13] According to the opinion of the author of the *Catalogue*, this piece may possibly have undergone an arrangement on the part of Bull. It is in the MS. 23623 that is to be found the *Juweel van Doctor Jan Bull* (1621), of which we have already spoken above, on the question of the origin of the *Fitzwilliam Book*.

The following sources, of less importance, also belong to the British Museum :—

6. Add. MS. 31403, dated about 1700, contains, *passim*, sixty-seven pieces for the organ or virginal, of which the first thirty only belong to the period in which we are interested. These have for authors, Bevin, Blitheman, Bull, Byrd, Gibbons, Soncino, and Tallis. (*Catal. of the MS. Mus. in the Brit. Mus.*, vol. iii., p. 90.)

7. Add. MS. 36661. This collection, dating from 1629-30, contains forty-two pieces for the organ or virginal. They are by Orlando Gibbons, Bull, [Robert] Johnson, [Edward] Bevin, Hugh Facy, Emanuell Soncino and sundry anonymous authors. (*Catal. of the MS. Mus. in the Brit. Mus.*, vol. iii., p. 84.)

8. MS. 31392. This MS. contains four pavans by Byrd, followed by their galliards. (*Catal. of the MS. Mus. in the Brit. Mus.*, vol. iii., p. 106.)

[13] On Hieronimo or Girolamo Ferabosco or Ferrabosco, see the article by Giovanni Livi in the *Musical Antiquary* of April, 1913 (*The Ferrabosco Family*, p. 121 ff. ; specially p. 137).

9. MS. 30485. According to Seiffert, this collection contains nothing but pieces taken from *Nevell's Book*. This is a mistake arising from the fact that the MS. has the inscription, *Extracts from Virginal Book—Lady Nevells* added in the 18th century, on what appears to have been the original cover. Actually, MS. 30485 borrowed a very small number only of pieces from *Nevell's Book*. Besides anonymous pieces, there are compositions by Tallis, Blitheman, Byrd, Bull, Marchant, Kinloughe, Fardinando [Richardson], Philip van Wilder, Bickerll, Renold, Alfonso[Ferabosco, sen.?], Jeames Harden, Alwoode, Tho. Weelkes, and [Robert?] Johnson. This MS. probably dates from the confines of the 16th and 17th centuries. (*Catal. of the MS. Mus. in the Brit. Mus.*, vol. iii., p. 104.)

10. MS. 29485. (Collection of Susanna van Soldt, of the date 1599.) This MS. contains thirty-five secular (various dances, &c.) and sacred pieces (arrangements of psalms of the reformed church for four voices).[14] Bassano alone is cited as author, with the exception of Orlando di Lassus, of whom the MS. contains an arrangement for the clavier of *Suzanne un jour*. (*Catal. of the MS. Mus. in the Brit. Mus.*, vol. iii., p. 104.)

11. MS. Harl. 7340 contains among other music an organ prelude by Edward Gibbons, elder brother of Orlando (between about 1565 and about 1650). This piece is published by Mr. John E. West in his *Old English Organ Music* (No. 20). (See *Catal. of the MS. Mus. in the Brit. Mus.*, vol. iii., p. 91.)

12. Add. MS. 29996. This MS., dated 1647, contains one hundred and two pieces, which for

---

[14] See notice on *Susanne van Soldt*, by Seiffert, in the *Tÿdschrift der Vereeniging voor Noord-Nederlands Muziekgeschiedenis*, Deel V., p. 139.

the most part appear to be arrangements for the virginal of compositions originally written for strings or for voices. But yet certain pieces seem to have been directly written for the virginal, as for example No. 97 (Variations on *John come kisse me now*, by John Tomkins); No. 101 (*Pavan* by [Orlando] Gibbons); and No. 102 (*Pavan* by Tho. Tomkins). (*Catal. of the MS. Mus. in the Brit. Mus.*, vol. iii., p. 85.)

13. Add. MS. 30486. Dates from the confines of the 16th and 17th centuries; contains fourteen pieces, partly anonymous, partly by Byrd. Three of these pieces are common to this MS. and the *Fitzw V. B.* (See *Catal. of the MS. Mus. in the Brit. Mus.*, vol. iii., p. 107.)

14. Add. MS. 10337 (Book of Elizabeth Rogers), dated 1656, contains seventy-nine pieces, belonging for the most part to a later time than that with which we are concerned. Among the exceptions is found, among others as No. 27, *The Battle*, by Byrd, taken from *Nevell's Book*. (See *Catal. of the MS. Mus. in the Brit. Mus.*, vol. iii., p. 107.)

15. Add. MS. 22099. Dates from the opening of the 18th century; contains under No. 69 a *Voluntary* attributed to Orlando Gibbons, which is identical with the *Preludium octavi toni* by Bull which is found in MS. 23623. (See *Catal. of the MS. Mus. in the Brit. Mus.*, vol. iii., p. 112.)

Mr. John E. West (article cited) mentions the existence of :—

16. A manuscript belonging to Dr. W. H. Cummings, dating from the 17th century (about 1660-70), containing, in addition to compositions of musicians belonging to more recent generations,

organ pieces of Byrd, Morley, Orlando Gibbons, and Christopher Gibbons, son of Orlando.

We must record also certain manuscripts which are to be found in the Continental libraries:—

17. MS. 191 fol. of the Royal Library at Berlin, containing among other works compositions by the following English musicians: William Brown, John Bull, James, J. Kennedy, Carolus Luython, Peter Philips.

18. MS. 888 of the Library of the University of Liége. We find, among others, pieces by P. Philips and Will. Brown.

19. MS. 17771 of the Imperial and Royal Library of Vienna contains compositions by John Bull.[15]

20. A manuscript (MS. of Vincentius De la Faille) belonging to M. Jules Ecorcheville, of Paris, the cover of which bears the date 1625. The pieces which it contains belong for the most part to the English school of virginalists. Transcribed by two or three different hands, they seem to date uniformly from the second quarter of the 17th century. Two only are accompanied by any mention of the composer's name: the two series of variations by John Bull on the Flemish sacred song *Een Kindeken is ons geboren.*[16]

---

[15] Nagel, *Gesch. der Musik in Eng.*, vol ii., p. 28, Note 7, gives detailed contents of this manuscript: 1. *Fantasia;* 2. *Fant(asia);* 3. *Salve regina;* 4. *Miserere mei;* 5. *Fant(asia);* 6. *Galliarda;* 7. *La Chasse du Roy;* 8. *Salve regina;* 9. *Fantasia;* 10-13. *Various Canons;* 14. *Thema cum notulis et ligaturis;* 15. *Canon;* 16. *(Fantasia?);* 17. *Revenant.*

[16] We must here tender our warmest thanks to M. Ecorcheville, who has been good enough to place at our service the MS. of V. De la Faille. This collection, which must be of Netherlandish origin, appears to have belonged in the first place to a family of amateurs who were themselves composers. Many of the pieces which it contains are simple arrangements for the clavier (harmonizations with and without coloratura, variations in the style of the virginalists) of themes well known during the first half of the 17th century. Everything in these arrangements betrays the hand of the amateur indifferently acquainted with

21. MS. 18546 of the Library of the Conservatoire of Paris. This MS. consists of 124 leaves, and contains pieces noted on two staves in different clefs. On the inside of the cover there is a dated inscription probably more recent than the MS. itself, an extract from which we give: *The Contents of this Book for the Virginal are the Compositions of Orldo. Gibbons, 1608; Will. Byrd, 1575; Dr. Bull, 1570* [followed by several other names, up to *Th. Tomkins, 1640*]. *Writen in 1635, in 1636, año 1638.*

22. MS. 18547 of the Library of the Conservatoire of Paris. This MS. has 190 pages. It bears on the back of the binding, which is ancient, this title and these dates: *Thomas Tomkins. Instrumental music. 1646, 1654.* The music which it contains appears more specially interesting for the organ than for the virginal.

musical technique, including notation. This is shown in *C'est trop courir les eaux* (melody taken from a ballet of Guédron) ; *l'Engloise* (a corante which strongly recalls those in the *Fitzw. V. B.*) ; *A galiard* (same theme as that of *Nowel's Galiard* by an anonymous writer in the *Fitzw. V. B.*) ; a piece without title and unfinished, the melody of which is really that of *Amarilli* by Caccini (*cf.* the variations of P. Philips on the same melody in the *Fitzw. V. B.*) ; a piece without title, also unfinished, the subject of which is obviously Italian, possibly Venetian. The variations by Bull, *Een Kindeken is ons geboren*, are apparently the same as those to be found under the same title in the MS. 23623 of the British Museum (1628), in which they were transcribed on the 4th and 5th of April, 1628, after the death of Bull. The variations on the melody *Une jeune fillette* (a melody already popular about the middle of the 16th century) are written in the purest virginal style, as are also a *Galiarde*, interesting from a rhythmical point of view, and the *Courante la Roÿne*, the subject of which is to be found in the *Harmonie Universelle* of Mersenne (1636) (the MS. No. 23623 of the British Museum contains a *Courante La Reine* by Bull, but we are unaware whether there is identity between the latter and that of the MS. of De la Faille). Let us quote lastly the *Galiarde pekel harinck* (pickle herring) ; *Cecilia* (a melody well known in the 17th and 18th centuries) ; and *Que je suis travaillé*, which show no peculiarities. As to the two remaining pieces of the MS., the *Sarabande Pinel* (Pinel was a celebrated French lutenist, whose activity was about the middle of the 17th century), has French rather than English leanings, and the charming piece without title forming the end of the MS., which consists of a *superius* only with unfigured *continuo*, seems to be an Italian Sonata for the violin, with an accompaniment for organ or clavicembalo,

23. MS. 18548 of the Library of the Conservatoire of Paris.   This volume contains, in addition to the engraved *Parthenia* (see p. 44), which takes the first 21 leaves, 348 pages of manuscript containing 141 pieces, the list of which is preceded by the note: *A Table of all ȳ Virginall Lessons contained in ȳ Booke.*

24. MS. 18570 of the Library of the Conservatoire of Paris.   This MS. has on the back of the binding, which is modern, the title *O. Gibbons, etc.   Pièces pour la Virginale.*   It is in fact a miscellaneous collection containing two manuscript collections of different " formats," one of 55, the other of 56 pages. Weckerlin, the former librarian of the Conservatoire of Paris, has added a note that the second collection " is an old transcript of the second part of the book of music for the virginal which belonged to Queen Elizabeth."   (He evidently meant the pseudo-*Queen Elizabeth's Virginal Book*, otherwise the *Fitzwilliam Virginal Book.*[17])

[17] We are indebted for the valuable information referring to the four MSS. of the Conservatoire of Paris to the kindness of the Librarian of that Institution, M. Julien Tiersot, to whom it becomes our duty to tender in this place our very warmest thanks.   M. Tiersot has in addition brought to our knowledge that in one of these MSS. there remains a sheet of paper containing the name of Mme. Farrenc.   The acquisition Nos. following exactly for the first three MSS., and the fourth following pretty closely, " it is evident," adds M. Tiersot, " that they are from the same source, and that that source was without doubt the Farrenc sale."   It thus follows that the Virginal MSS. of the Conservatoire of Paris are in fact indentical with those which Mme. Farrenc asserts (vol. ii. of the *Trésor des Pianistes*) that she acquired in various sales held in London, and from which she extracted the *Victoria* of Byrd, the *Courante* of Gibbons, and the two *Courantes* of Crofurd, all pieces published in the *Trésor des Pianistes*.

Mme. Farrenc asserts that Rimbault also became possessor of a certain number of MSS. of virginal music.   What has become of them?   Of this we have no certain information except as to *My Ladye Nevells Booke*, of which Rimbault was for a certain time the owner.   Again, Oscar Bie (*Das Klavier und seine Meister*, p. 14: Ed. Bruckmann, Munich, 1898) remarks that in addition to *Nevell's Book*, Rimbault had in his library a virginal book of the Earl of Leicester.

Along with these numerous manuscript sources, there exists a single and unique printed document dating from the time of the virginal composers. It is the celebrated collection entitled: *Parthenia or the Maidenhead of the first musicke that ever was printed for the Virginalls. Composed by three famous Masters: William Byrd, Dr. John Bull and Orlando Gibbons.* The first edition is dated 1611. There were reprints in 1613, 1635, 1650, 1655, and 1659.[18] It appears from the title that Byrd, Bull, and Gibbons were already in their lifetime looked on as masters of great reputation, worthy all three of the epithet " famous."

In the dedication addressed by the engraver Hole to Frederick, Elector Palatine of the Rhine, and his affianced wife, Elisabeth, daughter of the King of England, we find this opinion of music: " For Musick (like that miraculous tongue of th' Apostles) having but one and ye same Caracter, is alike knowne to all the sundry nations of ye world."

Among manuscripts containing virginal music, trace of which has been lost, there is one which formed part of the library of Count Zu Lynar, at Lübbenau. According to an index which has been preserved, it contained, among others, organ and clavier compositions by Philips, Bull, G. and R. Farnaby, and Wooddeson. This index is added to a transcript of a fragment of the manuscript, which transcript is to be found in the possession of the *Vereeniging voor Noord-Nederlands Muziekgeschiedenis*, since 1886 (see the Introduction, by Seiffert, to vol. i. of the complete works of Sweelinck, p. iii.). Professor Seiffert has kindly given us a list of the English keyboard pieces contained in the copied fragment, namely, *Rossignol di Orlando, intavolata da P. Philippi; Chi fara, Al. Striggio, Intavolata da P. Philippi; Pavana dolorosa da Philippi; Bonny sweet Robin, D. B(ull)*. (The first three are found in the *Fitzw. V. B.*, the fourth treats in variations the song which Munday and G. Farnaby varied in the pieces which form part of the *Fitzw. V. B.*; it is no doubt identical with the *Bonni Well (?) Robin* by Bull, which is No. 3 in the MS. 23623 (1628) in the British Museum. See *Catal. of the MS. Music in the Brit. Mus.*, vol. iii., p. 82.)

[18] In 1613, 1635, 1650, and 1659, according to Grove, *Dictionary* (art. *Parthenia*), and according to the preface by Rimbault to the modern reprint of *Parthenia*. In 1655, according to a *Catalogue of one hundred works illustrating the history of music printing from the 15th to the end of the 17th century in the library of Alfred H. Littleton* (Novello & Co., London, 1911).

In addition to the dedication, *Parthenia* contains also two poems addressed to Hole: one is by Holland, the other by George Chapman. The first cries up Byrd, Bull, and Gibbons by means of elegant plays on words: Byrd "doth vary his notes" so "daintily, as if he were the Nightingalls owne brother." Bull is compared to "the brave bull of mythology which did Europa cary." Orlando Gibbons is likened to that other Orlando, the great Belgian master, Orlando di Lassus.

The second poem praises the pieces of Byrd, Bull, and Gibbons as classic compositions, which the poet contrasts with the fantasies of the "moderne mere Phantastique *Tasters* (whose Art but forreigne Noveltie extolls)." This appreciation is not wanting in wisdom, for the twenty-one compositions included in *Parthenia* (eight by Byrd, seven by Bull, and six by Gibbons) seem to have been chosen expressly to show what is the most restrained, the purest and the most classic which the art of the virginal has produced. The person or persons who made the selection were assuredly people of taste, and artists fully aware of the beauty of the works to which they devoted their admiration.

B.—Modern Editions of Virginal Music.

To what extent have the treasures contained in the different sources which we have just enumerated become accessible ? For many years we had to be content with the few extracts given by Hawkins and Burney in their several histories of music (1776 and 1776-89), by John Stafford Smith in his

Musica Antiqua (1812), and by Busby-Michaelis in the *Allgemeine Geschichte der Musik*, published at Leipzig in 1821.[19]

Since 1847 we have been able to form an opinion of the contents of *Parthenia* by the publication of it in modern notation in that year by the *Musical Antiquarian Society* of London, under the direction of Dr. Rimbault.[20] Although the latter affirms in the preface that he collated the pieces in *Parthenia* with the same pieces contained in the *Fitzwilliam Virginal Book* and in other manuscripts, in order to produce versions as free from fault as possible, there exist in this new edition not only glaring printer's errors, but also many faults of detail which deprive it of a part of its value. Moreover, the arbitrary omissions of the signs of ornament has subjected him to just reproach.

Mme. Farrenc has incorporated all the pieces of *Parthenia* in vol. ii. (1863) of her *Trésor des Pianistes* (Leduc, Paris).[21] Pauer has done the

---

[19] In Hawkins (*A General History of the Science and Practice of Music*) we find : *A meane* by Blitheman (No. 31 in *Mulliner's Book*), *A poynte* by Shephard (taken from the same MS.), *A voluntary* by Allwoode (the one from *Mulliner's Book* republished by Mr. John E. West).

In Burney (*A General History of Music*) we find : *The Carman's Whistle* by Byrd ; a fragment of the second *ut, re, mi, fa, sol, la* by Bull and of the *Miserere in 3 parts* of the same master ; fragments of Dr. Bull's *Jewell;* an *Alman* by Rob. Johnson ; the subject and the words of *Fortune,* a popular song varied by Byrd, all these pieces belonging to the *Fitzw. V. B.* The *Musica Antiqua* of Stafford Smith contains a *Lesson* by Tallis, which Weitzmann reproduces in his *Geschichte des Klavierspiels,* 2nd Edn., p. 324 ; and also, according to Mme. Farrenc, preludes and other organ pieces by Gibbons ; lastly, three virginal pieces taken from the Roy. MS. App. 58 (*A Hornepype* by Ashton, *Lady Carey's Dompe,* and *The short mesure off my Lady Wynktyldes Rownde*). In Busby, the English historian, translated into German by Michaelis, we find *The Carman's Whistle* and *Dr. Bull's Jewell.*

[20] Vol. xix. of the publications of the *Musical Antiquarian Society.* Since 1847 this volume has been re-issued by Wm. Reeves, London.

[21] In this edition Mme. Farrenc has restored the graces of *Parthenia,* and has taken the trouble to secure a version less faulty and more faithful to the original than that of Rimbault.

same in his *Old English Composers for the Virginals and Harpsichord* (Augener, London).[22]

Lastly, the most important work of re-editing has been the publication in 1899 of the *Fitzwilliam Virginal Book* in its completeness by Messrs. Fuller Maitland and Barclay Squire (Breitkopf & Härtel, London and Leipzig). The editors have confined themselves to the reproduction in modern notation of all the pieces of this celebrated collection, in the order in which they occur in the manuscript, without attempting to group more or less methodically this confused and disorderly accumulation, in which are mixed up, without the slightest connection, pieces of different character and different origins.   In spite of the criticisms which have been brought against this publication[23] it none the less forms an extremely valuable document, and its appearance has been the chief starting-point of all the interest which virginal music has excited during the last few years.

Beyond the various editions of *Parthenia* which we have mentioned, and that of the *Fitzwilliam Virginal Book*, there is only a very small number of modern publications in which any pieces are to be found which do not form part of these two collections.   Thus, Mme. Farrenc reproduces in vol. ii. of the *Trésor des pianistes* a galliard (*Victoria*) by Byrd, two courantes of Crofurd, and a courante of Gibbons, taken from the old manuscripts which she possessed.[24]   Pauer publishes *Les Buffons* and the *Courante Jewel* of Bull in his

---

[22] Pauer is content to reproduce the version of Rimbault without any alteration, and without adding the graces.

[23] See Seiffert, *Geschichte der Klaviermusik*, p. 56, note 1.

[24] See above, p. 43, note 17.

Old English Composers for the Virginals and Harpsichord. In the complete works of Sweelinck, published under the direction of Seiffert, we find (vol. i., p. 125) a *Fantasia op de fuga van M. Jan Pieterss* (Sweelinck), *faecit Dr. Bull*, 1621, 15 dec., taken from MS. 23623 of the British Museum. Ritter, *Geschichte des Orgelspiels*, ii., p. 51,[25] gives us the version, in modern notation, of a *Fantasia* by Peter Philips, taken from the MS. 888 of the Library of the University of Liége. Lastly, we must mention the pieces published by Mr. John E. West in his *Old English Organ Music :* No. 25, the third part of a *Vexilla regis* of Bull, and a *Fantasia on a Flemish choral* by the same master, taken from the MS. 23623 of the British Museum; No. 14, a *Voluntary* of Orlando Gibbons belonging to the MS. 31403 of the British Museum; No 20, a *Prelude* of Edward Gibbons extracted from the Harl. MS. 7340; No. 28, a *Verse* of Christopher Gibbons.

All the other reproductions of virginal music are simply popular issues, and offer no new materials.[26]

[25] Max Hesse. Leipzig, 1886.

[26] The services they have already rendered, and which some of them may still render, induce us to draw up an inventory as below, which however, we do not give as complete :—

1. Farrenc, *Trésor des pianistes*, vol. ii. (1863). In it we find, in addition to the pieces from *Parthenia* and the compositions by Byrd, Crofurd, and Gibbons, cited above : *Prelude, The Carman's Whistle,* and *Callino Casturame* by Byrd.
2. Pauer, *Alte Klaviermusik*, 2nd series, 6th part : *Præludium* and *The Carman's Whistle* by Byrd; *The King's Hunting Jigg* by Bull; *Praeludium* and *Galliard* by Gibbons.
3. Pauer, *Old English Composers for the Virginals and Harpsichord.* In addition to the pieces from *Parthenia*, the *Courante Jewel*, and *Les Buffons* by Bull, we find *Sellenger's Round* and *The Carman's Whistle* by Byrd, and *The King's Hunting Jigg* by Bull.
4. Litolff's edition, *Les Maîtres du Clavecin* (Köhler) : *The King's Hunting Jigg* by Bull, *Prelude* and *The Carman's Whistle* by Byrd, *Prelude* and *Galiardo* by Gibbons.

Thanks to the modern editions of *Parthenia* and the *Fitzwilliam Virginal Book*, we are in a position to form a pretty complete idea as to what the virginal music of the second half of the 16th and the first quarter of the 17th century really was. We may fairly hope that what has been done for *Parthenia* and for the *Fitzwilliam Virginal Book* will also be done for *My Ladye Nevells Booke*, for *Forster's* and *Cosyn's Books*, as well as for the other manuscripts of the period.[27] In the meantime what we already possess

5. Peters' Edition, *Alte Meister des Klavierspiels* (Niemann) : *The King's Hunting Jigg* by Bull, and *The Bells* by Byrd.

6. Breitkopf & Härtel, *Encyclopédie classique du piano* (Aug. Dupont) 3rd part : Sundry pieces taken from *Parthenia; Victoria* by Byrd.

7. Breitkopf & Härtel : Messrs. Fuller Maitland and Barclay Squire have published in this edition two numbers comprising a selection of pieces taken from the *Fitzwilliam Virginal Book* : 5 of Byrd, 1 of Morley, 3 of Bull, 4 of G. Farnaby, 1 of Munday, 2 of Peerson, 1 of Philips, 1 of Robt. Johnson, and 3 anonymous. Although the selection is not always very happy, these two little books together give a fairly complete idea of the virginalists' skill in variation.

8. Augener, London, *Anthologie classique* : *The King's Hunting Jigg* by Bull and *The Carman's Whistle* by Byrd.

9. *Édition universelle, Les Anciens Maîtres* (Epstein) : *The Carman's Whistle* by Byrd and *Pavane* by Bull.

10. M. Kovacs published in 1910 or 1911, through Demets, Paris: *Barafostüs's Dreame*, anonymous, and *Quodling's Delight* by G. Farnaby.

11. Hugo Riemann reproduces several pieces taken from *Parthenia* (*Pavane* and *Galliard* by Byrd, a *Pavane* by Bull, and *The Queene's Command* by Gibbons) in his *Musikgeschichte in Beispielen* (Seemann, Leipzig, 1912).

[27] The question of *New Editions of English Virginal Music* has been the subject of a communication on the part of Max Seiffert at the Congress of the International Musical Society in London in 1911. The monthly journal of the I. M. S., XIII., iii., p. 101, reports as follows the views of Seiffert on this subject : " To continue to publish original manuscripts separately is neither desirable nor useful from a scientific point of view. It is much more urgent that we should have complete critical editions of the works of the principal masters of virginal music, such as Bull, Gibbons, &c., for which we possess a considerable amount of original material, whether on the Continent or in England."

enables us to form essential ideas on virginal music. Thus *My Ladye Nevells Booke* contains compositions by Byrd alone, to the number of thirty-seven : now, the *Fitzwilliam Virginal Book* alone gives us seventy compositions of his, a dozen of which are common both to the celebrated manuscript and the virginal book of Lady Nevell. *Forster's Book* contains for the most part the compositions of Byrd—thirty-three, nearly a third part of which are already to be found in the *Fitzwilliam Virginal Book*. Beyond this, we find a very small number of the compositions of Bull, who is represented by forty-four pieces in the *Fitzwilliam Virginal Book*. There remain two pieces by Morley, of whom the *Fitzwilliam Virginal Book* gives us eight compositions ; one piece by an unknown master, Englitt (possibly the Inglott of the *Fitzwilliam Virginal Book*) ; nine pieces by John Ward, which scarcely present any special interest for the reason that according to their titles they seem to be nothing but transcriptions of vocal music ; lastly, some anonymous pieces—simple dances for the most part. As to the virginal book of Benjamin Cosyn, it stands almost on the same footing as those of Lady Nevell and Forster, with this difference, that it contains a considerable number of compositions (twenty-six) of a master of great importance, Orlando Gibbons, of whom *Parthenia* and the *Fitzwilliam Virginal Book* give us but a limited number of works. So far then as regards this master we have to put up with a void much to be regretted—a void moreover more important from a purely æsthetic than from the actual historic point of view, for if this musician charms us by the originality of his musical ideas, he does not occupy, so far as regards the creation of virginal technique, the place of honour of a Byrd or a Bull. Coming after them, he was content to profit by the progress which they had already achieved in this technique, and to adapt it to his own way of feeling.[28]

[28] Dr. Naylor (*An Elizab. Virg. B.*, p. 4) is tacitly in agreement with us when he says : "It is not going too far to say that if all other remains of this period were destroyed it would be possible to re-write the history of music from 1550 to 1620 on the material which we have in the *Fitzwilliam Virginal Book* alone."

CHAPTER II.

THE VIRGINALISTS. AN ATTEMPTED GROUPING AND BIOGRAPHICAL NOTES.

IN order to form an accurate idea of the gradual development of virginal music from the middle of the 16th century until about the year 1630, above everything it is desirable to make a chronological and systematic table of the masters of the keyboard, who successively brought their activity into play during the course of that period. Max Seiffert has already attempted a sketch of such a table in his *Geschichte der Klaviermusik*.[1] We are about to attempt to enlarge it by entering into further details, which will enable us to give an accurate account of the part which these musicians filled in the development of the art of the virginal. We rely for biographical details on the most generally admitted facts, completing and correcting these in those cases where recent documents have succeeded in shedding fresh light. On the other hand, we

[1] Pp. 56 and 57.

shall include in this table only those virginalists whose works have been rendered accessible by means of modern reprints.

1. In the first place we find a group of musicians, the date of whose birth is anterior to 1550 :—

ROBERT PARSONS, the date of whose birth is unknown, but who died January 25, 1569 or 1570. He became a *sworn-gentleman* of the Chapel Royal October 17, 1563.

THOMAS TALLIS, born between 1510-20, died in 1585, as organist of the Chapel Royal.

WILLIAM BLITHEMAN, the date of whose birth is unknown. We know that he became organist of the Chapel Royal after the death of Tallis in 1585, and that he occupied that post till his own death in 1591. He must have been pretty old at that time, for he was already chief chorister of Christ Church, Oxford, in 1564.

WILLIAM BYRD, born about 1542-43,[2] died at a great age in 1623.

2. Then follows a numerous generation of virginalists, the date of whose birth falls, either with certainty or with probability, between 1550-70 :—

EDMUND HOOPER, born about 1553, died in 1621, organist of Westminster Abbey. He is mentioned as being a member of the English Chapel Royal in 1603, 1612, and 1618.[3]

WILLIAM INGLOTT, born about 1554, died in 1621.

THOMAS MORLEY, born in 1557, died probably in 1602 or a little later,[4] organist of St. Paul's Cathedral.

---

[2] Riemann (*Handb. der Musikg.* (1907), II., i., p. 339) gives 1543. Walker (*A History of Music in Engl.*) (1907), p. 53) suggests 1542 or 1543.

[3] See *The King's Musick*, by the Rev. H. Cart de Lafontaine, pp. 44, 50, and 52. Novello, London, 1909.

[4] According to Walker, *op. cit.*, p. 52.

E

FERDINANDO RICHARDSON,[5] born about 1558, died
in 1618. He was a pupil of Tallis, and became
Chamberlain to Queen Elizabeth in 1587.

PETER PHILIPS, born between 1550-60. Left
England probably about 1590, and settled
soon afterwards in the Netherlands for the
remainder of his life. He died in 1628.[6]

JOHN BULL, born about 1562, died in 1628. He
left England in 1613, and was organist to the
Archduke Albert at Brussels, up to 1617, from
which date he became organist of the Cathedral
at Antwerp.

THOMAS WARROCK, or WARWICK, became organist
of Hereford in 1586. The date of his birth
is probably between 1560-65. He was still
living in 1642. He certainly died before
1660.[7]

JOHN MUNDAY, became Bachelor of Music of the
University of Oxford in 1586, and married in
1587. As the Bachelor's degree was generally
taken between twenty and twenty-five years of
age, we may assume that this musician was
born about 1563-4.[8] He died in 1630.

GILES FARNABY, began his musical studies about
1580, and took his Bachelor's degree at Oxford

[5] The youthful name of Ferdinando Heyborne.

[6] According to a note which appeared in the *Musical Antiquary* of
July, 1911 (p. 241).

[7] The accounts of the English Court state that Warwick succeeded
Gibbons in 1624-25 as virginalist in the company of the *King's Musicians*
(*Musical Antiquary*, January, 1912, p. 114). It follows from these same
accounts (*Mus. Ant.*, July, 1912, p. 232) that he was still in the service of
the Court in 1641-42. On the other hand, the registers of the *Record Office*
(see *The King's Musick*, by the Rev. H. Cart de Lafontaine, p. 118),
mention that after his death he was replaced, at the time of the
Restoration, in 1660, by Christopher Gibbons.

[8] About 1566, according to the programme of the Historical Concert of
May 30, 1911, arranged in London on the occasion of the Congress of the
International Musical Society.

in 1592. We may therefore assume that he was born about 1569-70. All trace of him is lost after 1598.[9]

ROBERT JOHNSON was born in 1569, and died before November 26, 1633.[10]

JOHN PARSONS, who, if he was, as may be supposed, the son of the elder Robert Parsons mentioned above, must have been born before 1569 or 1570, the date of the death of Robert. He died in 1623.

3. We now come to a new generation, that of the virginalists who were born, either certainly, or probably, between 1570 and 1600:—

EDWARD JOHNSON took the degree of Bachelor of Music at Cambridge in 1594. Of him nothing further is known.

ORLANDO GIBBONS, born in 1583, obtained his Bachelor's degree at Cambridge in 1606, was organist of the Chapel Royal from 1604-25, and of Westminster Abbey from 1623-25. In addition he held the post of virginalist at the Court from 1619-25, the year of his death.[11]

MARTIN PEERSON became Bachelor of Music at Oxford in 1613, and died in 1650.

RICHARD FARNABY, of whom we know nothing unless he was the son of Giles Farnaby.

[9] G. Farnaby was a native of Cornwall. The fact that we find a great number of the compositions of this master in the *Fitzw. V. B.*, while he is unrepresented in the other collections of virginal music, is a fresh argument in favour of the compilation of the Cambridge manuscript by or for Francis Tregian the younger. It is obvious, in fact, that the latter would be specially interested in the work of a musician of importance born in the same region to which the Tregians belonged by birth.

[10] He was attached to the English Court as lutenist. After his death he was replaced by Nicholas Duvall, on November 26, 1633 (*The King's Musick*, p. 86).

[11] See *Musical Antiquary* of October, 1911 (p. 58), and of January, 1912 (p. 110 ff.).

THOMAS TOMKINS, of whom we know that he died in 1656, and that he was the son of one Tomkins, also a musician, who lived during the second half of the 16th century. He was organist of the English Chapel Royal.[12]

4. We next come to a series of musicians about whom we possess chronological details too vague for us to be able to class them with any one of the preceding groups:—

GIOVANNI PICHI, an Italian, represented in the *Fitzwilliam Virginal Book* by a single composition, was organist at the Casa Grande at Venice at the beginning of the 17th century. In 1621 he brought out a reprint—the only edition actually known—of his interesting *Balli d'Arpicordo* (Dances for the Harpsichord). In 1624 he took part in a competition for the place of second organist at St. Mark's, at Venice, and was unsuccessful.

FRANCIS TREGIAN, the probable compiler of the *Fitzwilliam Virginal Book*, died about 1619.

NICHOLAS STROGERS was an organist of the reign of James I. (1603-25).[13]

5. Lastly, there is a short series of composers, whose names only are known to us—Marchant,[14] Galeazzo, Oldfield, Oystermaire, Tisdall, and Crofurd.

---

[12] He appears for the first time in that position in the registers of the *Record Office* of 1625 (*The King's Musick*, p. 58).

[13] The article of Mr. Arkwright, *Early Elizabethan Stage Music*, which appeared in the *Musical Antiquary* of January, 1913, contains some interesting details about Strogers.

[14] In *Cosyn's Virginal Book* we find as No. 32, a piece entitled, *The Marchant's Dreame*. Does this refer to Marchant, by whom the *Fitzw. V. B.* contains an *Allemanda*, and whose name occurs among the composers of the MS. 30485 of the British Museum?

CHAPTER III.

————

ATTEMPT AT A CHRONOLOGICAL ARRANGEMENT OF THE WORKS OF THE VIRGINALISTS.

Having attempted to group according to chronological order, partly accurate, partly approximative, the composers who have written music for the virginal, it is desirable to make a similar attempt as to the works which they have left.

This chronological grouping will interest us only so far as it may help us the better to understand the evolutionary development of virginal technique. From this point of view it may be looked on as a settled fact that this technique was completely formed at the period of *Parthenia*—that is to say, about 1611. We may therefore, without inconvenience, dispense with further research of a date subsequent to that year.

From the period extending from the early sources of virginal music to 1611, information is furnished in the two following manners, firstly, by the fact that several pieces in the *Fitzwilliam Virginal Book* are dated in a manner either precise or inferential; secondly, that all the pieces by Byrd which are found in *My Ladye Nevells Booke* date at the very latest from 1591, the period at which the compilation of the manuscript was completed; it thus results that all the compositions of this master which we come across in the *Fitzwilliam Virginal Book*, and which are common to this manuscript and to the collection of Lady Nevell, are anterior to 1592.

The most ancient dated pieces to be found in the *Fitzwilliam Virginal Book* are two figurations of a plainsong by Tallis, entitled *Felix namque*. According to the written notes of the manuscript, the one (*Fitzwilliam Virginal Book*, i., p. 427[1]) is dated 1562, and the other (vol. ii., p. 1) 1564. From 1564 we make a jump to 1580, a date at which we find a *Pavane* by Philips (*Fitzw. V. B.*, i., p. 343), shortly followed by a *Fantasia* by the same composer, dated 1582 (vol. i., p. 352). We are now approaching the period of the compilation of *My Ladye Nevells Booke*, and we meet with a piece by Byrd common to the two manuscripts (*The Wood's so wild*, *Fitzw. V. B.*, i., p. 263), which is dated 1590. Here we are able to group all the pieces by Byrd not dated in the *Fitzw. V. B.*, but which are equally to be found in *Nevells Booke*. Twelve come under this category.[2]

[1] From this point the Roman and Arabic figures, preceded by the abridged words, *Fitzw. V. B.*, signify the volume of the modern reprint of the *Fitzwilliam Virginal Book* in which are published the pieces alluded to, and the page on which they will be found in the volumes.

[2] *The Carman's Whistle* (*Fitzw. V. B.*, i., p. 214): *The Hunt's up* (i., p. 218), *Walsingham* (i., p. 267); *All in a garden green* (i., p. 411); *The Mayden's song* (ii., p. 67); *Rowland* (ii., p. 190); *Pescodd time* (ii., p. 430); *Passamezzo Pavana* (i., p. 203) and *Galiardas Passamezzo* (i., p. 209); *Sellinger's Round* (ii., p. 248); *The Earle of Oxford Marche* (ii., p. 402); and *Treg. ground* (i., 226).

After 1590-91, so far as regards dated works, we have only arranged transcriptions of madrigals and variations of dances by Philips. The first are : *Le Rossignol* (1595) (*Fitzw. V. B.*, i., p. 346), *Bonjour mon cœur* (1602, *id.*, p. 317), *Amarilli di Julio Romano* (1603, *id.*, p. 329), and *Margott Laborez* (1605, *id.*, p. 332). The varied dances are : *Passamezzo Pavana* (1592, *id.*, i., p. 299), and the *Pavana dolorosa* (1593, *id.*, p. 321).

Let us remark further that the pieces which are common to the *Fitzw. V. B.* and to *Parthenia* are of the date 1611 at the very latest. Their number is but small. They are : a prelude by Byrd (No. 4 in *Parthenia, Fitzw. V. B.*, i., p. 83) ; a *Galiardo St. Thomas Wake*, by Bull (No. 11 of *Parthenia, Fitzw. V. B.*, i., p. 131) ; a second galliard by Bull (No. 15 of *Parthenia, Fitzw. V. B.*, ii., p. 249) ; *The lord of Salisbury his pavin*, by Gibbons (*Parthenia* No. 18, *Fitzw. V. B.*, ii., p. 479),—say, four pieces out of the twenty-one contained in *Parthenia*.

As no piece in the *Virginal Book* of Forster (1624) is dated, we are unable to find materials to fix accurately the date of the pieces common to that manuscript and the *Fitzw. V. B.* The same is the case with the *Virginal Book* of Benjamin Cosyn, the date of which is unknown, but which, as we have already seen, may be considered as having been collected at a period when the technique of the virginal was completely settled.

There remain a few particulars which serve to give us approximations as to the chronology of certain works. Thus the figured plainsong

In nomine (*Fitzw. V. B.*, i., p. 181) by Blitheman, dates at the latest from 1591, the year of the death of that master. For the pieces of that very finished virginalist, Giles Farnaby, it may be admitted that the most important among them are later than 1592, the date at which that musician acquired his degree of Bachelor. As to John Bull, who is of capital importance from the point of view of the progress of virginal technique, we have scarcely anything which can help us to establish, even approximately, the chronology of his virginal works; we may, however, suppose that it was only after he had obtained the degree of Bachelor, in 1586, that he set himself to compose those works the virtuosity of which has gained for him the title of the " Liszt of his time." [3] He had unquestionably made notable progress in that direction at the time when, having become a Doctor of the University of Cambridge, he was ordered by Queen Elizabeth (in 1595) to give two lectures on music weekly at Gresham College; and his technique was no doubt completely formed when in 1601 he undertook that extended travel on the Continent, in the course of which he astonished all those who heard him by his exceptional gifts of virtuosity. [4]

May we not deduce from these different particulars that it was approximately between 1590 and 1600 that were elaborated those daring innovations by which part of his work is distinguished? Finally, let us remark that the seven pieces by him which are found in *Parthenia*

---

[3] See Seiffert, *Geschichte der Klaviermusik*, p. 87, Note 2.

[4] See Seiffert, *Geschichte der Klaviermusik*, pp. 86 and 87.

are previous to 1612, as well as those by Byrd and Gibbons contained in the same collection.[5]

[5] Here are a few chronological details of less importance :—Byrd (*Fitzw. V. B.*, ii., p. 42), Morley (ii., p. 173), and G. Farnaby (ii., p. 472), wrote variations on the celebrated *Lachrymae* of Dowland, a vocal piece in the rhythm of a pavan, which appeared in the $S^{d.}$ *Book of Songs or Ayres* of that master in 1600. It is extremely probable that these three versions for the virginal are posterior to that date. It is very likely that the galliard which follows the version of Byrd (subject by Harding, *Fitzw. V.B.*, ii., p. 47), and that which accompanies the setting by Morley (*Fitzw. V. B.*, ii., p. 177), are also later than 1600.

It may be admitted also that the *Pavana Delight* by Byrd (*Fitzw. V. B.*, ii., p. 436), and the *Galiarda* which follows (*Fitzw. V. B.*, ii., p. 440), are subsequent to 1594, since they borrow their thematic material from Edward Johnson, who took his Bachelor's degree in that year.

We might make many other remarks of this nature. We confine ourselves for the present to these few examples, leaving us free to consider from time to time these questions of chronology when we take up the detailed analysis of virginalistic production.

CHAPTER IV.

THE NEW FIGURAL MATERIAL OF
THE VIRGINALISTS.

It may seem strange to treat of virginalistic figuration before we have studied the forms and styles of the music to which it was applied. This apparent anomaly finds its justification in the fact that this figuration does not consist in certain ornaments plastered afterwards on to virginal pieces, but actually of real material, the purpose of which is truly organic. In proceeding as we are about to do, we act in some sort as an architect who, finding himself in a country of which as yet he is ignorant, were to begin by making himself acquainted with the materials which were there in use, before undertaking to build. Knowing in advance the essential elements of virginalistic technique, we shall be in a better position to give an account of the way in which the English keyboard artists conceived and realised the plan of their musical edifices.

We are compelled, so far as is possible, to group the forms of virginal figuration in relation with certain principles which we find in the development of music in general. It is in relying on this foundation that we have drawn up the following table :—

I. Archaic figures (faux-bourdon; ternary figures; short detached counterpoints (hoketus) ; figural imitation).

II. Figures of a progressive character :—
  1. Melodic (embroidery ; sequence ; repetition of notes).
  2. Rhythmic (triolets and sextolets ; rhythmic figures, properly so called ; figures in cross rhythm ; symmetrical figuration).
  3. Harmonic (counterpoint in thirds or in sixths ; suspensions and appoggiaturas ; spreading or decomposition of intervals or chords).

III. Various figures (figures of Italian origin ; graces, &c.).

We will consider these various figures in turn, and analyse the many aspects under which they appear in the work of the virginalists.

I.—Archaic Figures.

If we consider their origins, the archaic figures may rightly be considered as *polyphonic*, as opposed to the melodic, rhythmic, or harmonic figures which we shall study later.   The first which we meet with is :—

(I.) FAUX-BOURDON.

Originally, faux-bourdon was not figural, but a form of polyphony which had its birth in England. It was formed in the Middle Ages in the following manner : upon a given *cantus firmus* (tenor) a counterpoint was created, which, starting from the octave above, to return to it at the conclusion of the musical phrase, followed step by step the *cantus firmus* at the sixth above, in all that part of the latter which lay between the first and last notes. Example :—

A very consonant form of polyphony was thus obtained, by the English called *gymel*, which means " twin voices," that is to say, strictly dependent on each other.

If, taking the *gymel* for foundation, an intermediary part is placed between the tenor and its counterpoint at the sixth,—this third part being placed at the fifth above the *cantus firmus* at the beginning and end of the phrase, and at the third above this same *cantus firmus* in the interval comprised between the first and the last chords,—we obtain what the English called *faburden* (*faux-bourdon* in French, and *falso bordone* in Italian). This invention having crossed the Channel, was rapidly adopted in France, the Netherlands, and Italy. Here is an example of faux-bourdon applied to the *gymel* above :—

It consists, as we see, of a succession of chords of thirds and sixths, very consonant in character,

encompassed in chords of three parts, in their
original position, but wanting their thirds (hollow
fifths).[1]

This is not the place to recall the important part
which faux-bourdon has played in the formation of
harmony, at a period when the theorists refused to
recognise a true consonance in the third.   What is
of interest to us is that the virginalists made use
of faux-bourdon as an element of figuration.   We
shall find it specially in the most ancient virginalist
of the *Fitzw. V. B.*, Thomas Tallis, in his second
figured plainsong, *Felix namque* (*Fitzw. V. B.*, ii., 1),
of the date 1564.   It there appears under the
following forms (pp. 4 and 5) :—

In the first example the lower part undergoes a
figuration by means of the neighbouring notes
(conjoint degrees) : curious appoggiaturas are the
result.   In the second example the lower part
undergoes a figuration by disjoint degrees, which
has the result of putting hollow fifths between

[1] See on this subject Riemann, *Handb. der Musikgeschichte* I., ii.,
p. 162 ff.

each of the chords of sixths, the succession of which forms the faux-bourdon.[2]

After Tallis, John Bull is the only virginalist who still used faux-bourdon as a means of figuration. It is curious to find that the man who most contributed to the advancement of virginalistic technique should have remained for so long a time attached to a formula of this archaic nature. We must not be too astonished; the learned Cambridge doctor delighted in showing the comprehensiveness of his knowledge; moreover, in his case we often find by the side of very spontaneous inspirations displays of a scholastic spirit tinged with a certain pedantry. It is also in the form of the figured plainsong that Bull has most often used the faux-bourdon as a means of figuration.

Example: Plainsong, *Salvator mundi* (*Fitzw. V. B.*, i., p. 163), p. 168:—

(Unfigured form of faux-bourdon. Notes of the Plainsong in the *superius*.)

---

[2] The figuration of the faux-bourdon goes back much farther than Tallis. Figured faux-bourdon is met with frequently in the motets of Dufay (15th century). Hugo Leichtentritt (*Gesch. der Motette*, p. 398, Breitkopf & Härtel, Leipzig, 1908) remarks that Tallis uses faux-bourdon abundantly in certain of his vocal sacred works.

Example: *In nomine (Fitzw. V. B.*, p. 34) p. 39:—

(Unfigured form, obtained by successive imitations, on the third and sixth of a rising scale. Notes of the plainsong in the bass.[3])

Bull also made use of the faux-bourdon in his variations on the scale of solmisation, *ut, re, mi, fa, sol, la (Fitzw. V. B.*, ii., p. 281), a scholastic piece, the interest of which is purely theoretical; there he generally uses it in the unfigured form. At the end of the piece (p. 291) he ornaments it with a light rhythmic figuration :—

(*Cantus firmus* in the *superius*.)[4]

(2.) TERNARY FIGURES.

Here again we are carried back into the actual Middle Ages, at the controversial period of mensural notation. Theory admits ternary values only, in

[3] We find besides in the same piece other examples of figural faux-bourdon more or less concealed under a figuration of the second power.

[4] The *figural* character of faux-bourdon is very plainly evident in Bull's music, since the master on every occasion uses this archaic formula to serve as accompaniment to a *cantus firmus*. With Tallis, on the other hand, passages in faux-bourdon are rather passages of transition which intervene in places where the *cantus firmus* is interrupted or seems to be interrupted.

conformity with the dogma of the Holy Trinity, and rejects binary values. But practice makes use of the latter without worrying about the speculations of the theorists, who themselves finished in the 14th century by bending to the fact and making their theories agree with the deductions of practice.

If to this strife between ternary and binary values we add the circumstance that in the polyphony of the Middle Ages the parts which formed the contrapuntal edifice possessed, apart from special cases such as organum, gymel, and faux-bourdon, a melodic and rhythmic independence as complete as possible one from the other, we easily come to understand why in polyphonic pieces of that time we meet so frequently with passages where the binary and ternary constantly alternate and at times run counter to each other in a very curious manner, the equivalent of which we find in certain ultra-modern compositions of to-day.[5] Here, for example, is a passage taken from a madrigal by Jacobus de Bononia, extracted from the *Codex Squarcialupi* and published in modern notation in vol. i. of the *Arte musicale in Italia* of Torchi:—

(The upper part advances by values sometimes ternary (triplets), sometimes binary; the second

---

[5] The French at the end of the Middle Ages called these rhythmic combinations by the name of *trayn* or *traynour*. See Riemann, *Handb. der Musikg.* II., i., p. 5. Johannes Wolf defines the idea of the *traynour* by means of examples in his *Geschichte der Mensuralnotation*, i., pp. 140 and 294.

part is in the same condition, but the alternations occur in different places.)

In the 15th century this state of things appeared very frequently, and we find numerous examples in the work of G. Dufay. Thus, in this curious passage of the song, *Belle, que vous ai-je mesfait*[6] :—

In these examples there is no question of figuration, but really of principal melodies, each having its own individuality and importance. We shall see that the virginalists utilised these curious combinations of rhythm in a manner purely figural; and they were not the only composers in the 16th century thus to make use of them. We find in fact several examples in the work of the Spaniard Cabezon.[7]

The oldest virginalist in whom we meet this kind of figuration is Blitheman. His figured plainsong, *In nomine* (*Fitzw. V. B.*, i., p. 181), offers an example at its very outset :—

[6] See *Denkmäler der Tonkunst in Oesterreich*, 11 Jahrg., 1 Teil, p. 77.

[7] See, among others, the *Tiento del segundo tono* (*in fine*) taken from the *Obras de Musica* (1578) and reproduced in modern notation as No. 1 in vol. iv. of the *Hispania Schola Musica Sacra*.

(The *cantus firmus* is in the alto. Figuration in triplets in the bass, then in the *superius*. Here we have no crossing rhythms.)

After Blitheman, William Byrd furnishes us with examples in a figured plainsong, *Miserere* (*Fitzw. V. B.*, ii., p. 230), and in his secular variations, *Walsingham* (*Fitzw. V. B.*, i., p. 267), and *The Mayden's Song* (ii., p. 67). These last two pieces are earlier than 1592.

Miserere :—

(There is here a contrariety of rhythm between the counterpoint in sextolets and the counterpoint in quartolets. *Cantus firmus* in the *superius*.)

Walsingham :—

(Triplets in opposition to duolets. *Cantus firmus* in the *tenor*.)

In *The Mayden's Song* we find curious complications of rhythm, among others :—

(In this case archaism unites with modernism,
owing to the subtlety of the rhythm in the very
middle of the ternary group.   *Cantus firmus* in the
superius.)

John Bull in the same way made use of these
ternary figures of the Middle Ages.   He in fact it is
who supplies us with the largest number of examples.
We find them in two of his figured plainsongs, in
two of his scholastic pieces, in a secular variation,
and in a gigue.   Although in this last piece we have
really to do with a figure in every way similar to
those which we have come across up to now, we may
fairly ask, the essentially secular and progressive
nature of the piece being granted, whether it is not
rather a subtlety of a modernist character, which in
the intention of the author has little to do with the
old formula of the Middle Ages?

A Gigge (*Fitzw. V. B.*, ii., p. 258) :—

In the plainsong *Gloria tibi trinitas* the archaic character is beyond doubt (*Fitzw. V. B.*, i., p. 160), as well as in the *Christe Redemptor* (*Fitzw. V. B.*, ii., p. 64), where we find the following curious passage :—

(*Cantus firmus* in the *tenor*.)

The two scholastic pieces, which consist of variations on the scale of solmisation, *ut, re, mi, fa, sol, la*, also offer characteristic examples of the use of this kind of figuration (*Fitzw. V. B.*, i., p. 183, and ii., p. 281). Lastly, in the thirty variations *Walsingham* (*Fitzw. V. B.*, i., p. 1), in which Bull has accumulated all the methods of figuration of his time, are to be found examples of ternary figures (var. 20 ff.), but they are complicated with such rhythmical subtleties that their archaism appears strongly modernised.[8]

[8] On this subject it is interesting to notice that on the borders of the 16th and 17th centuries there appeared throughout the whole of Western Europe, whether in the domain of rhythm or in that of harmony, a constant blending of ancient and modern notions. A sort of struggle took place between the comparatively free rhythm of the ancient polyphony, and the new idea of " square " rhythm, regulated by the measure of the bar. (See Leichtentritt, *Gesch. der Motette*, p. 301, à propos of the motets of Hassler.) Max Seiffert, who has closely studied the notation of the virginalistic manuscripts, remarks that triplets are indifferently expressed in them by the mensural methods of the Middle Ages and by modern methods (*Vierteljahrschrift für Musikwissenschaft*, 1891, p. 147, and *Introduction* to vol. i of the complete works of Sweelinck, p. ix.).

(3.) SHORT DETACHED COUNTERPOINTS (HOKETUS).

A single example will make us understand in what this third formula of archaic figuration consists. We borrow it from the first *Felix namque* of Tallis (1562, *Fitzw. V. B.*, i., 427) :—

(*Cantus firmus* in the *superius*.)

One has no trouble in tracing the origin of this figure to a manner of writing dating back to the 12th century, which bore the curious name of *hoketus, hoquet, hoccitatio*.[9] It consists in the fact that two parts, vocal or instrumental, became silent and re-entered alternately, at a very short interval, so as to form short melodic fragments, detached one from the other. Here is an example, taken from a motet by Guillaume de Machault (14th century) :—

[9] See Riemann, *Handb. der Musikg.*, I., 2, p. 212 ff.

This manner of polyphonic writing was practised throughout musical Europe, more especially between the 12th and the 14th century inclusive,[10] and there can be no doubt that the figure used by the virginalists was directly derived from it.

We meet it for the first time in the *Felix namque* of 1562 by Tallis. In this its value is purely figural; but there exists another piece by Tallis in which we see this manner of writing made use of with a melodic intention analogous to that which the polyphonists of the Middle Ages gave to it. We refer to the *Lesson* which Weitzmann published in the musical supplement to the second edition of his *Geschichte des Klavierspiels*.[11] This piece is an absolutely strict canon in two parts, which are joined, from the second third of the piece, by a third part which forms a figural bass. The whole of one part of the canon is conceived as a *hoketus* at once imitative and sequential :—

[10] Hugo Riemann (*Handb. der Musikg*. II., 1, p. 410) remarks that we still find it in use in the vocal music of the 16th century, particularly with the descriptive polyphonist *par excellence*, C. Jannequin. We have found a very expressive example in a polyphonic song of the Netherlands of the opening of the 16th century (*Een sotte cluytte;* see, *in fine*, the passage : *Aÿ mÿ*), taken by Johannes Wolf from Addl. MS. 35087 of the British Museum, and published in *Uitgave xxx.* of the *Vereeniging voor Noord-Nederlands Muziekgeschiedenis* (p. 26).
    As to the term " hoquet," we have found it used in its musical sense well into the 18th century, in a French satirical review, *L'Amour maître de langue* (1718). One of the characters offers himself as a master of Italian music, and represents himself as the " restorer of doubles, of ricochets, sighs and *hoquets*, the inventor of cantatas, tremblings, nightingalings, and mewings." It is not unlikely that "hoquet" coming immediately after " sighs " has preserved something of its ancient meaning (see *l'Année musicale* of 1912, Alcan, Paris, article by M. Cucuel, p. 151).

[11] This *Lesson* is taken from MS. 30485 of the British Museum.

After Tallis, the English virginalists of the 16th and of the beginning of the 17th centuries continued to make use of the figural *hoketus* under very various aspects, which often partook of imitation or of sequence.   There is no appearance of any development in its use.   Thus Byrd, the immediate successor of Tallis, hardly makes use of it at all, but we come across it pretty frequently with John Bull and with Giles Farnaby, although they belong to later generations.

Here are a few examples :—

Pavane by Philips (1580) (*Fitzw. V. B.,* i., p. 343):—

(Here the *hoketus*, appearing simultaneously in several parts, has a harmonic character.)

In nomine by Bull (*Fitzw. V. B.,* i., p. 35):—

(The *hoketus* is mixed up with imitation and the spreading of the chords.)

Christe redemptor of Bull (*Fitzw. V. B.*, ii., p. 64) :—

(Same remark as for the preceding example.)

Galliard by Bull (*Fitzw. V. B.*, i., p. 177) :—

(The *hoketus* affects a single part only, and assumes the appearance of a sequence.)

In nomine by Parsons (*Fitzw. V. B.*, ii., p. 135) :—

(The *hoketus* has a harmonic character, producing the effect of chimes.)

Tomkins uses the *hoketus* in four of the five pieces by him which occur in the *Fitzw. V. B.*

Example: *Worster Braules* (ii., *Fitzw. V. B.*, p. 269) :—

(The *hoketus* presenting rhythmic complications.[12])

(4.) FIGURAL IMITATION.

We must now dwell a little on this form of figuration, which by its constant use occupies so important a place in virginalistic material.

When or where arose the idea of causing one singing voice to be imitated by another singing voice, when the first has already made its entry, is a question which has caused much controversy, and on which it would be difficult to come to a decision. But from actual documents we are at any rate able to affirm that imitation was already cultivated in France in the 12th century, and very probably also in England at the same period.[13] It developed insensibly in the course of ages, to attain, with the Belgian Ockeghem during the second half of the 15th century, the summit of perfection and refinement. The imitative counterpoint of Ockeghem and of his Franco-Belgian pupils spread rapidly throughout all

[12] Cabezon more than once used the figural *hoketus;* see among others the *Diferencias sobre la pavana italiana,* taken from his *Obras* of 1578, in the *Hisp. Schol. Mus. Sacr.,* vol. viii., p. 6.

[13] The famous canon, *Sumer is icumen in,* dating from about 1240, presupposes from all the evidence a use of imitation at a period at least as remote as the preceding century.

Europe, and notably to England, to Italy, and to Spain. From vocal music it soon passed into the domain of instrumental music, in which it found its natural use in the strict forms of the *ricercare* or *tiento*, and of the *canzona francese*.

The English composers of the 16th century largely made use of imitation in their vocal works, whether they belonged to the austere sacred motet or Mass, or to the lighter *genre* of the madrigal.

The virginalists went further, in that they made use of imitation as a means of figuration. In what manner? An example will show us. Let us take the variations of Byrd on the song *John come kisse me now* (*Fitzw. V. B.*, i., p. 47):—

Announcement of the theme:—

Beginning of the second variation:—

(Two imitations at the octave, one without *stretto*, the other with *stretto*.)

Beginning of the fourth variation :—

(Two imitations at the ninth (or the second), one without *stretto*, one with *stretto*.)

We see that the subject submitted to variation is accompanied by short figures which give place to imitations.   Such is virginal figural imitation ; it shows itself always under this same aspect of little ornamental figures giving rise to imitations, on variable intervals, with or without *stretti*.   The inventiveness of the English musicians succeeds in an infinite variety of the inter-play of these little imitative combinations ; and they had the capacity of uniting under these conditions the nicest ingenuity with the most perfect spontaneity.

Has the use of imitative figures undergone a development ?   We may assert with certainty that there has been an actual development, in virtue of which the nearer we approach to 1610-20, the less were these little figures brought into use.   Byrd, one of the oldest masters, has a particular affection for them, and uses them systematically in almost two-thirds of those of his works which we have been able to analyse.   With Bull we only find them appearing not more often than in about a third of his pieces.   With Farnaby there seems to be a recrudescence : nearly half of his compositions give characteristic examples of imitative figures ;

and finally, in the forty-six anonymous pieces contained in the *Fitzw. V. B.*, which to all appearances belong to the 17th century,[14] there are only six cases in which we come across these figures. This tendency to a more or less increasing restraint in the use of imitative figuration coincides with the general bent of the period in favour of the harmonic idea, as opposed to the ancient polyphonic conception: and it is precisely from the moment that the new style of accompanied monody spread —that is to say, from the beginning of the 17th century—that we find arising a gradual abandonment of figuration based upon imitation. We shall see further on how gradually sequence took the place of the latter, and ended in a great measure in supplanting it.

In a certain number of pieces imitation shows itself under the appearance of an echo. Such is the case, for example, in *A Medley* of Byrd (*Fitzw. V. B.*, ii., p. 220) :—

[14] It is inconceivable, in fact, that the compiler of the manuscript could have included in it anonymous pieces dating from a period so remote from that of the compilation ; he was not influenced, in fact, by the prepossessions of antiquarian research. Moreover, the greater part of the anonymous pieces of the *Fitzw. V.B.* have actually the style and character of works written at the very period of the compilation of the manuscript.

[15] See, again, certain other passages of the same piece ; in addition, *Tregian's Ground* by Byrd (*Fitzw. V. B.*, i., p. 226) ; *Passamezzo Pavana* by Byrd (*Fitzw. V. B.*, i., p. 203), *Galiarda* by Bull (*Fitzw. V. B.*, ii., p. 251).
This effect of echo is taken from vocal music, more especially from the style in double chorus (see in the *Jahrb. der Musikbibliothek Peters* of 1909, an essay by Kroyer, *Dialog und Echo in der alten Chormusik*).

II.—FIGURES OF A PROGRESSIVE CHARACTER.

As we have seen, the figures of a progressive character group into melodic, rhythmic, and harmonic figures.

A.—MELODIC FIGURES.

The first melodic figure that attracts our attention is :—

(I.) EMBROIDERY.

Embroidery consists in the art of elaborating a mere simple melody by means of contours which give it a more ornamented and active appearance. In its origin this art is in reality very ancient; it might almost be maintained that it is as old as melody itself.[16] If, however, we have decided that we could rank the melodic embroidery of the virginalists among the figures of a progressive character, it is for a double reason : in the first place the widespread idea which it represents[17] prevents it from taking a place in the somewhat narrow limits which the term " archaic " suggests, and moreover the applications

---

[16] We find examples of embroidery which is at the same time rhythmical and melodic even in the songs of birds. B. Hoffmann (*Musikalische Frühlingswanderungen*, in *Die Musik*, XII., xviii., p. 334) records some very curious ones which he observed in the coletit (*Kohlmeise*) and the thrush (*Zippe* or *Singdrossel*).

The pretended polyphony of the Greeks seems to have been merely an elementary form of embroidery, applied to a monodic instrumental accompaniment, performed at the unison or the octave of the voice (Riemann, *Handb. der Musikg.*, I., i., p. 144 ff).

The Gregorian plainsong, from its very origin, made use officially of embroidery (*L'Art grégorien*, par A. Gastoué : Alcan, Paris ; p. 30 ff).

The Italian *frottola* of the 15th and the early 16th centuries gives us specially characteristic examples (*Die Frottole*, by R. Schwartz, *Viertelj. für Musikw.*, 1886, p. 463).

[17] It must not be lost sight of that embroidery is still at the present day one of the essential bases of musical development as much in the realm of dramatic and programme music as in that of absolute music.

which the virginalists have made of it are so novel
and so varied that it would be unjust not to look
on them as elements of progress in the development of instrumental music.

It is not implied that the English masters of the
keyboard were without precursors in this direction,
either in their own country or on the Continent.
At an earlier period the little English pieces for
the organ of the 14th century, analysed by
Wolf, present rudimentary examples of melodic
embroidery. At the rise of the 16th century
Hughe Ashton shows that this training had reached
a comparatively high degree of perfection.

Again, in Spain the lutenists of the first half of
the 16th century,[18] as well as Cabezon, practised
contemporaneously with those unknown virginalists
who formed the bridge between Ashton and Tallis,
an art of melodic embroidery which was very
refined, and thus contributed to a very important
extent in laying the foundations of the new kind of
instrumental variation.

An actual example will show us under what form
this pre-eminently melodic figuration shows itself
among the .virginalists. Here is a dance subject
treated in variation form by G. Farnaby :—

Spagnioletta (Fitzw. V. B., i., p. 199) :—

<hr />

[18] See Morphy, *Les luthistes espagnols,* in two volumes, 1902. "Lute"
and "lutenists" are here taken in quite a general sense, including both
the Italian *liuto* and the Spanish *vihuela.*

The musician varies the subject by embroidering it in the following manner :—

There is no difficulty in recognizing the original melody under this embroidery of regular quavers. Farnaby has allowed the principal features, *fixed points*, to remain,[19] and has filled up the voids by means of passing and other notes which, thanks to their subordinate melodic duty, do no violence to the essential features of the melody.   Later on the master varies the same theme by means of semiquavers :—

Here the melody has already become more difficult to recognize; thus in the second bar the essential note B, which is found on the first beat in the primitive melody, is transported half a beat ahead by means of the double rising appoggiatura G A.

We see by these examples how limitless is the field of possibilities in the art of melodic embroidery.   We see also that if the system is pushed to its extreme limits the melody ends by

---

[19] See specially the first beat of each bar, marked with an asterisk. The acute accents indicate the notes of the original melody which have been preserved.

being no longer recognizable under the profusion of ornaments with which it is overlaid ; that which originally should have been a figuration became in fact a veritable disfiguration. This happens frequently with the virginalists, especially when they allow themselves to be carried away by the notion of virtuosity : in that case their art is of no more value than that of the musicians of the present day who are carried away by the same temptation. It often happens, however, that these disfigurations or deformations end in melodic constructions altogether new, very original, and full of the unexpected ; the art of the virginalists is, from that point of view, very fertile in surprises.

But melodic embroidery is not applied to the principal melody alone when given to the *superius ;* it also affects the other parts, particularly the bass. Thus, in the *Spagnioletta,* the bass, which appears in this remarkable form at the beginning of the piece—

is transformed in the following manner in one of the variations[20] :—

[20] We already frequently meet with these figurations applied to the bass in the variations of Cabezon. See for example the *Pavana italiana* taken from the *Obras* of 1578, and reproduced in the *Hisp. Schol. Mus. Sacr.,* vol. vii., p. 73.

When, further on, we come to analyse the various kinds of variations of songs and dances which the virginalists have left us, we shall have occasion to consider more closely the various combinations to which melodic embroidery could give rise with the virginalists.

(2.) THE SEQUENCE.

Sequence or *progression* consists in the persistent and regular repetition of a short figure, on various degrees of the musical scale, whether ascending or descending. We may to a certain extent consider it as related to imitation. In common with this last it possesses in fact this important characteristic —the repetition of the same motive. But while imitation is in its very nature polyphonic, sequence is purely melodic.

Before being used as a means of figuration by the virginalists, it existed, in the current practice of vocal and instrumental music, as a device of melodic development. As such it is very ancient; it is be found as early as the 13th century with the French troubadours. The Florentines of the 14th century used it frequently.[21] In the 15th century Dufay and his contemporaries provide more than one example, and Leichtentritt[22] asserts that in England it is to be found very often in the immediate successors of Dunstable. At the end of the 15th century and at the beginning of the 16th it was cultivated by the greater part of the polyphonists of Western Europe, whether in the realm of religious music (*laudi spirituali*, Mass and motet) or in that of secular music (*frottola*, song, and madrigal).

[21] They also cultivated the purely figural sequence.
[22] *Gesch. der Motette*, p. 389.

G

At the rise of the 17th century it flourished more than ever under cover of the melodico-harmonic style of accompanied monody. As Heuss has very justly observed,[23] Monteverde at that period made use of it in a way which tended to transform it into an actual means of *thematic development*. Just as the development of a theme in the form of imitation prepares the road for the classic fugue, looked on as an adaptation of the ancient polyphony to the requirements of the new harmonic idea, so sequential thematic development forms one of the principal foundations of this purely harmonic manner of writing of which the sonata form was the outcome in the 18th century.

Thus we see the very great importance of the sequence taken in its widest sense. This sequence, not as yet figural, we meet with frequently among the virginalists, particularly in the dance forms, which call for a certain periodic symmetry. Let us look, for example, at this fragment of a corante by Hooper (*Fitzw. V. B.*, ii., p. 312) :—

[23] See *Die Instrumental-Stücke des Orfeo*, by Alf. Heuss, p. 12 (Breitkopf & Härtel, Leipzig, 1903). See also as to the sequence of the 17th century the interesting study by Wellesz on *Cavalli*, which appeared in the *Beiheft* I. of the *Denkm. der Tonk. in Oesterr*. The author considers the sequence as one of the most important elements of the dramatico-musical style (p. 17), and bases on this subject a most ingenious theory (p. 48 ff).

But what ought specially to interest us here is
that the virginalists have made of the sequence a
remarkable instrument of figuration.   We have
already met with it as such at the opening of
the 16th century in Hughe Ashton[24]; later it
reappeared in the first instance in William Byrd:
thus in his variations *The Wood's so wild* (*Fitzw.
V. B.*, i., p. 263) dating from 1590 :—

In the variations *John come kisse me now* (*Fitzw.
V. B.*, i., p. 47) it takes the appearance of a small
harmonic figure :—

The progression here is not of perfect regularity;
it is a quasi-sequence.   In a fantasy by Philips
(Ritter, *Geschichte des Orgelspiels*, ii., p. 51) the
sequence is nothing but the figuration of a fragment
of a scale :—

Bull gives us numerous examples of figural
sequences.   At one time he figures a fragment

[24] See his *Hornepype*, previously mentioned.   On the Continent we find
elementary sequential figurations not only in the organ music of
Arnolt Schlick the elder (1512), a contemporary of Ashton (see the
reprint of his organ pieces in the *Monatsh. für Musikgesch.* of 1869),
but as early as the *Buxheimer Orgelbuch* (of 1450-60, edited by Eitner in the
Beilagen der Monatsh., 1888), and in Conrad Paumann (about 1450) (reprint
of his organ pieces in the *Jahrb. für Musikw.*, ii., 1867, p. 182 ff).

of a scale as the steps of a ladder: *Christe Redemptor (Fitzw. V. B.*, ii., p. 64) :—

At another his sequences are complicated by elements of various rhythms :—

Example: Fantasia (*Fitzw. V. B.*, i., p. 138) :—

(Figuration of a fragment of a scale.)

Prelude (*Fitzw. V. B.*, ii., p. 248) :—

(The sequence in combination with the repetition of notes.)

Fantasia op de fuga van Sweelinck (Complete works of Sweelinck, vol. i., p. 125) :—

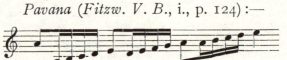

(Rhythmic figuration of a fragment of a scale.)

Pavana (Fitzw. V. B., i., p. 124) :—

Galiarde (Fitzw. V. B., i., p. 170):—

(Quasi-sequence combined with decomposition of chords and repetition of notes.)

After Bull the sequence occurs more and more frequently among the virginalists. We notice here the contrary to what we noticed when we fixed our attention on the development of figural imitation. With Byrd, the oldest master who has left us a large number of compositions, the sequence appears about once in four ; with Bull we notice it at least in half ; and with Farnaby in three-fifths. Finally, of the forty-six anonymous pieces in the *Fitzw. V. B.* a good twenty give us characteristic examples of figural progressions.

We have pointed out, in speaking of the disappearance of imitative figures from virginal music after the beginning of the 17th century, that the cause of it was to be found in the gradual replacement of the polyphonic idea by the harmonic. It may be said of the sequence that it is in many cases a form of adaptation of the ancient polyphonic imitation to the new conditions which had been brought about, at the confines of the 16th and 17th centuries, by accompanied monody based upon harmonic homophony.

There is another element which must not be lost sight of in coming to an understanding of this process of development: the comparative incapacity of the lute—the favourite instrument of the 16th century—to adapt itself to imitative playing. Imitation and sequence on the lute ended therefore by being hardly distinguishable. Composers for keyboard instruments, being aware how essentially favourable their instruments were for harmonic playing, followed the example of the lutenists and borrowed from them their methods of writing, among which they found the sequence as a substitute for imitation.

(3.) THE REPETITION OF NOTES.

We hardly ever meet with this system of figuration among the most ancient virginalists, especially with Byrd, even in those of his works which date probably from the first twenty years of the 17th century. John Bull, on the other hand, affords us numerous examples : they are to be found in quite a quarter of those of his pieces which we have been able to analyse.

Repetition of notes with him appears under very various aspects. Here is the simplest :—

Miserere in three parts (*Fitzw. V. B.*, ii., p. 442) :—

In the same figured plainsong we see also more rapid repetitions of notes :—

In the following instance we notice this form of figuration in two simultaneous parts, in combination with the decomposition of chords :—

Galiarde (Fitzw. V. B., p. 249; *Parthenia,* Rimbault, p. 33) :—

A piece of a descriptive character, *The King's Hunt (Fitzw. V. B.,* ii., p. 116), presents a passage where the same note is successively repeated ten times in very rapid semiquavers ; the intention to depict the movement of the chase is obvious.

Giles Farnaby makes use of the repetition of notes almost as often as Bull, and at times in a curious way.   Thus, in a *Fantasia (Fitzw. V. B.,* ii., p. 333), he makes one part imitate note for note the part in which the repetition appears.   In the following instance the repetition of notes is combined with the figuration of a fragment of a scale :—

Tell me, Daphne (Fitzw. V. B., ii., p. 446) :—

The successors of Bull and Farnaby also employed the repetition of notes, but less frequently, with the exception of Tomkins, the last of the virginalists (died in 1656), with whom we meet with it in four out of the five pieces by him in the *Fitzw. V. B.*

In all the cases we have examined up to now, the repetition of notes had a purely figural intention; but it also occurs with an actual melodic value. This happens sometimes with Farnaby, who, of all the virginalists, is the one who appears to have been the greatest borrower from popular music. Now the repetition of notes of a specifically melodic character appears pretty frequently in the English popular subjects of the 16th and 17th centuries, which sometimes imparts to them an element of vulgarity.[25] This is the case, among others, in the first subject of the *Meridian Alman*, varied by Giles Farnaby (*Fitzw. V. B.*, ii., p. 477) :—

The second subject gives opportunity, from its first announcement, for the repetition of notes, which have at once a melodic and a figural character :—

[25] The theorists of strict vocal counterpoint of the 16th century prohibit the repetition of notes as opposed to the calm and harmonious character which the line of melody should possess (see Schering, *Die Niederländische Orgelmesse im Zeitalter des Josquin*, pp. 6, 7, and 30, Breitkopf & Härtel, Leipzig, 1912).

Examples of the same nature are to be found in other compositions by Farnaby, and in more than one piece written by one or other of his contemporaries or successors.[26]

With the exception of a single instance, that of the *King's Hunt*, the repetitions of figural notes by the virginalists do not seem to have an actual expressional character. They are pure accidents of virtuosity, due no doubt to the fact that the composers for the virginal perceived that their instrument, unlike the organ, was essentially fitted to lend itself to this new effect.

Monteverde was the first formally to recognize the expressive fitness of the repetition of instrumental notes. He explains in detail his views on this subject in the preface, dated 1638, of his *Madrigali guerrieri e amorosi*. It is in this very interesting document that he proposes, with the view of interpreting musically the *stile concitato*,[27] of which he is the inventor, to make use of the rapid repetition of one and the same note, as the accompaniment of passages in the vocal text where the expressions of anger or hate prevail. When he wrote this preface he had already, fourteen years previously, composed his *Il Combattimento di Tancredi e Clorinda*, which gave him the opportunity, said he, "to set to music two contrasting moods of feeling: on the one side war, on the other prayer and death." "At first," he continues,—and the

---

[26] The Lute Book of Thysius, the collection of a Dutch lutenist about the early years of the 17th century, contains a dance (*Den Gulicker Dans*) made up almost entirely of repeated notes (see Land, *Het Luitboek van Thysius*, No. 292, p. 267 ; Muller & Co., Amsterdam, 1889). This lute book contains a great number of pieces of English origin, the themes of which were treated in the form of variations by the virginalists.

[27] An expression meaning "passionate, animated dramatic style."

matter specially interested those who were called on to perform the *basso continuo*,—" the fact of being called on to strike the string sixteen times during the continuance of a single beat, appeared to be more laughable than excellent, and therefore the performers cut down to a single note the numerous notes which ought to have been played during the length of a beat; thus they replaced the Pyrrhic rhythm by the *spondee*, and lost sight of the passionate character of the text."

From this it appears that, at least in practice, the English virginalists had for a long time realised the idea of the repetition of notes, even at a time when Italian performers of *basso continuo* were still in arms against this novelty on the score of its absurdity.[28] [29]

[28] *Il Combattimento di Tancredi e Clorinda* is dated 1624. According to the most recent researches, the first appearance in Italy of the repetition of notes (tremolo of the violin and of the *continuo*) dates from 1617. It is to be met with in the sonata, *La Foscarina*, of Biagio Marini (see Riemann, *Handb. der Musikg.*, II., ii., p. 100 ff).

[29] There occurs an isolated case of repetition of notes in an organ piece of Arnolt Schlick the elder (1512) (see musical quotation, p. 26).
We meet from time to time with the repetition of notes in Cabezon, but without any aim at virtuosity or expression. In a *Tiento del primer tono* (No. 3 of the *tientos* in vol. iv. of the *Hisp. Schol. Mus. Sacr.*) it is introduced as an element in the formation of an imitation or a sequence :—

This passage, obviously influenced by the music of the lute, is a good instance showing how an imitation which involves more than one part can transform itself into a sequence, which demands one only. The upper part imitates itself and becomes a sequence; on the other hand, it is in turn imitated by the second part, in accordance with the principles of the ancient polyphonic imitation.

The repetition of notes as practised by the virginalists, seems to have been a comparative rarity in the 17th century, for André Pirro (*Buxtehude*, Fischbacher, Paris, 1913, p. 151) notices as exceptional that Werner used "repeated notes in semiquavers" in a *Paduan* in his *Deliciae harmonicae* of 1657.

B.—Rhythmical Figures.

(1.) triplets and sextolets.

We have seen above that certain virginalists had occasionally made use of ternary figures which remind us of the Middle Ages. We at the same time remarked that in certain instances the archaic character of these figures was more or less questionable. But there exists a much larger number of instances with which this character has no connection, and where the triplet figures may be looked on as the special property of the virginalists of the 16th and the opening of the 17th centuries. The use of these figures has in such cases no other object than variety and virtuosity. This an example will explain. Let us take up again Byrd's variations on the song, *John come kisse me now* (*Fitzw. V. B.*, i., p. 47). In Variation 9, the bass is figured in quavers[30]:—

In Variation 10 the figure is more rapid, and takes the form of semiquavers; it is placed in the upper part, while the subject is in the tenor:—

---

[30] In the various quotations which follow, we suppress for simplification the parts which are neither the subject nor the figuration which concerns us.

Variation 12 presents us with a figuration in syncopated triplets, given to the *superius*, while the subject is placed in the tenor :—

Lastly, Variation 14 gives us regular sextolets in the *superius;* the subject is in the bass:—

We see by these examples that the aim of the musician has been gradually to enliven the figuration of the subject submitted to variation. Therefore it is especially in the style of variation of secular song or of dances that we find these ternary figures. Yet Peter Philips uses them often in his transcriptions of Italian madrigals and French songs; but in those cases they possess really an actual melodic value quite as important as their figural value. Thus in the varied transcription of the song of Orlando di Lassus, *Margott Laborez* (*Fitzw. V. B.*, i., p. 333) :—

We scarcely notice any development in the use of this kind of figuration. Byrd was probably the first to adopt it. Bull, G. Farnaby, and Tomkins are the principal masters who used it after Byrd and Philips.[31]

(2.) RHYTHMICAL FIGURES PROPERLY SO-CALLED.

Figurations in triplets and sextolets form part of the rhythmic idea, but they are not really rhythmic figures in the strict sense of the word. The latter appear as early as with Tallis, in whom we find them in his two figured plainsongs, *Felix namque* (*Fitzw. V. B.*, i., p. 427, and ii., p. 1). The form which they assume in those works may be represented by this scheme :— ♩. ♪ ♩. ♪[32]

[31] Cabezon made use of ternary figures of a progressive character in his *tientos* and his variations, but without any idea of virtuosity, and with an evident mixture of modernity and archaism (see for example the *Tiento del primer tono*, No. 3 of the *tientos* in vol. iv. of the *Hisp. Schol. Mus. Sacr.*).

[32] It is the "rythme saccadé," characteristic of the French overture of the second half of the 17th century, and of the first half of the 18th.

Cabezon already gives us numerous and remarkable instances of the use of this figure, notably in the *tiento* mentioned in the preceding note. In going further back we find examples, more or less rudimentary and scholastic, in the younger Schlick (1512, see first year of the *Monatsh. für Musikg.*), in the *Buxheimer Orgelbuch* (about 1450-60), reproduced by Eitner, *Beil. zu den Monatsh.*, 1888), and in Paumann (1452 ; vol. ii. of the *Jahrb. für Mus. Wiss.*, p. 182 ff). The *Buxheimer Orgelbuch* is specially rich in various rhythmical figures. But these figures do not possess the lively aspect, supple and varied, which later they assumed with the virginalists.

Example taken from the first *Felix namque* :—

(The *cantus firmus* is in the *superius*. The rhythmic figuration consists in thirds parallel in the other two parts.)

The doubling  is met with very frequently in some less ancient works; thus in Byrd's variations on the song *O Mistris myne* (*Fitzw. V. B.*, i., p. 258) :—

In the first bar the rhythmic figure is a simple figural counterpoint; in the second it is only a rhythmic figuration of the theme itself :—

The rhythmic figure or is the one which we notice the most frequently in the virginalists. But by the side of this fundamental formula we meet with many others which show to what a pitch of refinement the English

masters had arrived in the art of figural detail.
Thus the rhythm of the Canary or of the Gigue
taken more slowly makes us think of the Siciliana
♪.♫ ♪.♫ or ♩.♪ ♩.♪   We find it in
the *Galiarda Passamezzo* of Byrd (*Fitzw. V. B.*,
i., p. 209), which is earlier than 1592[33] :—

as well as in the inexhaustible *Walsingham* of Bull
(*Fitzw. V. B.*, i., p. 1) :—

We find also the following rhythmic design—
♫♪ ♩♫♪, which Bull uses in a systematic
manner in his *Quadran Pavan* (*Fitzw. V. B.*, i.,
p. 107) :—

(The rhythmic figure is combined with imitations,
sequences, and counterpoints in thirds.)

[33] In this example the rhythmic formula has a melodic rather than a
figural value.

Bull now and then gives to this design a waving character, very modern in appearance, which reminds us of Schubert: Variation of Galiard (*Fitzw. V. B.*, i., p. 173) :—

We find in the same master the following rhythmic figure :—

Thus in a Galiard (*Fitzw. V. B.*, ii., p. 125) :—

Bull is not alone in making use of these various rhythmic formulas, which for the period are so novel in design. Byrd offers us a number of examples of this sort of figuration. So does Giles Farnaby; the latter has in addition his own personal formulas, which possess the special humour which distinguishes him. In one of his fantasies (*Fitzw. V. B.*, ii., p. 347) he puts before us the following design :—

---

34 This formula is to be met with in organ music as early as the time of Paumann (*Jahrb. für Mus. Wiss.*, ii., p. 215 ff), but it has no part as a means of instrumental development; in fact, it appears only in the final cadences, as a sort of stereotyped ornament.

35 Would not one say that this is a passage taken from a joyful air in a Venetian opera of the 17th century?

In another fantasy (*Fitzw. V. B.*, ii., p. 313) he develops this design, at the same time rhythmic and sequential :—

Gibbons, in his *Fantasia* in *Parthenia* (p. 38, Rimbault), gives us these curious cross-times :—

Tomkins takes these up, and gives them to two parts in contrariety with each other :—

A Grounde (*Fitzw. V. B.*, ii., p. 87) :—

Further, certain virginalists use rhythmic figurations with a picturesque and expressive aim. This is what Byrd does in the piece where he is striving to reproduce on the virginal the sound of bells (*The Bells*, *Fitzw. V. B.*, i., p. 274). Bull, attempting in *The King's Hunt* (*Fitzw. V. B.*, ii., p. 116) to render the movement of a hunt, uses this rhythmic design :—

Ч

which further on he transforms in the following
manner, in order to give it more animation :—

And lastly, Munday uses different rhythmic
effects in his fantasy on 'faire wether, lightning and
thunder' (*Fitzw. V. B.*, i., p. 23). He thus represents
the sudden light of flashes of lightning :—

Here there is sequence at the same time as
rhythmical figuration.

(3.) FIGURES IN CROSS-TIME.

We find this sort of figuration as early as the
second figured plainsong, *Felix namque* of Tallis
(*Fitzw. V. B.*, ii., p. 1). Thus in the following
passage :—

(The *cantus firmus* in the tenor. Tied cross-time
between the *superius* and the bass.)

Later we find cross-time appearing under very various forms among the principal virginalists, especially with Byrd, Bull, and Farnaby: it is with these last two that we find the greatest number of examples.

Pavana Sir William Petre, by Byrd (*Parthenia*, Rimbault, p. 2):—

(Cross-time between tied notes.)

In a fantasy by Byrd (*Fitzw. V. B.*, ii., p. 406) the notes in cross-time are only tied in one of the two parts:—

This is also the case in *Callino Casturame* (*Fitzw. V. B.*, ii., p. 186), in which the notes in cross-time are detached in a picturesque manner, on a drone bass:—

With Bull, the figurations in cross-time are now and then complicated with harmonic elements

more definite than those of Byrd. Thus in the
Gaillarde Lumley (*Fitzw. V. B.*, i., p. 54) :—

(In this case there is also a decomposition of
chords.)

We have just seen, in *Callino Casturame*,
cross-time introduced as a picturesque element.
Bull gives us more definite elements in this respect
in his *King's Hunt* (*Fitzw. V. B.*, ii., p. 116), where
he makes use of chords or fragments of chords in
cross-time to express the panting huntsmen :—

Another master, Peerson, describes the falling of
the leaves (*Fitzw. V. B.*, ii., p. 423), and makes
use, with that view, of broken chords, the fragments
of which make cross-times between themselves :—

Lastly, the figures in cross-time are used also to express the vague, the undefined. Thus in his last variation on the scale *ut, re, mi, fa, sol, la* (*Fitzw. V. B.*, i., p. 395), Byrd produces a charming effect of *perdendosi* by means of indeterminate syncopations [36] :—

(4.) SYMMETRICAL FIGURATIONS.

Finally, the virginalists make us acquainted with rhythmic combinations which aim at absolute regularity and symmetry. We shall scarcely meet with this preoccupation except in Bull, G. Farnaby, and Gibbons, but it is very characteristic, and shows itself in the systematic use, in two different parts, of unequal durations the contact of which, however, leaves the impression of perfect symmetry. Bull affords scholastic examples of this form of figuration in a *Miserere in three parts* in the *Fitzw. V. B.* (ii., p. 442). This piece consists of a liturgical melody treated in the form of variation. In the first variation,

[36] The rudiments of melodico-figural cross-time are to be found in No. 5 of the *Diferencias* of Cabezon, reproduced at p. 20 of vol. viii. of the *Hisp. Schol. Mus. Sacr.* We meet with them also in a very interesting prelude for the lute (*Ein sehr kunstreicher Preambel*) of the German H. Neusiedler, dating from about 1535, and published by Körte in his essay, *Laute und Lautenmusik bis zur Mitte des xvi. Jahrh.* (Breitkopf & Härtel, Leipzig, 1901), p. 138 ff (see more especially p. 143).

Paumann frequently uses syncopations in his organ pieces, but with no special figural character ; they have moreover an archaic character completely in conformity with the vocal music of the period (1452).

the two parts in free counterpoint which accompany the subject present themselves in the shape of an alto part in regular crotchets standing out over a bass part in even quavers :—

(*Cantus firmus* in the *superius*.)

In the second variation the disposition is the same, but the values of the contrapuntal notes are halved :—

In the third and last variation, the *cantus firmus* being in the tenor, the counterpoint in regular quavers passes to the bass, and the semiquavers go to the *superius* :—

The grand variations, *Walsingham*, by Bull (*Fitzw. V. B.*, i., p. 1), also contain examples of this form of figuration.   In a prelude also by Bull (*ib.* ii., p. 259), it is applied to fragments of the scale in thirds, and contains at the same time broken intervals in one of the parts :—

37

C.—Harmonic Figures.

We come now to a kind of progressive figuration of the highest importance—that is to say, the group of figures which claim a harmonic origin.   Before analysing the various aspects which they may assume, we propose to make a few preliminary remarks of a general nature, which will help us the better to understand their meaning.

We have already pointed out above the influence which the music of the lute had in the formation of an instrumental style independent of imitative polyphony.   An instrument more capable of producing varied successions of chords than of

---

37 There are traces of symmetric figuration in Cabezon (see *Diferencias*, p. 20 of vol. viii. of the *Hisp. Schol. Mus. Sacr.*).   The *Preambel* of Neusiedler, of which we have spoken in the previous note, gives a very typical example (pp. 142 and 143 of the work of Körte).

rendering the subtle play of imitation, the lute formed for itself, little by little, in the 16th century a repertory in which the ancient polyphony was undermined by the rising harmony. On the other hand, when the lutenists had to transcribe for their instrument works belonging to the ancient vocal polyphony, they got over the difficulties of execution by eliminating certain details which formed an obstacle to the free expansion of the technique proper to the lute, in other words, by reducing the work to its harmonic elements. Although theoretical harmony was far from being established in the 16th century, every polyphonic composition of that period might in strictness be looked on as a succession of chords, very obvious in the case of homophony, but more or less disguised under the form of imitation in the case of the polyphonic style of the Netherlands. In the first case the task of the lutenist was of the easiest; in the second he was brought face to face with a less easy duty, which consisted in drawing the parts closer together in such a manner that the work, although undergoing modifications of detail, was not distorted in its general appearance.

In what did these modifications consist? It must suffice to state that the principal consist in an attack directed against the strict movement of the parts. If at a given moment it is convenient to suppress one or several notes belonging to one or other of the parts, they suppress them; if, on the other hand, in order to strengthen a chord it suits to add a note and thus to increase their number, they do not hesitate to do so. This special technique, adopted by the lutenists in their transcriptions of vocal music, is used *a fortiori* in their free compositions.[38]

Since stringed instruments provided with keyboards share with the lute the comparative incapacity of the latter to treat successfully the imitative style, it is not astonishing that the masters of the keyboard should have borrowed from the lutenists their habit of making quite free with the number of polyphonic parts. This is notably the case with the German "colourists" of the end of the 16th century in their tablatures, as Seiffert has well explained in his *Geschichte der Klaviermusik* (p. 21).[39]

The English virginalists followed the same road, but with greater independence, and with a clearer intelligence of the resources appropriate to the keyboard. Thus they succeeded much more rapidly than the Continental musicians not only in breaking away from the leading-strings of vocal and organ music, but in creating a technique of the keyboard in which their borrowings from the lute soon bore but a very secondary part. It is in this fact that we must recognize the chief reason why English lute music of the time of Shakespeare lived in a measure under the shadow

---

[38] The *Hortus Musarum* of 1552-53 gives some specially interesting examples of the reduction of polyphonic vocal music for the lute, in accordance with the special resources of the instrument (see *Sammelbände* of the International Musical Society, VIII., ii., art. by M. Quittard on the *Hortus Musarum*, p. 267 ff).

[39] This practice dates as far back as the 15th century; in fact, we find in the *Buxheimer Orgelbuch* (about 1450-60, republished by Eitner in 1888), a number of pieces (varied transcriptions of polyphonic songs) in which parts have in places been added or suppressed for the sake of the instrumental effect. We notice the same thing in Paumann and his contemporaries (see especially the song, *Mit ganczem willen* and the *Praeambulum super F*, pp. 204 and 223 of the *Jahrb. für Musik. Wiss.*, vol. ii.).

of virginal music, and is on that account but very little known in our day.[40]

If we wish to consider the violence done to the strict movement of the parts in English clavier music, it is scarcely necessary to take trouble to find numerous examples. Already, at the rise of the 16th century, Ashton gives us one in the *Hornepype* which we have analysed above (see p. 23). Subsequently this practice came to be a rule of such general application that even in the pieces with the second title, " for 3 " or " for 4 parts," signifying that the musician has undertaken to conform to a certain polyphonic rigour, the number of parts indicated is never observed with absolute strictness: thus the *Miserere* in three parts by Bull (*Fitzw. V. B.*, ii., p. 442) winds up with a chord of G major consisting of six notes: the G is twice doubled in the octave, the D once. The same remark may be made on the *Miserere* in three parts of Byrd (*Fitzw. V. B.*, ii., p. 230). In the *Miserere* in four parts of this latter master (*Fitzw. V. B.*, ii., p. 232) a fifth part insinuates itself into the polyphonic tissue from the penultimate bar onwards, an octave being doubled; while the final chord has six parts. The *Fantazia* in four parts by Gibbons (*Parthenia*, Rimbault, p. 38) in like manner concludes with a chord of six notes, comprising two doublings of the octave.

[40] On this question see the *résumé* of the communication of Mr. Norlind to the Congress of the International Musical Society (London, 1911), *English music for the lute in the time of Shakespeare* (*Zeitschrift* of the Society, XIII., ii., p. 75). See also Chilesotti's *La Rocca e 'l fuso* (*Rivista musicale italiana*, vol. xix., No. 2, 1912), in which is reproduced a letter from Mr. Dent, asserting that the library of the University of Cambridge possesses a quantity of English lute music, mostly contemporary with the *Fitzw. V. B.* There is also a large number of collections of lute music of the time of the virginalists in the British Museum (see *A Catal. of the MS. Music in the Brit. Mus.*, vol. iii., p. 57 ff).

If we set aside this *genre* of composition, and study the inner structure of the pieces where the number of parts is not settled by any express indication, we shall be led with Seiffert [41] to the following opinion :—" The polyphony of the virginalists is apparent only, not merely in their pieces specially designed for the keyboard, but also in their fantasies in the figured style. It is extremely rare for the same number of parts to be maintained from one end to the other of a piece ; this number is sometimes increased, sometimes diminished on the road, according to the demands of the harmony. Here and there we see free parts superadded ; elsewhere there is a crossing of parts, resulting in a confusion under cover of which the parts that entered sportively lose themselves by degrees or disappear suddenly. At other times, again, there pass through all the parts lively figures executed partly by the right hand, partly by the left. The result of all this is a wayward and fantastic musical tissue, in which it becomes impossible to discover which is *superius, alto, tenor,* or *bass.*" [42] Here we have, in fact, a free polyphony evolving in the direction of harmony. Its existence coincides with the general tendency which at the turn of the 16th and 17th centuries was drawing music in the direction of harmony. The most obvious manifestation of this state of things is the continued bass, that was definitively established in Italy during the early years of the 17th century, and passed very quickly into England, where we find, from 1601 onwards, collections of *Ayres* with continued bass.

[41] *Gesch. der Klavierm.*, p. 63.
[42] Seiffert in this last phrase reproduces the words used by Samuel Scheidt in the preface to his *Tabulatura nova* (1624).

This leaning towards the harmonic idea is singularly evident in a somewhat large number of pieces for the virginal, where the part given to the bass is noticeable for its clear breadth, which anticipates the measured movement of the bass of the classic period of harmony.[43] It is more especially in dance music that this particularity is noticeable; thus, for example, in a galliarde by Bull, following the pavane of *My Lord Lumley* (*Fitzw. V. B.*, i., p. 54):—

Tonic.　　Dom.　　　　　Tonic.

Subdom.　　Tonic.　　Dom. Tonic. 6 Dom. Tonic.

We see, not only in the progress of this bass, but in addition in the chords actually placed on it, that we have here a real attempt at tonal equilibrium, founded on the several relations of the tonic, dominant, and subdominant. This succession of notes forms, in fact, the essential foundations of the key of G major; and the opening of the galliarde produces the actual impression of this tonality, if we set aside certain passages where the F sharp becomes natural.[44]

[43] This sort of quasi-harmonic bass, in which the tonic, the fifth, and the fourth play the most important part, is already to be met with in the Italian *frottola* of the 15th and the opening of the 16th centuries (see *Die Frottole*, by R. Schwartz, 1886, pp. 458 ff). But they are far from being so frequent and so characteristic there as with the virginalists.

[44] Examples of this nature might be multiplied (see, among others, *Monsieurs Alman*, by Byrd (*Fitzw. V. B.*, i., p. 234); the *Duke of Brunswick's Alman*, by Bull (ii., p. 146); *Alman* by Byrd (ii., p. 182); *Pavana* by Tisdall (ii., p. 307), &c.

It is desirable to pause a little longer on this question of the tonality of virginal pieces. In truth, at the period when these works were composed, musicians still lived, in theory, under the authority of the Church modes. The result is that the greater part of them are written without being furnished with any key, whatever the tonic may have been. When the piece bears a flat in the signature—which often happens—or two flats, which is much less common, this in no respect indicates that in the musician's thought it was in F major or D minor, or in B flat major or G minor, but that it is written in a Church mode transposed either a fourth higher or a fifth lower, which requires a flat in the signature, or two fourths higher or two fifths lower, requiring two flats in the signature.

However, if the greater number of pieces for the virginal give us no absolute impression of the modern major and minor, it is only very exceptionally that they recall the Church modes in their primitive purity; that is to say, without chromatic alteration of this note or that. On the contrary, we notice that numerous alterations occur in the course of these pieces, and thus tend to give them a physiognomy which to a certain degree suggests the modern major and minor. We find ourselves, therefore, in the presence of a transitional idea of harmony, in which, still clinging to the past, composers are groping towards new horizons. This is not a condition which belongs specially to the English virginalists. The Italian madrigalists of the second half of the 16th century present exactly the same spectacle, and it may be said that what in large measure constitutes the charm of Italian and English music of the end of the 16th century and of the opening of the 17th, is precisely this uncertain tonality, this comparative harmonic freedom, which, in the hands of artists of genius, produces exquisite feelings of poetry and fantasy.

Let us take a few examples. The first piece which we meet in the *Fitzw. V. B.*, vol. i., p. 1, is Bull's *Walsingham*. It bears no signature whatever. The end of the first variation tells us that we are in the mode of A. But the numerous changes which we meet by the way show us that there can be no question of the old Church mode A. Are we in A major or A minor? The opening of the variation offers us little help on the point; it gives us, however, a general impression of A minor, which impression is strengthened in the following bars, thanks to the appearance of a chord of the dominant provided with G sharp. At the end of the variation this very vacillating A minor is transformed into a characteristic A major, owing to the presence of the F sharp, C sharp, and G sharp.

The second piece of the *Fitzw. V. B.* (i., p. 19) is a *Fantasia* by Munday. There is no key-signature. The final cadence reveals to us the key of A. Numerous alterations prevent us from recognizing the ecclesiastical mode of A. But nothing in the use and the succession of these alterations allows us to say that we are in the modern A major or A minor. Again, the final chord A, C sharp, E, that which precedes it being granted—a bar in which we meet C sharp, B flat, and not F sharp and G sharp—ought rather to be looked on as a chord of the dominant in the key of D minor, than as a chord of the tonic in A major.

Skipping forty pages, we fall (p. 65) on the first piece in the collection which has a flat in the signature ; an *Alman* by an anonymous writer. The flat in the signature in no respect shows that we are in F major or in D minor, but actually that it means the Church mode in D, transposed a fourth higher; that is to say, in G. But a great number of chromatic alterations of various kinds have the result, from one end to the other of the piece, of changing the character of the old mode, without, however, giving us the feeling of either one or the other of our modern tonalities. At the opening we have the feeling of G minor without E flat, but already at the second bar an E flat intervenes, and we come upon pure G minor ; third bar, suspension on the chord of the dominant of G major ; fourth bar, F sharp becomes F natural ; we are suddenly transported into F major, to be shortly brought back, in the final bar which follows, to the key of G minor without E flat.

Let us go on to page 291 ; there we find for the first time a virginal piece bearing two flats in the signature (*Pavana Pagget*, by Philips). This by no means implies that we are in B flat major or G minor, but rather that the piece is written in the ecclesiastical mode of D, transposed two fourths higher ; that is to say, in C. But frequent alterations occur which again prevent the key of D appearing in its complete purity. The first bar gives us the actual impression of the modern C minor, thanks to a natural added to the B ; this impression disappears after the second bar, in which, in consequence of the absence of any other alteration than B flat and E flat, the old mode in D transposed seems to resume its rights. The third bar leaves us the passing feeling of G minor, thanks to the introduction of F sharp; this feeling ceases for a moment at the confines of the third and fourth bars, where the E flat and the F sharp are modified by a natural; but the feeling reappears in the middle of the fourth bar, and soon merges into that of the purest G major (end of the fourth bar and first half of the fifth). Then we have the C minor again (second half of the fifth bar and beginning of the sixth). We might pursue this analysis to the very end of the piece; it would have no other result than to show once more that the virginalists adopted an extremely free harmony released from the tyranny of the Church modes, and not as yet entangled in the trammels of classic harmony.

These various examples have allowed us to glance in passing at the numerous possibilities of modulation which the art of the virginalists involves; but we have at the same time seen that the modulations used by these masters are purely empirical in origin, and in no respect derived from rules already accepted. There is one case only in which we find a preconceived intention of modulation, and the methodical realisation of that intention: it is the first *ut, re, mi, fa, sol, la* by Bull (*Fitzw. V. B.*, i., p. 183). We will not dwell for the moment on this piece of an exceptional character, to which we shall have occasion to return, and of which we shall then make a detailed analysis.

One of the harmonic anomalies which we meet with most frequently in the virginalists consists in

false relation.[45]   Here is an example taken from
the *Galiarda to my Lord Lumley's Pavan* by Bull
(*Fitzw. V. B.*, i., p. 54) :—

There is a false relation between the F sharp of
the first beat of the bar and the F natural of the
second beat; that is to say, contrary to the rules of
classical harmony, the chromatic descent F sharp-
F natural takes place not in a single part, but
is carried through two different parts.   The
theorists of classic harmony see in these false
relations an unacceptable element of harshness and
roughness.   The virginalists did not share this way
of looking at it, if we may judge by the countless
instances where they make use of false relation
without having the slightest idea that it might be
in any way abnormal.   It is always well to
note, with Messrs. Fuller Maitland and Barclay
Squire (preface to the modern edition of the *Fitzw.
V. B.*, p. xviii.), that the unequal temperament of
the instrument must have helped in fining down
the harshness of these false relations, because it
became nearer to being in tune by means of perfect
fifths than would equal temperament.[46]   However

[45] Leichtentritt, *Geschichte der Motette* (p. 404, Note 1, following
Walker), draws attention to the frequency of false relations in the English
music of the 17th century.

[46] It is precisely for this reason that we so frequently meet with false
relations in the vocal music of the period, which in itself was entirely
independent of the question of temperament, equal or unequal.

I

that may be, the false relations of the virginalists none the less produce, even on our modern keyed instruments in equal temperament, effects which are very curious and seldom unpleasant.

False relations do not appear to have been the object of criticism on the part of the theorists of the second half of the 16th century and the early part of the 17th. On the other hand, parallel fifths and octaves were severely banished from contrapuntal vocal music.[47] The virginalists, following in that the example of the lutenists, felt no compunction in violating that rule. At first it was often a necessity, resulting from the fact that in the transcription of vocal music for an instrument it was impossible on account of the uniformity of *timbre* to take advantage of the crossing of the parts by means of which parallel fifths and octaves were avoided in the original vocal works.[48] But apart from these circumstances, the virginalists frequently made use of consecutive fifths and octaves, without seeing the least harm in it. Here, by way of example, are a few bars from the anonymous piece *The Irish Ho-Hoane*:—

---

[47] See Seiffert, *Geschichte der Klaviermusik*, p. 23.

[48] In his preface to the *Concerti ecclesiastici* of 1605, Viadana insists (9th instruction) on the absolute necessity of avoiding parallel octaves and fifths in the vocal parts, but he allows them in rendering the *continuo* on the organ.

(*Fitzw. V. B.*, i., p. 87) in which the use of parallel fifths seems to be adopted out of bravado. [49]

After these long preliminaries relating to the absolutely empirical idea of harmony of the virginalists we are well armed to resume what is really the principal object of our investigation; that is to say, virginalistic figuration so far as it borrows its elements from a harmonic source. In this connection we meet in the first place with :—

(I.) COUNTERPOINT IN THIRDS OR IN SIXTHS.

Let us remark in the first place that it is no question here of counterpoint in *thirds and sixths*, which would bring us back to faux-bourdon. Counterpoint in thirds or in sixths is, on the contrary, a form of figuration which, although related to faux-bourdon, owes its origin much more to the charm which belongs to it, and in its happy adaptation to instrumental music of a progressive nature, than in an old tradition which had been preserved and more or less developed.

Counterpoint in thirds or in sixths occurs frequently with Cabezon. Among the virginalists we see it appearing concurrently with faux-bourdon

---

[49] *The Irish Ho-Hoane* appears to be of purely popular origin. Now it is asserted that the popular music of the period, so far as it made use of polyphony, had no objection to the effect of consecutive fifths. That was the case not only in England, but equally in Italy, where we meet with numerous examples of parallel fifths in the *Villanelle alla Napolitana* as well as in the *Laudi spirituali* (see Alaleona, *Studi sulla storia dell' oratorio musicale in Italia*, p. 102 ff, ed. Bocca). False relations abound also in these little compositions in the popular style.

as early as 1562, in the first *Felix namque* of Tallis (*Fitzw. V.B.*, i., p. 427) :—

(*Cantus firmus* in the *superius*. Counterpoint in thirds. By transferring one of the two parts to the higher or lower octave they become counterpoints at the tenth, the character of the consonance being unchanged.)

(*Cantus firmus* in the *superius*. Counterpoint in sixths.)

The frequency of this kind of counterpoint in this piece, the origin of which is comparatively ancient, seems to conform more or less to the predilection which the English always had for consonances of thirds and sixths. In this respect it may be said that in certain transitional works, such as this plainsong, their presence signifies, in spite of everything, some bond with the past. The *Meane* of Blitheman (No. 31 of *Mulliner's Book*), which Hawkins publishes in his *History*, and which

we have analysed above (p. 19), contains no
figuration properly so called, but the three parts
forming the contrapuntal material display a
real obstinacy in creating successions of sixths or
thirds between each other. What is novel with
Tallis is the application of these successions of
consonances to instrumental figuration.[50]

After Tallis, we see the other less ancient
virginalists use currently counterpoints in thirds or
in sixths as a means of figuration. No development is observable in their practice. Byrd uses
them in the oldest of his pieces the date of which
we know : for example, in a part of those which are
common to *Fitzw. V. B.* and to *Nevell's Booke*
(1591). Philips seems to have a particular love
for them, and so has Giles Farnaby. John Bull
at times makes them into an object of virtuosity
by confiding them to the left hand in a quick
movement.[51] A few examples will give an idea of
this method of figuration :—

Passamezzo Pavana by Philips, 1592 (*Fitzw. V. B.*,
i.. p. 299) :—

---

[50] Groups of figural thirds or sixths are already frequently met with
along with other figures in the German organ tablature of Kleber, about
1520. (See the Organ pieces of Kleber, published as a supplement in *Das
Buxheimer Orgelbuch*, by Eitner, *Beil. zu den Monatsh.*, 1888.)

[51] For example, in his twenty-three variations on the scale of solmisation
ut, ré, mi, fa, sol, la (*Fitzw. V. B.*, ii., p. 281).

Walsingham by Bull (*Fitzw. V. B.*, i., p. 1),
26th variation :—

Used in certain ways, the counterpoint in thirds
or in sixths produces most charming effects of
expression ; thus, in a passage of the *Wooddy-Cock*
of G. Farnaby (*Fitzw. V. B.*, ii., p. 138), they
give the impression of the murmuring of a
brook :—

Further on they suggest the Elysian Fields of
Orfeo and the enchanted gardens of *Armida* :—

In *The King's Hunt* (*Fitzw. V. B.*, i., p. 196), also by Farnaby, the lively counterpoint in thirds produces a picturesque effect of movement :—

Further on :—

Lastly, with Tomkins, we find a case where the counterpoints in thirds and sixths are used simultaneously, resulting in successions of chords of sixths which have no real connection with the ancient faux-bourdon, as much on account of the general character of the piece as of the context :—

The Hunting's Galliard (*Fitzw. V. B.*, ii., p. 100) [52] :—

[52] Similar examples are often furnished us by classical composers ; thus Beethoven in his Quartet, Op. 59, No. 1 (first movement), and in his Pianoforte Sonata, Op. 2, No. 3 (opening of the *Finale*). We find it also in the ultra-modern musicians ; for instance, in the *Rosenkavalier* of Strauss (pp. 184 and 301 of the German score for voice and pianoforte, Ed. Fürstner).

(2.) SUSPENSIONS AND APPOGGIATURAS.

In theory, suspensions and appoggiaturas are ideas inseparable from classical harmony. But, in fact, long before the last was established these accidents of harmony were in current use in practice; the polyphonic vocal music of the 16th century drew from them the most characteristic effects of dissonance. Certain Italian organ pieces of the commencement of the 17th century,[53] in which suspension was systematically used, bore a special name, *Toccate di durezze e ligature*, which sanctioned by its signification the theoretical recognition of this effect, which was so singular and so remarkably expressive.

The virginalists constantly made use of suspension and appoggiatura, but they did not employ it simply as an element indispensable to the variety of harmonic successions which formed the thread of their pieces; they also used it as a means of figuration. The case is uncommon, and shows, in the rare passages where we meet with it, an unusual refinement in the art of figuration.

Byrd gives us an early example in his *Galiarda Passamezzo* (*Fitzw. V. B.*, i., p. 209), dating from before 1592 :—

[53] See Torchi, *L'Arte musicale in Italia* (vol. iii., pp. 231 and 370).

We notice in two instances in this passage a suspension of the fundamental primitive C of the chord of the fourth and sixth , a suspension obtained by holding on the D of the preceding chord.

Of Morley we have a very characteristic example in his second variation on the song *Goe from my window* (*Fitzw. V. B.*, i., p. 42):—

Here we have a figural succession of suspensions, appoggiaturas, and passage notes, the effect of which is most charming.

Bull's figured plainsong *In nomine* (*Fitzw. V. B.*, ii., p. 34) presents us with successions of suspensions of the highest interest.   The following quotation will give an exact idea of it:—

(*Cantus firmus* in the bass.)

Bull also gives us examples of suspensions and appoggiaturas as figuration in his variations on the *Quadran Pavan* (*Fitzw. V. B.*, i., p. 107). Lastly, Farnaby (*Pavane, Fitzw. V. B.*, i., p. 141), Gibbons (*Pavane, Parthenia*, p. 42, and *Prelude, Parthenia*, p. 49), and Tomkins (*Worster Braules, Fitzw. V. B.*, ii., p. 269) furnish us with a few very interesting examples, in which, however, the figural character is not so obvious as in the preceding quotations.

(3.) SPREADING OR DECOMPOSITION OF INTERVALS

OR CHORDS.

We now come to an extremely important method of virginalistic figuration—the spreading or decomposition of intervals or chords. As regards the spreading of intervals it may be maintained with a good show of reason that its harmonic origin is to be looked on with caution, and that it is nothing but a variety of melodic embroidery. But in fact it is practised according to principles absolutely similar to those which are used in the spreading of chords ; and moreover, the particular effects resulting from the one are in every way similar to those of the other. This gives us the opportunity of grouping these two forms of figuration under one and the same heading.

What does the breaking of intervals consist in ? Bull offers striking examples of it. Desiring to give more animation to this succession of notes :—

and to confer on it a more striking instrumental character, he duplicates them in this way :—

(Figured Plainsong : *Gloria tibi Trinitas* (*Fitzw. V. B.*, i., p. 160).)

In the plainsong *Salvator mundi* (*Fitzw. V. B.*, i., p. 163) Bull treats in the same way a series of notes that succeed each other by degrees partially disjoint and partially conjunct :—

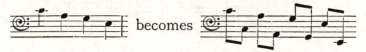

In the same plainsong the following fragment :—

as the result of a more complicated figuration becomes :—

Worster Braules of Tomkins presents breakings of intervals the specific virginalistic character of which is singularly marked :—

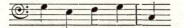

From an example of this nature it is evident how far the virtuosi of the virginal took advantage of the compass of their instrument and succeeded in creating works forming a complete contrast to the smooth constructions of strict polyphony.

In certain cases the breaking of intervals shows itself by a sort of "beating" of the bass, in which we can see—just as in the rapid repetition of one and the same note—the origin of the tremolo basses of the classical period. Thus in the variations by Gibbons on the song, *The wood's so wild* (*Fitzw. V. B.*, i., p. 144) :—

This beating has a descriptive signification in *The King's Hunt* by Bull (*Fitzw. V. B.*, ii., p. 116) :—

In other cases we have to do with more complicated figures, that are half-way between the breaking of intervals and embroidery in the sense in which we have previously used that word. Thus in a variation of a *Pavan* by Richardson (*Fitzw. V. B.*, i., p. 29) :—

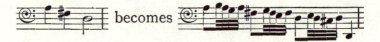

In a variation of a *Galliard* by Bull (*Fitzw. V. B.*, i., 177) :—

In *The Duchesse of Brunswick's Toy* (*Fitzw. V. B.*, ii., p. 412), Bull again figures this succession of notes :—

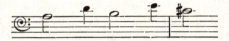

in the following way :—

From these latter examples it is obvious what an important part passing-notes play in figural combinations.

The spreading of chords shows itself under various forms; the simplest, which is at the same time the most frequent and the most characteristic of the virginalistic style, is the decomposed fifth. We have already seen it used at the beginning of the 16th century by Hughe Ashton. William Byrd adopts it subsequently, and makes frequent use of it. We have noticed it in more than half of the compositions of his which we have been able to analyse.

It shows itself generally under a rhythmic form, of which this is the usual type :—

Fantaisie by Byrd (*Fitzw. V. B.*, i., p. 37) :—

and it is most often in final cadences that we see it occur. Its origin must be looked for in an effect peculiar to the brass instruments used in war and the chase, instruments on which the fifth, the third sound of the harmonic scale, was the sound most frequently used, concurrently with the tonic. The confirmation of this origin may be found in a piece by Byrd, *The Earle of Oxford's Marche* (*Fitzw. V. B.*, ii., p. 402), of earlier date than 1592, in which the numerous decomposed fifths are evidently intended as an imitation of warlike fanfares.[54] The decomposed fifth seldom wanders from the little rhythmic formula by Byrd of which we have given an example. In a *Galliard* of Gibbons (*Parthenia*, p. 35) the rhythm disappears, and we have :—

The virginalists other than Byrd do not seem to have had the predilection of their elder for

[54] Formulas of this character are met with in the polyphonists as early as the 14th and 15th centuries. Thus, for example, in the counter-tenor part of the rondeau in canon *Ma fin est mon commencement* by Machault (about 1300 to later than 1371), reproduced in the *Gesch. der Mensuralnotation* of Johannes Wolf (vol. ii. and iii., No. 22), and in the *Et in terra pax ad modum tubae* of G. Dufay (about 1400-74), reproduced in the *Denkm. der Tonkunst in Oesterr.*

the decomposed fifth.   Philips uses it very seldom, Bull scarcely at all in one-fourth of his pieces, and Farnaby in a very limited number.   No doubt it may have become the object of a certain disfavour towards the opening of the 17th century, by reason of the increasing development of the harmonic feeling, and of the tendency to look on the chord of three tones no longer as a mere polyphonic accident, but rather as an actual harmonic entity.[55]   It is very natural to think that from the moment when the virginalists became aware that they could obtain effects admirably suited to the resources of their instrument by spreading chords in different ways, they abandoned with a light heart the primitive and slightly monotonous little figure which consisted in decomposing the open fifth.[56]

Examples of chords of three notes decomposed are to be found as early as 1564 in the second *Felix namque* of Tallis :—

[55] In accordance with the theory of Zarlino (*Istitutioni harmoniche*, 1558).

[56] In fact, this little figure hardly ever produces the real effect of the naked fifth, for the reason that the third of the chord is almost always found in another part, devoid of any figuration :—

Ex.—*Fantasy* by Byrd (*Fitzw. V. B.*, i., p. 37) :—

Byrd gives us a very limited number; in seventy-seven of his compositions we scarcely notice more than five where we come across this kind of figuration. Bull, on the contrary, uses it in nearly two-fifths of his pieces, and Farnaby in almost half. We discover it less frequently among the anonymous authors, but that is because they specially cultivated short dance pieces, which did not lend themselves so well to broken chords as did the variations of secular songs.

Here follow a few particularly interesting examples :—

Galiard to the Quadran Pavan by Byrd (*Fitzw. V. B.*, ii., p. 111) :—

(In this example the decomposition of chords has a true melodic value.)

Galiard Mrs. Brownlo by Byrd (*Parthenia*, p. 10) :—

Pavane by Richardson (*Fitzw. V. B.*, i, p. 87) :—

(Arpeggio effect.)

In a variation of this pavan this outline is complicated with passing-notes of the most charming effect :—

In another variation (*Fitzw. V. B.*, i., p. 90) the complication is still greater :—

(The third chord is a chord of the dominant seventh, somewhat rare for the period.)

Plainsong, *Salvator mundi*, by Bull (*Fitzw. V. B.*, i., p. 163) :—

(A rhythmic element intervenes here.)

Miserere in three parts by Bull (*Fitzw. V. B.*, ii., p. 442) :—

(The *cantus firmus* forms a sort of interior pedal; the decomposition of chords is formed by the simultaneous concourse of the bass and the *superius*.)

K

Prelude by Bull (*Fitzw. V. B.*, i., p. 158) :—

Bull's *Walsingham* (*Fitzw. V. B.*, i., p. 1) offers us numerous examples of the decomposition of chords. Let us remark especially the following, in which the break is made by means of arpeggios given to both hands and disposed in contrary movement :—

This figure is found again in other pieces, notably in a *Toy* by G. Farnaby (*Fitzw. V. B.*, ii., p. 421).

In the following example, taken from the variation of the *Quadran Pavan* by Bull (*Fitzw. V. B.*, i., p. 107), the object of the break is to palliate the effect of the parallel fifths :—

A *Fantasy* by Farnaby (*Fitzw. V. B.*, ii., p. 82) presents this interesting arrangement :—

The piece for two virginals by G. Farnaby (*Fitzw. V.B.*, i., p. 202) is equally worthy of remark for its breakings of chords :—

(The first virginal decomposes the chords in a simple form. The second applies to these same chords more complicated forms of spreading.)

It happens also that the decomposition of chords assumes a picturesque character. Thus in a

Pavane by Bull (*Fitzw. V. B.*, i., p. 124) it produces a vague and distant effect[57] :—

In *The King's Hunt* by Farnaby (*Fitzw. V. B.*, i., p. 196) the jarring of a bass figure in the shape of the decomposition of a chord against a B flat in the alto leaves a singular impression of wildness :—

Lastly, there are certain embroideries connected with the form of figuration of which we are treating, which may be looked on either as spreadings of chords of three notes complicated by passing-notes, or as spreadings of chords of more than three notes. Such is this example taken from the *ut, mi, re* of Byrd (*Fitzw. V. B.*, i., p. 401) :—

[57] Identical effects are to be met with in various other cadences of this pavane.

In *The Bells* of Byrd (*Fitzw. V. B.*, i., p. 274) a figure of this nature presents a character purely descriptive[58] :—

[58] It is interesting to inquire what part was contributed by certain Continental musicians who were contemporary with the English virginalists in the formation of the spreading of chords—which is, in the end, the most progressive method of figuration of the period.

Cabezon, who was contemporary with Tallis, and died in 1566, already gives us a few examples of the decomposition of chords which are worthy of notice :—

Canto del Cavallero (*Hisp. Sch. Mus. Sacr.*, viii., p. 3).

Variations : *De quién teme* (*ib.*, viii., p. 13).

(See also *Diferencias* (*ib.*, viii., p. 20), opening of the second variation, and first part of the third.)

III.—Various Figures.

(1.) Figures of Italian Origin.

In truth these are distinguished less by definite formal characteristics than by a general physiognomy which makes one think of the figural art of the Italians of the end of the 16th century, especially of the writers of toccatas, such as the two Gabrieli and Claudio Merulo. When we read certain virginal pieces and witness the

Among the Italian toccata writers of the end of the 16th century, characteristic examples are not uncommon. They are already to be met with in Andrea Gabrieli, who died in 1586 :—

Intonation from a collection of 1593 (No. 27 of the *Beilagen* of Wasielewski, *Gesch. der Instrumentalmusik im xvi. Jahrh.* Berlin, 1878).

Passemezo antico, from a collection of 1596 (Torchi, *Arte musicale in Italia*, iii., p. 71).

The other examples which we might give are of less interest, since it is impossible to prove that they are anterior to the death of A. Gabrieli. To all appearances they date from a period when the practice of the decomposition of chords had come into current use. They are to be

unfolding of the fantastic arabesques with which they are decked out, we cannot help thinking of the fanciful and somewhat decadent art of the virtuosi who made the vaults of St. Mark resound with their improvisations.

The intrusion of the Italian musical spirit into England is due to various causes. In the Introduction to this work we have seen that from the opening of the 16th century Italian artists

found in Giov. Gabrieli, in sundry toccatists of the *Transilvano* (1597-1609), and in Merulo. The second book of toccatas by the latter (1604) contains several remarkable cases of broken chords. Thus:—

Final cadence of the *Toccata del nono tono* (Torchi, iii., p. 99).

Toccata del 2ndo tono (Torchi, iii., p. 123).

Recent researches tend to prove that the breaking of chords or of intervals must have its roots very far away in the past. Thus we discover very curious rudiments of it in the bass parts of the motets of the Netherlands of the period of Josquin des Prés; that is to say, in a realm to which it seems entirely foreign (examples in the article of Schering, *Die Notenbeispiele in Glarean's Dodekachordon. Sammelbände* of the International Musical Society, XIII., iv., p. 575 ff).

frequented the English Court.[59] Still later, musicians from beyond the Alps, especially players of bowed instruments, were more and more in favour there, and finally gained such a footing that in the Chapel Royal certain posts were held almost exclusively by them.[60] Among the violinists we remark, along with others, the names of Albert of Venice,[61] died in 1560; of Francis of Venice, died about 1587-88; of Ambrose of Milan, died about 1590-91; several members of the Lupo family, &c. &c.[62] The Ferrabosco family, the principal representatives of which were composers of great merit, also played some part in England during the second half of the 16th and the first half of the 17th centuries.[63] Finally, we find at the English Court the important family of Bassano, the five brothers of which occupied musical posts there from 1539 onwards. This family being very numerous, the number of Bassani settled in England became in the end very considerable.

[59] See p. 2. Besides Sagudino there was Memo, a Venetian musician, who was attached to the English Court between 1515 and 1520 as organist and virginalist.

[60] See the list of royal musicians in the accounts published by the *Musical Antiquary* from October, 1909.

[61] The MS. Roy., app. 74, 76, of the British Museum, dating from 1547-48, contains a *Pavin of Albarte* for five instruments, probably viols. Mr. Hughes-Hughes supposes that this Albarte is possibly Albert of Venice.

[62] No. 24 of *Cosyn's Book* is a galliard by Thomas Lupo, arranged for the virginal by Cosyn.

[63] On the Ferrabosco, see *Notes on the Ferrabosco Family*, by Mr. Arkwright (*Musical Antiquary*, July, 1912); *The Ferrabosco Family*, by Giov. Livi (*Musical Antiquary*, April, 1913); *Alfonso Ferrabosco the Younger* (anonymous notes in the *Musical Antiquary* of April, 1913, p. 189 ff); *Alfonso Ferrabosco and Alfonso Ferrabosco III.* (notes by Mr. Arkwright and J. S. Shedlock in the *Musical Antiquary* of July, 1913, pp. 260 and 263).

In 1685, under Charles II., we still find a Bassano among the musicians in the King's service.[64]

The influence of Italian music in England is readily understood when we consider the position which these numerous settlers occupied. To this it must be added that several English musicians of the period travelled in Italy, notably Philips (in 1595, according to Fétis), Dowland (between 1584 and 1588), and Morley.[65] Without doubt it is in the domain of vocal music—madrigal or *Ayre* with continued bass—that Italian influence is most strongly felt. But instrumental music also did not escape it, obvious proof of which we can already see in the *Fitzwilliam Virginal Book*, in which not only have the compositions of two Italian musicians, Pichi and Galeazzo, been included, but a very characteristic Italian terminology bears sway; thus Courantes are always designated by their Italian titles of *Corranto* or *Coranto*. The greater part of these are attributable to anonymous authors, and there are many which recall those of Frescobaldi to such an extent that it would not be astonishing if they were of Italian origin. Moreover the Italian forms, *Pavana*,[66] *Galliarda*, *Galiarda*, *Galiardo* are met with at least as often as the English forms

[64] On the Bassano family see *Notes on the parish registers of St. Helen's, Bishopsgate, London*, by Mr. G. E. P. Arkwright, in the *Musical Antiquary* of October, 1909, p. 40 ff, and in the same periodical, July, 1913, p. 260, the Note on *Marke Antoney* by Mr. Arkwright.

[65] Morley himself tells us, in the preface to *The First Book of Songes of foure parts* (1597), that he stayed in Italy (at Venice, Padua, Genoa, Ferrara, Florence, &c.), where he had very friendly intercourse with Luca Marenzio and Giovanni Croce (see Naylor, *An Elisab. V. B.*, p. 30). Possibly it is to this intercourse that we owe the publication in London in 1608, by Thos. Este, of the *Musica Sacra : to six voyces, composed in the Italian tongue by Giovanni Croce. Newly Englished*.

[66] *Pavana* is also the Spanish form.

Pavan, Pavin, Paven, and *Galliard.* Lastly, we find again in the *Fitzw. V. B.* the Italian terms *Allemanda, La Volta,* and *Passamezzo.* In *Parthenia* the words *Pavana* and *Galiardo* recur continually; once only do we meet with the English form *Pavin.* The fashion of Italianising names appears in *Orlando* Gibbons and *Ferdinando* Richardson.

It is very natural that Peter Philips, who travelled in Italy and who cultivated the transcription of Italian madrigals for the virginal, should have used in his instrumental versions figural forms in the Italian manner. From that habit to the use of them in original compositions there was but one step; indeed we meet in a part of the latter with a "figural atmosphere" which is quite Italian. Thus in a *Fantasia* (*Fitzw. V. B.,* i., p. 335) we find, among others of the same kind, this passage of a character purely Italian :—

We see, again, a large number of touches of virtuosity in the Italian style in a fantasy by Philips which forms part of a manuscript at

Liége of 1617 (Ritter, *Gesch. des Orgelsp.*, ii., p. 51).
Moreover this piece has all the characteristics of an
instrumental madrigal.   From the very first bars
we are struck by the Italian character of its
figuration :—

Throughout the whole of this piece we recognise
the presence of embroideries of this kind, which
seem directly taken from the toccatas of the
Gabrieli or of Merulo.

Byrd, in spite of his leanings towards a certain
English tradition, seems also to have been touched
by the Italian influence in a certain number of his
compositions which appear to date from after 1600.
Thus in his version with variations of the *Pavana
lachrymae* of Dowland (*Fitzw. V. B.*, ii., p. 42) he
makes use of Italian cadence formulas ; for
example :—

Thus again in another *Pavane* (*Fitzw. V. B.*, ii.,
p. 394) and in a *Pavana Fantasia* (*Fitzw. V. B.*,
p. 398).[67]

[67] The "Italianisms" of Byrd contain nothing which ought to
surprise us, in view of the fact that he wrote more than one Italian
madrigal, or in the Italian style, as may be proved by the collections of
madrigals by different authors published by Nicholas Yonge (*Musica
transalpina*) and by Thomas Watson, respectively in 1588 and 1590, through
the publisher East, in London (see *A catalogue of a hundred works*, &c.,
by Alfred H. Littleton, pp. 30 and 31).

Several pieces by Morley also exhibit traces of Italian virtuosity. Now we know that as madrigalist this master was strongly influenced by Italy. In his variations *Nancie* (*Fitzw. V. B.*, i., p. 57) the figuration, which gradually becomes richer and more animated from the beginning to the end of the piece, is an interesting mixture of English and Italian formulas, with a predominance of the latter.

Nor did Bull escape the influence of Italian virtuosity. Two of his *Preludes* (*Fitzw. V. B.*, ii., pp. 22, 23) and his *Fantasia* on a fugue by Sweelinck, dated 1621, and published by Max Seiffert in the complete works of the Dutch composer (vol. i., p. 125), according to all the evidence borrow certain elements from the toccata of the Venetian organists.

In two anonymous preludes in the *Fitzwilliam Virginal Book* (i., p. 80, and ii., p. 40), we recognise borrowings of the same kind. The second takes the shape of a little toccata with a fugued interlude: perhaps we may assume from this that it is of Italian origin.

We have just seen that one of the pieces in which the influence of the Italian toccata is most noticeable is the *Fantasia* composed by Bull in 1621 on a fugue by Sweelinck. This is the place to observe how important a part the Dutch master took as an intermediary between the Italian organists and the English virginalists, particularly those, such as Philips and Bull, who dwelt in the Netherlands during the latter part of their lives.

Born in 1562, Sweelinck pursued his musical studies from 1578 to about 1580 at Venice, where it seems certain that he had personal relations

with A. Gabrieli and Cl. Merulo. Besides this
he was also in touch with the art of the virginalists,
of whose conquests he did not hesitate to take
advantage; so that as a pupil at the same time of
the Italian as well as the English school he gives
us in his work for the organ and the clavier a
synthesis of the art of the Venetian organists and
of that of the virginalists across the Channel.
Since he enjoyed great celebrity until 1621 it is
highly probable that the larger part of his works
came to the knowledge of musicians such as Bull
and Philips, and that the Italian influence which is
traceable in the compositions of the two last
is in part the result of this knowledge. This
supposition becomes a certainty as regards the
fantasy by Bull on a fugue of Sweelinck.[68]

(2.) GRACES.

Strictly speaking, graces are not contained in
the forms of figuration, in a measure organic,
which we have studied so far. We will include
them, nevertheless, for the convenience of our
general plan, and because we really see no better
place to consider them than this.

According to Mme. Farrenc (preface to vol. ii.
of the *Trésor des Pianistes*), the graces used by the

[68] As further proof of these suggestions, we may refer to the following
facts:—1. The *Fitzw. V. B.* contains four compositions by Sweelinck;
2. Sweelinck knew and valued the works of Philips, since he wrote, under
the title of *Pavana Philippi* (compl. works, vol. i., p. 107), variations on the
subject of a pavan treated by Philips himself in 1580, which is to be
found in the *Fitzw. V. B.*, i., p. 343; 3. Sweelinck wrote variations on an
English popular song, *Fortune*, which Byrd has also treated (*Fitzw. V. B.*,
i., p. 250); (compl. works of Sweelinck, vol. i., p. 127).

Max Seiffert thinks, moreover, that the relations between Bull and
Sweelinck were in all probability very close. (*Vierteljahrschr. für
Musikwiss.*, 1891, p. 153).

virginalists are indicated by means of the three following signs :—

According to her, the first ♪ ought to be interpreted as a *beat* (the German *mordent*) :—

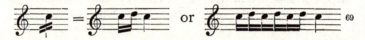

The sign ♯ represents a trembling or trill, without termination (the German *pralltriller*, the English *shake*, the Italian *trillo*) :—

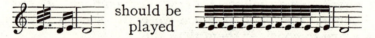

Lastly, ♯ represents a prolonged shake, bearing a melodic resolution, which we often find written out [70] :—

should be played

According to the Introduction of Messrs. Fuller Maitland and Barclay Squire to the modern reprint of the *Fitzw. V. B.*, this third ornament is not met with in that celebrated manuscript.[71] We find the first two only, and in

[69] The number of beats varies according to the particular case.

[70] Taken from the *corante* by Gibbons, published by Mme. Farrenc in vol. ii. of the *Trésor des Pianistes*.

[71] Mme. Farrenc was the possessor of manuscripts of virginal music in which this unusual ornament was met with.

very rare cases a third, which assumes this form : ⨎ . The two commentators think that the two little vertical bars with which it is furnished are a simple mark of correction, warning the performer that the sign ⊤ has been placed on a note by mistake, and that in consequence this note should be played without any ornament whatever.

So far as concerns the interpretation of the signs ⊤ and ⨎, Messrs. Fuller Maitland and Barclay Squire are not in complete agreement with Mme. Farrenc. Depending on the work of Dannreuther, *Primer of Ornamentation*, p. 18 (Novello), they consider that the sign ⊤ —which occurs much more rarely in the *Fitzw. V. B.* than ⨎—ought to be interpreted as a *slide*, a little figure taking its starting-point from the third below the note to which this sign is applied. Example :—

This is, as we see, a *double appoggiatura* (the *Doppel-Vorschlag* of the Germans). In certain cases, they add, we may see in this sign an indication of a *mordent*.

As to the sign ⨎, they think it represents a shake more or less long, or a *mordent*, or even a *Pralltriller*.[72]

---

[72] Other signs of graces are found in the MS. 31403 of the British Museum, where explanations are given as to their execution (see *Introduction* by Seiffert to vol. i. of the complete works of Sweelinck, p. xv.).

This MS. is of about 1700, as we have seen above ; that is to say, a period already somewhat removed from that of the virginalists.

From the multiplicity and the comparative confusion of these interpretations, we may come to the conclusion that the question of deciding how virginalistic graces ought to be executed is still far from being settled. Moreover, the problem is of no very great importance; we have, in fact, a conviction that the graces are purely superficial ornaments only, the presence of which has no determining influence on the stylistic physiognomy of virginal compositions. In that particular the latter differ entirely from the French pieces for the harpsichord of the epoch of Couperin, in which the graces have generally a decorative duty or an expressive meaning which confers on them a true and actual value. It suffices to read just as they are—that is to say, deprived of their ornaments—the pieces contained in the modern reprint of *Parthenia* (Rimbault), to come to the conclusion that these compositions are wholly sufficient in themselves, and that the mordents and shakes add nothing to their beauty.

Again, in analysing the pieces of the *Fitzw. V. B.* from the point of view of the grace signs, we find that the distribution of these little ornaments is often very arbitrary, and displays a pronounced taste for excess; so that we end by asking whether these indications are not simply the work of a transcriber who had an exaggerated affection for these trifles. Therefore a reticence is necessary if we desire to execute these pieces according to the dictates of good taste; reduced in this manner to wiser proportions, and interpreted according to the demands of the context, virginalistic graces are capable of producing the most pleasing effects.

(3.) DIFFERENT WAYS OF WRITING.

We may affiliate with figuration—by a very weak and very artificial bond, it is true—certain methods of writing practised by the virginalists, which show their ingenuity in the use of the most various resources of their instrument.

We have already had occasion to notice that the English masters profited largely by the compass of the keyboard. Now one of these methods of writing consists in the fact of assigning to the hand—left or right—the brisk passage from one fixed register of the keyboard to another, far removed from the first. Thus, in a *Fantasia* by G. Farnaby (*Fitzw. V. B.*, ii., p. 270), we have this series of rapid skips from the lower part to the middle and from the middle to the lower part assigned to the left hand :—

We find an identical example in another *Fantasia* by Farnaby (*Fitzw. V. B.*, ii., p. 347). We notice, again, in a prelude of the same master (*Fitzw. V. B.*, ii., p. 372), this extraordinary passage, in which a rapid figure winds up on a note situated three octaves below the position which it ought normally to occupy :—

L

Tomkins similarly gives us some examples of this way of writing. His variations *Barafostus Dreame* (*Fitzw. V. B.*, ii., p. 94) contain various uses of it :—

Further on :—

The *Hunting Galliard* of the same master (*Fitzw. V. B.*, ii., p. 100) also contains a few :—

73

One of the most characteristic of Domenico Scarlatti's ways of writing consists in the necessity for crossing the hands. Now it may be asserted

---

73 We also find other examples, pretty numerous, of these brisk skips, both in the left hand and the right. We shall instance several in analysing the virginalistic pieces, which we shall do in the following chapter.

that more than a century before that master the
virginalists practised this way of playing. Thus, in
Walsingham (*Fitzw. V. B.*, i., p. 1) by Bull we meet
with this passage :—

74

Farnaby gives us an example no less interesting
in *Bony sweet Robin* (*Fitzw. V. B.*, ii., p. 77) :—

75

If we take a glance back on the various forms of
figuration which we have attempted to record and
to comment upon, we shall come to the conclusion
that the English virginalists, thanks to those
novelties which they had in great part conceived
without foreign help, were admirably equipped for
creating a repertory absolutely appropriate to the
resources of their instrument. In truth the source

---

[74] According to a communication of Mr. Fuller Maitland, the crossing
of hands in this passage is not only indicated by the notation, but also
expressly pointed out by a × in the margin.

[75] These are the only two examples of crossing of the hands to be
observed in the *Fitzw. V. B.*; but this method of performance does
not seem to have been exceptional, for we find, for example, in *Cosyn's
Book*, No. 14, a galliard which bears in the table of contents the
significant title of *A cross-handed galliard*.

of the whole technique of the pianoforte must be sought for among them. Moreover, it seems that this technique was not exceeded until Domenico Scarlatti. It may even possibly be maintained that after the grand period of virginalistic efflorescence there was an actual retrogression as far as concerns real virtuosity. Neither Frescobaldi in Italy, nor Scheidt nor Froberger in Germany, nor the French harpsichord players, forerunners of the great Couperin, present us with examples of figuration so varied and so original as the English of the first third of the 16th century. Continental artists, it is true, furnish us with happy compensations in the progressive refinement of musical forms ; thanks to them the variation, the suite, the toccata, the fugue become little by little better balanced constructions, answering better to the conception of an organism and a style. But they do not possess that blooming freshness, that expansion, that is characteristic of somewhat unregulated *primitifs*, and their creations have not that perfume of the wild flower, that playful and fantastic physiognomy by which the work of the virginalists, looked on as a whole, is distinguished.

CHAPTER V.

—

THE MUSICAL FORMS AND STYLES
CULTIVATED BY THE VIRGINALISTS.

It is by design that we associate the terms musical
"forms" and "styles"; nor shall we attempt
to define these terms more precisely. Our aim is
indeed to take them as the basis of a purely
empirical classification. This becomes necessary
in music of this nature when we consider the variety
of aspects under which virginalistic production in
its entirety shows itself, and the impossibility of
establishing absolute boundaries between them.
Moreover, the analytical study which we are
proposing to make of them will give us, as we
proceed, all the necessary elements for the
separation between what attaches to the idea of
"form" and what attaches to that of "style."

As we drew up a systematic table of the various
methods of figuration made use of by the
virginalists, in the same way we are proposing to
establish in the following pages a logically

arranged inventory of the various forms and styles practised by these musicians :—

I.—" Coloured" transcriptions of vocal pieces.

II.—Figured Plainsong.

III.—Forms under the laws of imitative counterpoint.

IV.—Fantasia.

V.—Prelude and Toccata.

VI.—Variation of secular songs and variation of dances.

VII.—Scholastic pieces.

VIII.—Various forms or styles.

IX.—Descriptive music.

The essential characteristic of this grouping consists in the fact that it does not lean to that strict classification which may be set up for the musical forms in use on the Continent during the 16th and at the beginning of the 17th centuries. We find, in fact, in Continental Europe, on the one hand, forms *dependent on vocal music;* on the other, forms *independent of vocal music.* In the first category we distinguish *figurations of plainsongs,* and *" coloured" transcriptions of songs and of secular dances.* In the second we see contrasted *forms subjected to the rules of imitative counterpoint—ricercare* and *canzona,* and *forms freed from this strictness—prelude, toccata, variation.*

England on the contrary presents us with the appearance of much greater confusion—to such an extent that it would be difficult, not to say impossible, to force virginalistic musical forms into the synthetic outline which obtains in Continental countries. Thus, for example, forms subjected to the rules of imitative counterpoint do not, so to speak, exist in England, whilst they assume a capital importance on the Continent (Italy and Spain); and when, by exception, they force themselves into the repertory of the virginalists, it is most often with a crowd of restrictions arising from the mingling of elements taken from forms freed from imitative polyphony.

(1.) "COLOURED" TRANSCRIPTIONS OF VOCAL PIECES.

"Coloured" transcriptions of vocal pieces are small in number, and the great majority of them have Peter Philips as author. All those which we have been able to analyse are contained in the *Fitzw. V. B.*, where their vocal origin is for the most part expressly mentioned. They consist of madrigals and polyphonic songs by Marenzio, Striggio, Orlando di Lassus, &c.,[1] to which the transcriber has adapted coloratura of his own. In addition Philips has made a "coloured" transcription of a madrigal for a single voice with continued bass, by Julio Romano,[2] who is identical with Giulio Caccini. The piece

---

[1] The three parts of the madrigal *Tirsi*, by L. Marenzio (*Fitzw. V. B.*, i., pp. 280, 283, 286); *Fece da voi a 6.* (*Fitzw. V. B.*, i., p. 288); *Chi fara fede al cielo*, by Alessandro Striggio (i., p. 312); *Bonjour mon cueur*, by Orlando (i., p. 347, dated 1602); *Margott Laborez*, by Orlando (i., p. 332, dated 1605); *Le Rossignuol* (by Orlando, i., p. 346, dated 1595). Mr. Barclay Squire states (Grove, *Dictionary*, 1907 edition) under *Philips*, that "the curious volume of mechanical devices which the celebrated engineer Salomon de Caus published in 1615, under the title *Les Raisons des forces mouvantes*, contains part of a Fantasia by Philips (for a barrel-organ turned by water), on Alessandro Striggio's five-part madrigal, *Chi fara fed' al ciel*." This is evidently the one of which the *Fitzw. V. B.* contains a transcription for the keyboard.

[2] *Fitzw. V. B.*, i., p. 329. (This piece is dated 1603.)

is taken from the *Nuove Musiche* (1601). Three other transcriptions of vocal music are by Giles Farnaby. They also belong to the *Fitzw. V. B.*, in which they are designated by no title,[3] but their vocal origin is proved: for the first by Messrs. Fuller Maitland and Barclay Squire, who show that it is simply a virginalistic adaptation of a *canzonet* by Farnaby himself, "*Ay me, poore heart*"; for the last two by the fact that their internal structure is in entire agreement with that of the first.

If we attempt to form an opinion of the value of the "coloured" transcriptions of Philips and Farnaby from the point of view of figuration, it may be said that on the whole they appear to be superior to those of the Continent: superior to the German transcriptions, the coloratura of which is stiff and stereotyped; superior to those of the Italians, whose fantastic ornamentation sins by excess of virtuosity; superior to those of the Spaniards, which, more severe and refined than those of the Italians as far as regards taste, still end by being tiresome on account of a noble monotony.

The cause of this superiority is that the virginalists used colorature which at most times consist in a combination of the brilliant and expert figuration of the Italians with new elements taken from English figural material, and that the latter modified the former and deprived it of whatever excess of formality it may have possessed.

If it is really the case, as Fétis asserts, that Philips went to Italy in 1595, we have in the transcription which the master made of the

[3] *Fitzw. V. B.*, ii., pp. 330, 333, 340.

Rossignuol of Orlando di Lassus (*Fitzw. V. B.*, i., p. 346), which is actually dated 1595, a document all the more interesting since, by comparison with other transcriptions—also dated, but more recent—it seems to a certain extent to be a first attempt to appropriate the Italian coloratura : an honest yet timid attempt, which, apart from a few ternary figures in the English style, is content to borrow the elegant embroideries, the rapid rising and descending scales and formulas of cadence which we meet again, for example, in the *Canzon ariosa* or the *Canzon francese deta ung gai berger di Crequillon* by Andrea Gabrieli.[4]

Ten years later, in 1605, Philips wrote the last dated transcription in the *Fitzw. V. B.* (i., p. 332). Here again it takes for subject a song by Orlando, *Margott Laborez*. The general feeling of the figuration in it still maintains an Italian cast, but features specially English are introduced ; we find, notably, the breaking of chords and of intervals, little rhythmic figures of the type ♪♫ ♪♫ [5] to say nothing of the inevitable ternary figures.

Margott Laborez forms a remarkable example of the comparative superiority of the English coloratura to that of the Continent. This superiority is in a great measure owing to the fact that the method of figuration adopted by Philips is more appropriate than that of the Continent to the homophonic style of the chanson of Orlando. The decompositions of chords in the bass are peculiarly fitted to bring out the harmonic

---

[4] See Wasielewski, *Gesch. der Instrumentalmus. im XVI. Jahrh., Beilagen*, pp. 57 and 66.

[5] We find them already in the *Rossignuol*, but more isolated.

essentials of the piece,[6] which acquires from this fact a very modern character.

The other transcriptions of Philips, whether dated or not, with the exception of *Bonjour mon cueur* by Orlando (1602), all present an Italian rather than an English appearance; moreover, they are instrumental versions of madrigals by Marenzio, Striggio, &c., the harmonic successions of which have already in themselves a coloration entirely Italian. The few English figures to be found in'them do not suffice to efface it.

However elegant may be the clothing of coloratura applied to these songs, it does not succeed in embellishing them. We must not deceive ourselves; these brilliant transcriptions stand on the same footing as those of a Thalberg or a Herz—"disarrangements" which mostly belong to the realm of pure virtuosity. They are the less justifiable since they are not applied, like those of the 19th century, to works whose artistic value is in most cases virtually *nil*, but to compositions of which the æsthetic merit cannot be contested. No doubt the vocal originals were themselves also treated in performance with an ornamentation of which no written trace has been preserved for us in documents of the period. But it is beyond doubt that this vocal coloratura was less elaborate and consequently less disfiguring than the instrumental; further, we know by numerous testimonies that the masters of that time lost no opportunity of protesting against the abuse of coloratura, by which the bad taste of singers made their works suffer.

[6] Certain passages already hint at the "Alberti bass" of the 18th century.

One of those who expressed themselves with the greatest energy on this subject was actually Giulio Caccini, whose madrigal *Amarilli* (*Fitzw. V. B.*, i., p. 329), Philips transcribed with colorations. This transcription, dated 1603, has this point of interest, that it takes for its foundation not a polyphonic work, but a monodic song with continuo to be filled in by the accompanist. The work of Philips therefore consisted—unless he found the realisation already made, which, for that epoch, is improbable—in completing the harmonic filling-in of the middle parts between the melody and the bass, and in " colouring " the whole.

When the transcription of the English master is compared with the original version as it is arranged by M. Parisotti,[7] we see that, apart from a few alterations of detail, Philips has preserved intact, but with "colourings," the melodic outline of Caccini's madrigal ; the divergences proceed either from slight rhythmical modifications, or else from the filling-in of certain inner parts rising in places above the original melodic line. We notice also little divergences between the conduct of the bass in the original and in the transcription, which involves a few differences in the harmonic effects.[8] In addition the bass, like the upper part, is treated with coloratura in the transcribed version. Finally it is an element which brings the latter near to the style of variation. Caccini's madrigal is of the following structure : A, B, B, the second B being a simple repeat of the first, but provided with

[7] *Arie Antiche, Libro secundo*, p. 20 (Ricordi, Milan).

[8] It is, moreover, very probable that there were in circulation in the time of Philips versions of *Amarilli* more or less differing from that in the *Nuove Musiche* of 1601.

an ornamental cadence which forms a *Coda*. The transcription by Philips follows the same plan, but with the addition to A of an episode A¹, which is a variation of A, while the reprise of B is conceived as a variation B¹. Moreover, the *Coda* is suppressed.

The comparison between the transcription and the original is all in favour of the latter, the noble and delicate simplicity of which cannot help being lost when encumbered with a tangle of colorature. Yet these are fairly sober, and do not sin by an excess of virtuosity. They show a free use of methods of figuration specially English.

It remains to examine the " coloured " transcriptions of Farnaby. The first is arranged, as we have said, from the *canzonet*, " *Ay me, poore heart !* " (*Fitzw. V. B.*, ii., p. 330).[9] Compared with the transcriptions of Philips, those of Farnaby show less predilection for virtuosity, and a better preservation of the balance between the original and its figured version, in the sense that the figuration, although still excessive, does not interfere with the melodic and harmonic advance to the point of encumbering it and in some degree obscuring its general outline.

The figuration of the " coloured " pieces of Farnaby is more English than Italian; in the second (*Fitzw. V. B.*, ii., p. 333), we come across, among others, the most virginalistic of all the figures, the rapid repetition of one and the same note. In *Ay me, poore heart!* we notice the sudden skips of the left hand from the middle of the instrument to its lowest extent.

[9] We are here speaking of one of the compositions of the collection *Canzonets to foure voyces, with a song of eight parts*, published by Farnaby in 1598.

(2.) FIGURED PLAINSONG.

A general remark in the first place becomes necessary in analysing the different aspects of English figuration of the choral ; it is that, contrary to what took place on the Continent, this form seems to have had as much if not more to do with the clavier than the organ. Outside England in the 16th century figured plainsongs and secular songs and dances are usually crowded indiscriminately into the tablatures intended both for the organ and the clavier. If among these pieces one asks which are intended for the organ and which for the clavier, we have to resort immediately to the distinction between " sacred " and " secular," being compelled to admit that the figured plainsongs naturally had their place in church, that is to say, on the organ, whilst the transcriptions of secular songs and dances were more suitable to the intimacy of the home, that is to say, to the clavier. Moreover, when one examines more closely the figured plainsongs it becomes obvious by their very technique that they are more suitable for the organ than the clavier.[10]

In England this is not the case. In the first place, the English plainsongs are on a scale which excludes the possibility of their execution in the course of divine service; further, many seem to be simply scholastic contrapuntal and figural exercises; lastly, there exists in the greater part of them a figuration better adapted to the clavier than to the organ.

[10] See especially, in Ritter, *Gesch. des Orgelspiels*, second part, the figured plainsongs of the tablatures of Schlick (No. 59) ; Kleber (No. 61) ; Ammerbach (No. 64) ; B. Schmid, senr. (No. 65) ; Paix (No. 67), &c.

The figured plainsongs of the English virginalists may be arranged in three distinct groups:—

A.—Plainsongs in which the liturgical melody is treated in its full extent;

B.—Plainsong variation;

C.—Various forms, not included in the two preceding categories.

A.—Plainsongs in which the Liturgical Melody is treated in its Full Extent.

Plainsongs belonging to this first category [11] have for *cantus firmus* a melody taken from the Gregorian repertory. They treat it in its full extent, with the result that they are occasionally of an unreasonable length. They are distinguished by a title which forms the opening of the Latin text, for example, *In nomine*, [12] *Felix namque*, &c.

[11] The following is a list of those which are to be found in the *Fitzw. V. B.*: *Felix namque* I. by Tallis (i., p. 427); *Felix namque* II. by Tallis (ii., p. 1); *In nomine* by Blitheman (i., p. 181); *Miserere* of three parts, by Byrd (ii., p. 230); *Miserere* of four parts by Byrd (ii., p. 232); *In nomine* I. by Bull (i., p. 135); *In nomine* II. by Bull (ii., p. 34); *Gloria tibi trinitas* by Bull (i., p. 160); *Christe Redemptor* by Bull (ii., p. 64); *Fantasia* by Bull (i., p. 138); *Veni*, anonymous (i., p. 421).

[12] Grove, *Dictionary*, under *In nomine*, says that *In nomine* is a vague word, used by the old English musicians to signify a certain kind of motet or antiphon composed to Latin words. Originally it was only employed for pieces the text of which actually began with the words *In nomine*, but afterwards the meaning was extended to other pieces, vocal and instrumental.

According to Dr. Naylor (*An Eliz. V. B.*, p. 177), *In nomine* became synonymous with *hymn*. He derives this meaning from the fact that no very long time since, the dialect word "A nomminy" was still applied to certain religious songs in the north-east of Yorkshire.

The expression *In nomine* appears at times with very remarkable orthography; for instance, *Parsons Innominey* (No. 46 of *Forster's Book*), or else *Inno myne*. In the latter case it is applied to a galliard (!) in the lute book of Thysius (see *Land, op. cit.*, No. 71, p. 82). Nagel (*Gesch. der Mus. in Eng.*, ii., p. 151) mentions Add. MS. 31390 of the British Museum as containing quite a series of *In nomine*.

We have here, when all is said, a true musical form, the history of which it would be interesting to follow up.

It is a question therefore of melodies specially Catholic, not ancient Gregorian melodies simplified with a view to the Anglican form of worship, and provided with English texts, such as we find in the *Book of Common Prayer* of Marbeck (1550). From this fact we may detect a new element of proof in favour of the Catholic origin of the *Fitzw. V. B.*

These plainsongs amount to the number of eleven in the *Fitzw. V. B.*, and have for authors Tallis, Blitheman, Byrd, Bull, and an anonymous writer. In five of them the *cantus firmus* takes the upper part, in five others an intermediate part between the *superius* and the bass, and in one single case the bass. Before proceeding to the analysis of the inner structure of these plainsong figurations, it is desirable to draw attention to certain outward particulars which distinguish certain of them.

The first plainsong of Tallis on the melody *Felix namque* (*Fitzw. V. B.*, i., p. 427) is preceded by two short preludes in the style of a ricercare or a voluntary. His second plainsong is written upon another melodic version of the *Felix namque* (*Fitzw. V. B.*, ii., p. 1). It also opens with two preludes of an imitative character, and winds up with rapid figures in the style of a toccata ; this is particularly interesting on account of the date of the piece (1564), which is anterior to that of all the available evidence which the Italians have left us in the realm of the toccata. Moreover, in England itself this postlude is the most ancient written and dated example of the application of the style of free improvisation.

The choral *Gloria tibi trinitas* of Bull (*Fitzw. V.B.*, i., p. 160) also has a prelude (*Fitzw. V.B.*, i., p. 158);

but in this case it forms no part of it, as in the two plainsongs of Tallis, and is composed in a free style, very modern in character. Its connection with the plainsong which follows it is inferrible, according to the notes of Messrs. Fuller Maitland and Barclay Squire, from a document of the 18th century which qualifies it as *Preludium to Gloria tibi trinitas.* It seems, in addition, that there is some resemblance between the few figured notes with which the tenor of the prelude opens and the melody of the choral.[13]

In what manner are the figured plainsongs of the first kind treated from the point of view of musical architecture ? On the selected *cantus firmus* the composer erects a multiplicity of little counterpoints which form a clothing of incomparable richness, but now and then of a heaviness and a complexity which take away all true beauty from the edifice as a whole.

When the *cantus firmus* occupies the upper part it retains something of its individuality. But when it is given to another part it disappears almost entirely under the more or less rapid figuration which surrounds it; its long notes, perceptible only to the eye, become in performance as though submerged under the moving flood of figured counterpoints. Even where the composer has duplicated them, with the design of not letting them be forgotten too soon, or in order not to lose the needful resting-places, the effect is scarcely more successful in bringing the melody into relief. Tallis

---

[13] Let us observe, however, that the prelude and the plainsong are not in the same key : the first is in the mode of D, and the second in the mode of A. This difference seems somewhat unusual for two pieces depending on each other.

in this way duplicates the notes of the first
Felix namque :—

becomes [14]

Bull at times introduces an element of rhythm
in this duplication. In the choral *Gloria tibi trinitas*
(*Fitzw. V. B.*, i., p. 160) he transforms this succession
of notes :—

in the following way :—

Elsewhere (*Fitzw. V. B.*, ii., p. 34) the
fragmentation of the same motive appears with
this singular rhythmical character :—

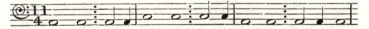

These duplications and fragmentations do not in
execution prevent the *cantus firmus* from seeming
to be an accessory, whilst the figural scaffolding
takes the principal place and draws all the attention
to itself. In other words the melody becomes only a

[14] The pieces in which these duplications are introduced are the
two *Felix namque* of Tallis (*Fitzw. V. B.*, i., p. 427, and ii., p. 1);
In nomine (i., p. 135, and ii., p. 34); *Gloria tibi trinitas* (i., p. 160);
Christe redemptor (ii., p. 64); and *Fantasia* (i., p. 138), of Bull.

M

technical starting-point, the support of an edifice to the construction of which it is indispensable, but in the whole effect of which it has a very small share, just as the foundations of houses do not form any element in the beauty of their general appearance.

It can hardly be objected that it was lawful for the performer to bring the *cantus firmus* into relief by using the resources peculiar to his instrument. If the pianists of the present day have at their command a keyboard on which it is more or less easy to bring out a part in long notes above the rapid figuration with which it is surrounded, if modern organs possess the advantage of a number of combinations which allow one part more important than another to be brought to the front, it could not, without doubt, have been the case at the period when these pieces were played, either on a little clavecin of homogeneous tone-colour, or on an organ which had a single row of keys only, and no pedals.

Among the figured plainsong melodies of the first kind, the most important from an historical point of view are the two *Felix namque* of Tallis, dated respectively 1562 and 1564.[15] This importance arises at the same time from their antiquity, and from the fact that we find in them elements of virginalistic figuration very remarkable for the period: actual rhythmical

---

[15] A rather large number of figured plainsongs entitled *Felix namque* are to be found in the English manuscripts of organ or virginal music of the 16th and 17th centuries. Thus, for example, in the MS. Roy. App. 56 (No. 1, *Felix namque* anonymous); in *Mulliner's Book* (*Felix namque* by Farrant); in Add. MS. No. 29996 (No. 47, *Felix namque* by Redford; Nos. 51 and 55 to 61, various *Felix namque* by Thomas Preston (?)); in the Add. MS. 30485 (No. 20, a *Felix namque* by Tallis, differing from those in the *Fitzw. V. B.*).

figures, symmetric figures, spreading of chords, &c., by the side of figures of more ancient origin : faux-bourdons, *hoketus*, short imitations, &c. All these scattered about with a profusion which at last becomes tedious, and which ends by producing an impression of monotony analogous to that experienced in the execution of the interminable *ricercari* of the period of Buus and Willaert. The most interesting problem arising from this richness of figuration is that of its antecedents. Was it Tallis who invented all these combinations, or was there already in England a figural tradition which he had only to follow and develop ?—a problem till lately insoluble, in view of the absence of actual evidence, but which is becoming clearer by some gleams of light since Johannes Wolf has called attention to the works of Hughe Ashton, and has thus proved that from the very opening of the 16th century there existed in the British Isles a figural technique which was exceptionally advanced for the period. It is allowable, therefore, to think that in the space of the half-century which divides the virginal pieces of Ashton from the plainsong melodies of Tallis, this technique insensibly developed in the direction of a gradually increasing variety, in such a manner that it becomes impossible to consider the figuration of these melodies as an instantaneous creation.

Another thing strikes us when we compare certain passages of the two pieces of Tallis with the works of Cabezon written in the style of variation: that is, the resemblance in general physiognomy between the said works of the Spanish master and that of these English fragments. Cabezon came to England in 1554 with his master,

Philip II.; he must certainly have had occasion to appear at the Court, to which Tallis was at that time attached as a member of the Chapel Royal. Did he perhaps reveal to the English master the secret of those elegant figurations with which he adorned his variations? This we cannot actually decide in view of the double fact that the compositions of the Spanish organist are not dated, while the plainsong melodies of Tallis, which are earlier than the death of Cabezon (1566), present a greater richness of figuration than the most advanced variations of the latter. We are rather tempted to believe that during his stay in England Cabezon assimilated the traditional figural technique of the virginalists, and that on his return to his own country he made use of it in his own works, with the taste and sense of proportion which we appreciate in him, and which place him well above Tallis[16] as a creative artist in instrumental music.[17]

The first plainsong melody of Tallis is, as we have said, preceded by two preludes; the opening prelude is separated from that which follows by a cadence which forms the close. The second is attached without any break to the opening of the melody. This is treated from one end to the other in the *superius*. The second plainsong presents

[16] Tallis is especially great in polyphonic vocal composition.

[17] Let us remark that we find in the variations and the *tientos* of Cabezon pieces of a character sometimes archaic, at others on the way to being modern. It is in the last only that we meet with forms of figuration in the English style. Possibly we might fairly decide that these dated from the later years of the master, that is to say, from the intermediate period between his journey to England (1554) and his death (1566). This hypothesis seems all the more plausible since all the pieces of this character are contained in the *Obras* of 1578, published by the son of the artist; whilst the *Libro de Cifra*, which was published in 1557, contains only works of a much more ancient appearance.

exactly the same structure, with the exception that it winds up with a *Coda* in free style, and that the *cantus firmus* occupies the tenor; moreover, the *cantus firmus* is already sketched out at the beginning of the second introductory prelude. This is a procedure often found in the organ choral of the Continent.

The religious melody is treated at full length, and with each of its notes repeated in both the two works; it appears surrounded with extremely varied figurations, into the details of which we cannot enter. A detail peculiar to the Gregorian original is that it contains fragments which give occasion for repetition. During the repetition the figuration assumes a different appearance, so that we find ourselves in this case in the presence of an element which has some affinity with variation.

In spite of the charm of detail in the figuration of the two *Felix namque* it must be recognised that the whole is long, heavy, and monotonous. These defects are the more apparent since the preludes are of a very sober and refined art. But from the moment when the inspiration of the musician is led by the long Ariadne thread of the Gregorian melody, stripped of its inner rhythm and of the words which give it life, a heavy constraint seems to rest on the melodic and harmonic progress of the two melodies, and it is impossible to listen to the end without a feeling of weariness.

The other figured plainsong melodies of the first category included in the *Fitzw. V.B.* will not delay us so long. With rare exceptions they appear to have as their most prominent feature a scholastic stamp. This is notably the case with the following :—

In nomine by Blitheman (*Fitzw. V. B.*, p. 181), where, the *cantus firmus* being placed in the alto, the figuration consists from one end to the other of regular triplets, without any interruption of the rhythm by the intervention of binary values.

The *Miserere* of three parts by Byrd (*Fitzw. V. B.*, ii., p. 230), where the melody occupies the *superius*, is a very dry study of figural counterpoint without virtuosity. We find in it several examples of contrasted rhythm (ternary values superimposed on binary values).

The first *In nomine* of Bull (*Fitzw. V. B.*, i., p. 135) uses the same subject as that by Blitheman, but in the *superius;* it is a curious exercise in syncopations; the figuration, somewhat modest, is not interesting from the virginalistic point of view, except towards the end. On the other hand, in the *Gloria tibi trinitas*, also by Bull (*Fitzw. V. B.*, i., p. 160), the virginalistic figuration is carried to the highest pitch; at each step we meet with new figures, archaic or almost modern. It is a veritable *étude de piano* which even in the present day might serve to make the fingers of the left hand supple. The *cantus firmus* is in the *superius*.

The plainsong melody for three voices, *Christe Redemptor*, by Bull (*Fitzw. V. B.*, ii., p. 64), is again a pure exercise of virginalistic figuration. The melody, given to the middle part, is surrounded with regular counterpoints, partly symmetrical. The conclusion offers curious examples of cross rhythms.

The Fantasia upon a plain song[18] by Bull (*Fitzw. V. B.*, i., p. 138) offers almost the same characters (three parts, theme in the intermediate part, regular figurations, partly symmetrical; no cross rhythms).

Lastly the anonymous *Veni* (*Fitzw. V. B.*, i., p. 421) is of all these plainsongs the one in which the scholastic character is the most apparent. Treated in two parts almost up to the end, the *cantus firmus* keeps itself apart in the *superius*, upon a figuration in absolutely regular semi-quavers, which persist up to the last bars, where triplets in quavers replace the semiquavers.

Up to this point we have reserved two figured plainsongs of the first kind, which are free from this scholastic appearance: the *Miserere* in four parts of Byrd (*Fitzw. V. B.*, ii., p. 232), and the second *In nomine* of Bull (*Fitzw. V. B.*, ii., p. 34), which treats the same subject as the first.

In the *Miserere* by Byrd the subject, given out in the alto, is insensibly lost in the figuration ; the result is that the constraint to which we have alluded in the case of the plainsongs of Tallis here disappears, giving place to a freer inspiration. The figuration of this piece is scarcely virginalistic ; it consists of very simple counterpoints, which combine among themselves with that charm of poetic sweetness and comprehensive tenderness which we shall have on more than one occasion to remark upon as being among the characteristic aspects of the genius of Byrd.

In the second *In Nomine* by Bull, the liturgical subject occupies the bass, and undergoes the curious

[18] It has no title in the *Fitzw. V. B.* ; but according to the notes of Messrs. Fuller Maitland and Barclay Squire, it is called in another document a *Fantasia upon a plain-song.*

rhythmical breaking up, which we have noticed above (see p. 165). On this solid and level foundation Bull constructs an edifice of free counterpoint of great variety, in which are heaped up, without excess, the greater part of the treasures of virginalistic figuration. The work in its entirety produces an impression of real beauty; far from having the effect of inexpressive monotony, the *cantus firmus* gives the feeling of a picturesque peal of distant chimes.

B.—Plainsong Variation.

The qualification of Plainsong variation is justified by the fact that in this kind of plainsong melody the musician chooses a religious subject and treats it in successive repetitions, in which it is each time furnished with a new figuration; this is a process absolutely in conformity with the secular variation.

The *Fitzw. V. B.* contains only two typical examples of the plainsong variation, of both of which Bull is the author. The first is a *Salvator mundi* (*Fitzw. V. B.*, i., p. 163), the second a *Miserere* (ii., p. 442). They are absolutely scholastic in character, and have no real æsthetic interest. In the *Salvator mundi*[19] Bull treats the subject successively in two, three, and four parts in three variations, in which he brings the most various virginalistic figures into play with a stiffness which takes from them any sort of charm. Notice the figurations in regular quavers or semi-quavers, the symmetrical figurations, the breaking

[19] The melody is that of the well-known Gregorian hymn, *Veni creator*.

of intervals and of chords. The *cantus firmus* is in the *superius* in each variation.

The *Miserere* is still drier. Written from one end to the other in three parts, it comprises three variations. In the first the subject is found in the *superius*, and is accompanied by a symmetrical figuration in the two other parts; crotchets in the alto, quavers in the bass. The second variation treats the *cantus firmus* once more in the *superius*, with, in the two other parts, a symmetrical figuration of quavers in the alto and semiquavers in the bass. Finally, in the last variation the melody is in the tenor, and undergoes a symmetrical figuration of semiquavers in the upper part and of quavers in the bass. The whole work has a thoroughly geometrical appearance, and all inspiration is wanting.

Outside the *Fitzw. V. B.*, we find another piece by Bull which is connected with the plainsong variation : this is the *Fantasia* on the Flemish melody, *Laet ons met herten reyne*, which Mr. John E. West has published in Part 25 of his *Old English Organ Music*.

This piece is taken from No. 23623 in the British Museum (1628). Mr. West observes [20] that it is expressly written for the organ, since it bears several indications of registration. It is very probably the first English piece so treated. It is, moreover, highly probable that it dates from the time when Bull was established in the Netherlands, and that it was written for an organ on the Continent. The work is absolutely beautiful by its general balance, and the sobriety of its figuration. The vocal original is a Flemish

[20] *Art. cit.*, p. 214.

religious song, the words of which celebrate the birth of the Saviour.[21]

The work opens with a prelude in the style of a voluntary, the subject of which is taken from the opening of the melody—a prelude of a solemn and sweet charm, noticeable for its harmonic elegances.[22]

The Flemish original may be represented by the following diagram :—

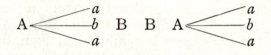

Bull treats it in its full extent, according to the following plan :—

The figures are of a simplicity and of a taste which show the great virtuoso in an entirely new light. Having come to the end of his career (he died in 1628), he seems to some extent to have renounced that over-rich figuration which he had practised in the earlier period of his life, and to have retained only just so much of it as was necessary to bring into relief in the most expressive manner the themes which he varied. This change is

---

[21] **Van Duyse** publishes at p. 1856 of his great work, *Het oude Nederlandsche Lied* (Nijhoff, The Hague, 1904), the text and music of this song.

[22] We meet, among other things, with augmented fifths.

no doubt due to Continental influences, more especially that of Sweelinck.[23]

C.—Various Forms not Included in the Two Previous Categories.

The *Fitzw. V. B.* gives us but two examples of this third kind of plainsong: a piece entitled *Heaven and Earth* (*Fitzw. V. B.*, i., p. 415) and bearing as author's name the three letters " Fre," an abbreviation which Messrs. Fuller Maitland and Barclay Squire interpret as possibly standing for Francis Tregian, the supposed collector of the *Fitzw. V. B.;* and secondly an *In nomine* signed Parsons (*Fitzw. V. B.*, ii., p. 135), of which the author is either Robert Parsons the father, or else his son John.

Heaven and Earth[24] is similar to the figured plainsong of the first kind in that it treats a religious melody in its full length. But in this case the melody no longer takes the part of a mere thread which forms a pretext for contrapuntal developments; on the contrary it occupies the first place, and is developed under the form of a homophonic hymn in four parts, one of which is figured by the use of animated colorature. The figured part is generally either the bass or the *superius*.

[23] An elementary form of the variation of plainsong is to be found as early as the younger Schlick (1512). See his organ pieces published in the first year of the *Monatsh. für Musikg.*, p. 17 ff., of the *Beilagen*. In the Plainsong *Da pacem* the subject is successively treated in the *superius* (in 3 parts), in the alto (in 4 parts), and in the bass (in 4 parts). The accompanying counterpoint is modified at each resumption of the subject. It is written in shorter notes than the latter, and comprises animated colorature specially instrumental in character.

[24] The unusual nature of the English title is worthy of notice.

The whole is a construction which recalls both the figured successions of chords of the Italian toccatists, and certain "coloured" homophonic hymns by Cabezon.[25]

In his *In nomine* Parsons apparently treats the same subject as Blitheman and Bull in their plain-songs bearing the same title. But the subject appears from its very outset so disguised under its accompanying counterpoints that it is almost impossible to recognise it. It has the appearance of being in quest of itself, and it is only at the end of the piece that we see it revealed clearly in long notes in the alto part. Thus we have again to do with a plainsong which resembles those of the first kind. The fact that the theme is announced without clearness in the concert of parts is alone sufficient to induce us to put it in a separate category.[26] The figuration has a somewhat unusual character. It looks as if the musician wished to suggest by his curious use of the *hoketus* the aerial polyphony of a multitude of bells. The effect produced is more curious than beautiful. At the outset this *In nomine* produces such an impression of modernity that one hesitates to attribute it to the older Parsons, who died in 1569 or 1570. Yet the roughness and the primitive heaviness of its harmonies, and in addition the analogy of certain of its figures with those of the plainsongs of Tallis, end by

---

[25] See, for instance, in the *Hisp. Schol. Mus. Sacr.*, vol. viii., p. 44, the plainsong *Dic nobis, Maria*.

[26] The *Miserere* in four parts of Byrd, which we have analysed above (see p. 171), shows a structure more or less analogous, but inverse, in the sense that the subject, clearly given out in the beginning, is finally lost in the midst of the figuration.

convincing us that that attribution would not be too adventurous.[27]

We may also connect with the figured plainsong of the third kind the *Vexilla regis prodeunt* of Bull (third part) which Mr. John E. West reproduces in Part 25 of his *Old English Organ Music*,[28] a work of a severe style from which all coloratura is banished, recalling the *ricercare* and the motet of the Netherlands from which the latter took its origin. Yet it is in appearance only that the piece is conceived in this form. In reality there is no question here of contrapuntal development of one or of several thematic fragments, but actually of a liturgical theme treated in its entirety; what makes one think of a *ricercare* is, in addition to the gravity of the style, the imitative use of fragments

[27] *Forster's Book* contains (No. 46) a piece by Byrd called *Parsons Innominey* (*sic*). According to a communication from Mr. Barclay Squire, this piece takes as its foundation the *In nomine* of the *Fitzw. V. B.* This being granted, there are the more grounds for believing that the latter is by Parsons the father, for it is doubtful if Byrd could have taken as subject for development the work of Parsons the son, who was, according to all probability, younger than himself (both were dead in 1623, but Byrd at that time was more than eighty years of age). At the moment of correcting the proof of this note, we learn from Mr. Barclay Squire that the *Innominey* of *Forster's Book* is, in fact, a new version, due to Byrd, of the *In nomine* by Parsons to be found in the *Fitzw. V. B.* On the other hand the Add. MS. 29996 of the British Museum contains under No. 70 an *In nomine* of R[obert] Parsons, followed by *Another* by Byrd; these two pieces seem to be one with the *In nomine* by Parsons of the *Fitzw. V. B.*, and with the *Parsons Innominey* by Byrd of *Forster's Book*. If this turns out to be the case, and if the initial " R " has not been placed carelessly before the name of Parsons, there can be no longer room for doubt that the *In nomine* of the *Fitzw. V. B.* is the work of the elder Parsons.

The late Mr. W. H. Husk (see his notice of *Parsons, Robert*, in Grove's *Dictionary*, ed. 1907) also believed that the *In nomine* of the *Fitzw. V. B.* is by Parsons the father.

[28] This piece is taken from MS. 23623 of the British Museum. Bull treated the subject of the *Vexilla regis* in " four settings," which occupy Nos. 53-56 inclusive of the MS. The first version comprises three sub-divisions, the three others four sub-divisions (*Catal. of the MS. Mus. in the Brit. Mus.*, vol. iii., p. 82).

of the liturgical theme as counter-subjects or as accompanying counterpoint.

The religious melody which forms the base of the piece still in our own day forms part of the official Gregorian repertory, where it appears in the category of "hymns."[29] Having given the opening of the subject to the tenor, Bull takes it up again in the alto, which develops it to the end, scarcely modifying its original form. The accompanying counterpoint is almost invariably imitative. The whole is perfectly beautiful, and makes us think of the Spanish masters of the 16th century, but the austerity of the latter is here tempered by that harmonic sweetness which characterises the English.[30] One must recognise the result of a Continental influence, more especially that of the German organ chorale, in the exceptional character which the structure of this work presents when compared with that of the other English figured plainsongs.

(3.) FORMS UNDER THE STRICT LAWS OF IMITATIVE COUNTERPOINT.

We have now arrived at the third kind of musical forms practised by the virginalists : those which are governed by the strict laws of imitative counterpoint. We shall not have to dwell long on

[29] It is a hymn to the Holy Cross.

[30] By way of comparison, see the *Vexilla regis* treated by Bermudo in his *Declaración* of 1555 (Kinkeldey, *op. cit.*, p. 233). The liturgical subject is treated almost in the same manner as by Bull. Given out at first in the bass and tenor, it is afterwards taken up by the upper part, which develops it to the close in free counterpoint, in which the numerous crossings of the parts show strong vocal influence. The general effect is that of a rugged mysticism, further accentuated by the predilection which the musician shows for the lower part of the instrument.

them, for, as we have already said, they are far from being an English specialty. With the English virginalists we do not meet with the words which serve to distinguish them on the Continent ; *ricercare, canzona, tiento* are terms foreign to the vocabulary of the virginalists.[31] One term alone, which is more or less synonymous in Spain with *ricercare* or *tiento*—the word *fantasia*,—is frequently employed by them. But, as we shall see further on, it is applied by them to somewhat various forms, with this interesting circumstance that the most frequent and the most characteristic form may be looked on as derived from the *ricercare*.

The chief reason which justifies the absence of preference of the virginalists for the strict forms exists, no doubt, in the fact that the purely polyphonic style of the *ricercare* and the *canzona* has only distant relations with those methods of figuration thanks to which they have in so happy a manner adapted their repertory to the resources of their instrument. When we meet in their works with pieces more or less wanting in this figuration, we may affirm that these are intended for the organ rather than for the clavier; the *voluntary*, which approaches the *ricercare* by its imitative style, free from all ornament, is essentially organ music.

We very seldom meet, therefore, among the English, with pieces which appear to resemble the

---

[31] We meet, in truth, with the term *ricercare* on several occasions in the MS. 23623 (1628) of the British Museum, which contains compositions by Bull only. But we must not lose sight of the fact that this MS. was made, probably in the Netherlands, just at the time of the death of Bull. Now at that time the master had been settled for many years on the Continent, and was therefore under strong foreign influence.

ricercari, and when, by exception, the virginalists occupy themselves with the development of a subject which presents a more or less strict character, there is always one or another obstacle preventing the complete carrying-out of this resemblance.

Thus the *Lesson* of Tallis which Weitzmann publishes[32] is a strict canon in two parts, one of which is given to the soprano and the other to the alto ; but starting from the second third of the piece a specifically virginalistic element appears which to a certain extent breaks this strictness. A third part, conceived in the style of embroidery, forces itself into the bass and serves as an accompaniment to the canon up to the conclusion. The embroidery comprises numerous sequences. It is curious to see this combination of a very ancient form, the canon, with an element of so progressive a nature.[33]

The *Fitzw. V. B.* gives us (i., p. 335) a Fantasia by Peter Philips which develops one identical subject thirty-nine times.[34] At first sight one thinks involuntarily of those long *ricercari* of the period of Willaert and Buus, in which one sees a single subject form the pretext for long imitative developments. Let us remark that in Italy the term *fantasia* seems to have been applied

[32] *Gesch. des Klavierspiels*, 2nd edition, p. 324.

[33] Oscar Bie (*Das Klavier und seine Meister*, p. 23) has given an excellent analysis of this *Lesson*.

34

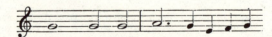

The manuscript carefully numbers the thirty-nine entries of the subject. This is treated sometimes in the original key, sometimes in the dominant ; once also in the subdominant. Byrd composed a *Fantasia* on the same subject (*Fitzw. V. B.*, ii., p. 406).

more especially to the *ricercare* on a single subject.[35] Another point in common between the work of Philips and certain Italian *ricercari* is that the subject with him is treated sometimes in the original values, sometimes in augmentation, sometimes in diminution.[36]

But when we examine matters a little more closely, we find noticeable differences between these two orders of composition. In the *ricercare* the theme is for the greater part of the time subject to re-entries which form *stretti*, and surround themselves with counterpoints which in most cases play only a purely accessory part. In the *Fantasia* by Philips we find only two re-entries in the form of *stretti*. The majority of the re-entries occur not only after the announcement of the theme in its completeness, but again by means of transitions in free counterpoint which often take up several bars. Finally, the accompanying counterpoints acquire so much importance, and so evidently aim at producing their own effects, that the subject ends in many cases in occupying quite a secondary position. We may perhaps liken this piece of Philips to a special class which the English call *ground*, which we shall have to consider later; it consists of variations on a subject (*ground*) the original form of which is never altered, and serves as a foundation, either in the bass or in some other part, for counterpoints and figures the aspect of which continually alters from variation to variation. But the similarity would not be complete in every case, for the *ground* does not

---

[35] See Seiffert (*op. cit.*, p. 34).

[36] See, for example, the *Ricercar del primo tuono*, by A. Gabrieli. (Wasielewski, *op. cit.*, p. 45, of the *Beilagen*.)

N

recognise either the principle of augmentation or of diminution of the subject, nor the practice of transitions between the various entries of the latter.

The *Fantasia* of Philips is very long, and could not be performed in its entirety without inducing weariness. But yet the figural graces which surround the subject avoid anything like scholastic virtuosity as well as all false brilliancy, and display an elegance which is quite Italian.

In the *Fantazia* of Bull, *Op de fuga van M. Jan Pieterss* (Sweelinck), (*Œuvres complètes*, vol. i., p. 125), we meet for the first time with a true *ricercare* or *fantasia* on a single subject. The principle of close imitation, with or without *stretti*, is completely maintained in it. But where the master departs from the original Italian model is in the figuration, which from the great simplicity of its opening increases more and more as it proceeds, even almost to the suggestion of a *toccata*, nevertheless returning at the end of the piece to a sobriety more in keeping with the style of the *ricercare*. The work offers but little attraction in spite of the exceptional effects resulting from the chromatic movement of one part of the subject.[37]

A composition which appears at first sight to belong to the strict forms is the *Fantasia of foure parts* of Gibbons, to be found in *Parthenia* (p. 38 of Rimbault's edition). One would call it at first a *ricercare* with three subjects, in which the principal essentials of that kind of composition are maintained: constant re-entries of the subjects, most

37
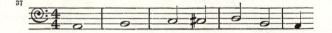

frequently in the form of *stretti ;* free counterpoints only slightly ornamented, and not interfering with the clearness of the development of the subjects. But if all this is noticeable in the first part of the piece, it is no longer the same in the second, in which the development ceases to be imitative and becomes sequential, and thus departs from the archaic strictness of the *ricercare.* The result is that this *Fantasia* in reality takes an intermediate place between the strict forms and certain freer forms which we shall have to study further on. From the point of view of its æsthetic value it possesses the unexpectedness and the harmonic charm which constitute one of the distinctive signs of the art of Gibbons.

We may again class among the works which belong to the strict forms the *Voluntary* of Orlando Gibbons which Mr. John E. West published in the 14th number (p. 1) of his *Old English Organ Music.* It is a piece more especially laid out for the organ than the clavier, as appears from its title of *voluntary* as well as from its severe polyphony and the sacred feeling which pervades it and gives it its character. In its structure it would be an absolute *ricercare* with a single subject [38] if through the whole of the second part of the piece the development of this subject did not give place to free counterpoints formed by means of rising scales.[39]

---

[39] We sometimes find this practice in certain authors of the Italian *ricercari* of the end of the 16th and opening of the 17th centuries.

(4.) THE FANTASIA (FANCY).

It is the same with this word *fancy* (*fantasia*) as with many other English words which are used to distinguish musical compositions; that is to say, it is not applied to a single clearly determined form only, but to various forms at times considerably differing from each other. The English fantasias may be classed in three distinct groups :—

(A) The fantasia-adaptation to the clavier of the style of the madrigal;

(B) The fantasia-amplification of the *ricercare*;

(C) The fantasia agreeing with neither of these in structure.

(A)—FANTASIA-ADAPTATION OF THE MADRIGAL STYLE TO THE CLAVIER.

Just as the *ricercare* and the *canzona*, considered as independent instrumental forms, are adaptations to the organ and the clavier of the vocal style of the motet and the French *chanson*, so the English *fantasia* of the first type appears to be the product of the translation into the instrumental realm of the freer and more fanciful style of the madrigal, or of those forms of composition which resemble it, such as the English *canzonet*.

The *Fitzw. V. B.* contains two compositions which fall into this category: a *Fantasia* of Byrd and one of Morley. That of Byrd (*Fitzw. V. B.*, i., p. 406) is remarkable for the charm of its harmonies and the tasteful sobriety of its colorature. A penchant towards homophony accentuates the grace of it, and confirms the fact that it forms an adaptation to the virginal of the vocal style most in favour at the end of the 16th and the opening of the 17th centuries.

Morley's *Fantasia* (*Fitzw. V. B.*, ii., p. 57) shines by the delicacy of its harmonies and by a very pleasant figuration, although it has more pretensions to virtuosity than that of Byrd. Certain passages have an exceptionally modern turn.

The fantasia-madrigal of Philips, taken by Ritter[40] from the Codex of Liége, has not the æsthetic merit of the pieces by Byrd and Morley. Constructed on a similar plan, it is ornamented with dry and stereotyped colorature, to which the madrigal style is hardly adapted.

B.—Fantasia-Amplification of the Ricercare.

This form of *fantasia* is the most typical and the most usual. It is certainly to it that Sir Hubert Parry alludes in an article in the *Musical Times* of April, 1900, reproduced in part in an article by Dr. Maclean[41] which appeared in the *Monthly Bulletin* of the I.M.S. of March, 1911 (p. 149). According to Sir Hubert Parry, the English *fantasia* or *fancy*, of which an innumerable number of examples exist, dating from the period extending from the opening of the 17th century up to the end of the Republic (1660), consists mainly of exercises in contrapuntal skill, without either method or system, and serving only to exhibit the learning and dry scholasticism of the composers. There are, he adds, exceptions to this dryness, and he quotes as examples the pieces of Orlando Gibbons, which are to be found in

[40] *Gesch. des Orgelspiels*, ii., p. 51.
[41] *A New Form in English Music.*

Parthenia,[42] and a few other little specimens of the same master contained in the *Virginal Book* of Benjamin Cosyn, which are of extreme delicacy and refinement.

The fantasia-amplifications of the *ricercare* contained in the *Fitzw. V. B.* answer pretty well to the definition of Sir Hubert Parry; they are, in fact, contrapuntal edifices in which the strict method which presides over the construction of a *ricercare* does not bear sway, and in which the composer allows himself in a way to follow the improvisation of the moment in the choice, the treatment, the succession, and the figuration of the subjects. In the first place he develops a subject in somewhat strict imitative style, but usually more ornate than is that of the *ricercare*. At one time this subject is the only one employed in the work; at another it is followed by one or

---

[42] In speaking of the *examples* of Gibbons's *Fantasias*, Sir Hubert Parry is mistaken. *Parthenia* contains, in fact, but the single and unique *Fantasia of foure parts* which we have analysed above (see p. 182).

Sir Hubert Parry is probably alluding to nine *fancies* in three parts (for stringed instruments) of Gibbons, the original manuscript of which is to be found in the library of Christ Church, Oxford, which were republished by Rimbault in one of the volumes of the Musical Antiquarian Society. This, at least, is what seems to result from an article by Dr. E. Walker, which appeared in the *Musical Antiquary* of January, 1912—in which that writer analyses a volume of *Fancies* belonging to that library; the volume in question contains 233 *Fancies*, transcribed in score by Dean Aldrich, on the confines of the 17th and 18th centuries. These *Fancies* date from the first part of the 17th century. Many of them are transcriptions of Italian or English madrigals. From this we may conclude that the concept of "fantasy-madrigal" which we propose to adopt is not hazardous. The conclusions of Dr. Walker concerning the structure of the *fancies* which are not simply transcriptions, agree with those of Sir Hubert Parry. Chappell (*Popular music of the olden time*, p. 470) gives some interesting particulars about the *Fantasies of three parts (for viol) composed by Orlando Gibbons*, published early in the reign of James I., and republished by Rimbault. He describes them as examples of the strict contrapuntal style. The first are composed in a very severe style, and still remain faithful to the Gregorian modes. The last have a more rhythmic and more popular character, and are freer from a harmonic and modulatory point of view.

several other subjects treated in the same style. But in both cases it seems that at a particular moment the author becomes weary of the imitative style, the strictness of which fetters his imagination; we find him then insensibly modifying the conduct of the *fantasia*, which then tends, by means generally of sequential figures, towards a less and less severe style, in which the imagination of the artist gives itself free play, as does also his leaning towards virtuosity. Thus the greater part of the fantasias of this type wind up with rapid and brilliant figurations, recalling the Italian toccata.

The *Fitzw. V. B.* contains in all fifteen *Fantasias* belonging to this last kind: eight by Giles Farnaby, three by Byrd, one by Philips, one by Munday, one by Richard Farnaby, and one by Strogers.

Of the three fantasias of Byrd, the first (*Fitzw. V. B.*, i., p. 37) is a very characteristic example. In it the composer develops eight subjects, or fragments of subjects, in imitative style. But the nearer he approaches the end of the piece the more does his style tend to become homophonic. After much play of sequences, the piece concludes with toccata figures. It possesses that poetic charm which we have more than once already observed in Byrd, which blossoms out by means of very consonant harmonies that are never overweighted by an excess of figuration.

The second *Fantasia* of Byrd (*Fitzw. V. B.*, i., p. 188) is perhaps still more interesting.[43] Formally

---

[43] Let us notice that the *Fitzw. V. B.* contains (i., p. 394) a prelude by Byrd separated from that fantasia, but expressly intended by its title to belong to it.

it is divided into four parts indicated[44] in the modern edition by double-bars. There exists no thematic bond between them. The first in itself forms a fantasia of the second type, in which several subjects are developed before the conclusion, which assumes the free homophonic style, figured or sequential. The second scarcely uses imitation, preferring the sequence and the echo, and also develops in the direction of figural homophony. The last two are throughout composed according to the system of figural homophony. The conclusion bears a resemblance to the style of the toccata.

It may therefore be considered as a work of important dimensions, which we may in a measure look on as an enlargement of the fantasia-amplification of the *ricercare*. Almost every page offers technical and expressive details that give it an exceptional value; thus towards the middle of the first section there is a long passage in two parts of extreme delicacy, anticipating the *Inventions* of J. S. Bach in the art with which the two voices are combined.[45] The second part gives us some charming effects of echo, and towards the end some counterpoint which seems to imitate distant trumpet blasts. A persistent bass, forming a drone, gives to the third a pastoral character. Moreover, this atmosphere dominates the whole piece; we are thus tempted to class it with programme music, so completely does it

[44] Very probably in agreement with the original MS. (according to the recollection of Mr. Barclay Squire, who, not having the document at his immediate disposal, has not been able to give the present writer an absolutely affirmative answer on the point).

[45] Partially in canon.

suggest a pastoral landscape, delicately tinted, and, as it were, bathed in sunshine.

The third *Fantasia* of Byrd (*Fitzw. V. B.*, ii., p. 406) develops several subjects, the first of which gives occasion for twelve entries, expressly numbered.[46] These are followed by sequential figures erected on a foundation more and more homophonic, and by way of conclusion an episode in the free toccata style. The work possesses that poetic sweetness which we meet with so frequently in Byrd; but the monotony of its harmony at last becomes wearisome.

The *Fantasia* which Peter Philips has left us (*Fitzw. V. B.*, i., p. 352) is dated 1582, a date comparatively early for a piece the form of which has an appearance of modernity. This piece, however, is not very interesting. Its somewhat hybrid construction places it on the border-line between the madrigal type and that of the *ricercare*. With the exception of the opening subject, which gives an opportunity for some not very strict imitations, what we notice most prominently is a succession of rather heavy harmonies, which colorature of the Italian stamp endeavour in vain to adorn and lighten. Too numerous figured cadences always of the same pattern introduce, in addition, an element of dryness and monotony.

The fantasia of Munday (*Fitzw. V. B.*, i., p. 19) is, on the contrary, a charming piece, which marks a considerable step in advance. In its main lines it conforms to the usual type of the fantasia. Opening with four fugal entries, in which the two

---

[46] On the margin of the piece there is found inscribed in the manuscript : *Vide P. Philippi sopra la medesima fuga, p. 158.* In fact, Philips treated the same subject in that fantasia (*Fitzw. V. B.*, i., p. 335), which we have reckoned among the strict forms (see p. 180).

answers are on the subdominant of the subject, it proceeds by various episodes in which short imitations, or, to be more exact, sequences, are prominent, formed by means of short melodic fragments. In one place there is a change of rhythm ; the $\mathbb{C}$ becomes $\frac{9}{8}$, and at that point the fugal development seems about to begin again. But after two entries of the subject, we are given another display of very animated sequential figurations, which make us think of the lively preludes of the *Well-tempered Clavichord*.

This fantasia is on other accounts a striking example of truly virginalistic figuration. Of all the compositions included in the *Fitzw. V. B.*, it is assuredly one of those most fitted for the instrument. The figuration is light and elegant, and endues the piece with a charm full of grace and playfulness.

Among the virginalists it is Giles Farnaby who is most devotedly attached to the fantasia of the second type. It moreover appealed in a very special manner to his temperament and his powers. A genius essentially spontaneous, an exquisite melodist, he reminds us of Schubert, of whom he possesses at once the qualities and the defects : on the one hand that delight in song, which gives to everything he does a character of generous verve the like of which we do not find in the other virginalists ; on the other hand a facility so great that it does not always afford him the leisure to control the quality of his inspirations, the result of which is often a negligence of form which takes from the value of his works.

We meet also with several of his fantasias in which it is impossible to discover real elements of interest. It is thus with the three examples to be found in the second volume of the *Fitzw. V. B.*, pp. 313, 343, and 347. In spite of the charm of detail which they show, the general impression remains confused, on account of the immoderate use of figurations.

On the other hand what a delicious perfume of Anglo-Italian sweetness is exhaled by a work such as the fantasia on p. 82 of the second volume! It begins like a graceful *ricercare* on a single subject, delicately coloured, and dotted with harmonies which recall the penetrating Monteverde of the madrigals. The continuation consists of different episodes, somewhat unskilfully connected, but interesting for their intrinsic qualities. We notice in it effects of echo, melodic sequences, curious experiments of rhythm, figurations happily graduated, a finale in the style of the toccata, and a concluding cadence containing a very bold double appoggiatura :—

The fantasia on p. 270 of the second volume does not yield in beauty to the one just described. Possibly it has even more charm and originality. The plan is that of the usual type of the fantasia with a single subject. This is developed by not very strict imitations, and surrounded with light and graceful figurations; it then loses itself insensibly in free counterpoints, which, gradually gaining the upper hand, dominate the piece to the end, taking for the most part the form of sequences. The general feeling is that of a delicate and fragile grace, with a mixture of playfulness and tenderness. For technical details we notice, starting with the sixteenth bar, a curious passage of modulation of two bars, in which we come across an example of the enharmonic (D sharp taken as E flat). The double appoggiatura of the final cadence recalls that of the previous fantasia. Lastly we find in profusion the sudden skip of the left hand from the heights of the middle of the keyboard to its lowest region, and vice versa.[47]

Another *Fantasia* of Farnaby (*Fitzw. V. B.*, ii., p. 320) has this characteristic, that the part in free counterpoint follows without transition, so to speak, the imitative part, which, taken by itself, consists of a *ricercare* with two subjects, without colorature; it is filled with a strangely seductive feeling of serenity and restfulness. Among the free figurations we notice repetition of notes, and an example of a rapid skip of the right hand from the middle to the top of the keyboard :—

On p. 323 of the second volume is a piece by G. Farnaby which has no title in the manuscript. It is really a fantasia-amplification of the *ricercare*. It is more interesting for its richness of figural detail than for its value as a whole. The opening is formed by the somewhat florid imitative development of three subjects, the first of which is the most important. In the continuation the

---

[47] See other examples of the use of this practice in the following fantasias of Farnaby : vol. ii., pp. 313, 323, 343, 347.

sequential figuration gradually prevails over the imitation ; the style becomes more and more free until the end, which is in the form of a toccata. At p. 328 we notice repeated notes that have a true melodic and rhythmic value and fine opportunities for imitations. We find also in this piece a rapid skip of the right hand from the middle to the top of the keyboard.

Let us in the last place point out the curious fantasia in vol. ii., p. 489, in which Farnaby again gives us an example of the usual pattern. It is not distinguished by any particular æsthetic merit, but we find in it the resolution of an interesting rhythmical problem, which consists in the succession and alternation, through more than the half of the piece, of movements in ₵ and in $\frac{6}{4}$, with this peculiarity, that the semibreve of the ₵ is to be understood as having the same duration as the dotted semibreve of the $\frac{6}{4}$. For example :—

and so on.

(The second bar has the same duration as the first).

There occurs, lastly, in this fantasia a fresh example of a sudden passing of the right hand from the middle to the top (p. 490), and in addition, at the end of the piece, the double appoggiatura dear to Farnaby.[48]

A little composition in two parts, entitled *A duo* (*Fitzw. V. B.*, ii., p. 374), by Richard Farnaby, the son of Giles, has the appearance of a miniature fantasia, of only moderate interest.

Nicholas Strogers is represented in the *Fitzw. V. B.* (i., p. 357) by one fantasia of the second

[48] The same ending in the fantasia of p. 347 in vol. ii.

kind only. In this short piece the principal subject makes fourteen entries, which are numbered in the original; the style of the imitative part is severe and unadorned; it is distinguished, among other things, by some very close stretti. From the purely virginalistic point of view this piece is of little interest, but its exceptional harmonies—we notice in particular a diminished octave—give it a very modern character and a romantic colouring which make it a curious and attractive work.

C.—Forms Agreeing with neither of the Foregoing in Structure.

This third group will not detain us long, for the reason that the greater part of the fantasias which are neither the adaptation of the madrigal nor the amplification of the *ricercare* fall, in fact, into the categories of other musical forms which we have already studied, or which we shall have occasion to study later. Of this kind are the fantasia of Bull *Upon a plain song*, and the fantasia on the Flemish chorale *Laet ons met herten reyne*, which are simply figured plainsongs (see pp. 171 and 173); the fantasia of Bull *Op de fuga van M. Jan Pieterss* (see p. 182); the fantasia of Philips in which a single subject enters thirty-nine times (see p. 181); and the fantasia in which Munday represents fine weather, thunder and lightning. We shall have to consider this fantasia when we come to treat of descriptive music.

Finally there is a fantasia by Bull (*Fitzw. V. B.*, i., p. 423), almost entirely written in two parts, which we might, in view of its structure, refer to the second type, if it did not exhibit the strange particularity of replacing the episode in which free counterpoints with sequential figuration usually appear, by a series of altogether unexpected variations on a persistent bass of a character still more unexpected :—

This curiously-designed bass is repeated twelve times in the sequel, in each case with fresh figural counterpoints in the right hand. Here we have a somewhat uncommon application of the principle of the *ground*, to which we have alluded above. Apart from this singularity, the piece has few elements of interest.

(5.) PRELUDE AND TOCCATA.

Thus far we have studied among the virginalistic musical forms, firstly, those depending on vocal music or which are connected with it by their origin (figured plainsong) or their style (fantasia-madrigal); secondly, those which undergo imitative counterpoint, or which in the main use it as a starting-point. We have met, in this latter order, with a form specifically English, the *fantasia-amplification of the ricercare*, in which we have observed a development in the direction of a freer and freer style, based in the main on a sort of figured homophony. We now pass on to the study of the free form *par excellence*—that of the prelude or the toccata.

Prelude and *toccata* are musical forms reaching back to a somewhat distant date. Italy has furnished us with the most interesting examples of them at the period of the Gabrieli, of Merulo, and of the *Transilvano*—that is to say, the end of the 16th century. The prelude or preamble is a piece of short dimensions, consisting of a succession of chords figured by means of rapid arabesques, intended in Church to give the intonation to the choir or to the officiant; hence the name of *intonazione* which the Gabrieli appropriated to it. The toccata is simply an amplification of the prelude. In most cases of much greater extent than the latter, it at the same time differs from it by its more pronounced character of virtuosity, and becomes in many cases, notably with Merulo, complicated in its inner structure by the intrusion of one or of several fugal interludes.

The virginalists do not give us in this form the great variety and fanciful originality of the Italians. Nothing in the *Fitzw. V. B.* corresponds to those grand toccatas of virtuosity by Merulo, which astonish us by their boldness, at the same time that they impose upon us by an exaggeration of bulk and by a somewhat decadent virtuosity. The actual word *toccata* is only used twice in the Cambridge manuscript; the first time in the case of a work of Sweelinck entitled *Praeludium Toccata* (vol. i., p. 378), in which we recognise all the essentials of the Venetian toccatas of the end of the 16th century, among them certain imitative elements; the second, in a composition of Giovanni Pichi, which has the appearance of an elegant toccata, perfectly Italian in procedure and in spirit, and provided with a little fugued interlude.

In the *Fitzw. V. B.* we meet with a composition of another Italian, Galeazzo. In spite of its title of *Praeludium*, it is really a toccata, on account of its length and of a central episode which comprises imitations and sequences (*Fitzw. V. B.*, i., p. 391).

Lastly, we find in vol. ii., p. 40, of the *Fitzw. V. B.* an anonymous *Praeludium* which has, in fact, all the appearance of a little toccata with a fugued interlude. It might very well, like the two previous pieces, be the work of an Italian.

Except these few examples, which apart from their appearance in the *Fitzw. V. B.* seem to have no connection with England, in this precious manuscript and in *Parthenia* we only meet with short preludes, the general characteristics of which may be thus determined : their most frequent form is that of the *intonazione* of the Gabrieli, but with a more modern character, due partly to the fact that their harmonic structure is less dependent on the Church modes, and partly to the fact that their figuration is strengthened by the new formulas devised by the virginalists.

Let us examine rather more closely a few of these little compositions. The *Fitzw. V. B.* and *Parthenia* together give us nineteen in all, the composers of which are Byrd (3), Bull (8), G. Farnaby (1), Gibbons (1), Oldfield (1), while five are anonymous.

Among the preludes of Byrd there is one (*Fitzw. V. B.*, i., p. 394) which is mentioned in the manuscript as forming part of one of the fantasias of the master.[49] Apart from the harmony, which is more modern, and has a leaning towards modulation, this little piece strongly recalls the intonations of the Gabrieli.

On the other hand the prelude to be found on p. 8 of *Parthenia*, and on p. 83 of vol. i. of the

[49] See note 43, p. 187.

O

Fitzw. V. B.,[50] has nothing Italian about it, and presents a curious specimen of music truly English by reason of its stately solemnity, of its development, and the somewhat mannered richness of its essentially virginalistic figuration.

The third prelude of Byrd (*Parthenia*, p. 1) is much shorter, but it is of perfect beauty, brought about by the balance maintained between its harmonic basis and its figuration. Here, again, we have to do with a work of a character specially English, in which a solemn gravity is united with a delicate feeling for harmony.

The eight preludes by Bull[51] are distinguished by their tendency towards virtuosity, and by the use of numerous virginalistic figures, among which is included the most curious of all, the repetition of notes. The first of these (*Fitzw. V. B.*, i., p. 158) has already received our attention (see pp. 163 and 164), from the fact that it may be considered as connected with the figured plainsong which follows it—*Gloria tibi trinitas*. The figuration of this prelude offers interesting instances of the repetition of notes, and especially of the spreading of chords.

In the prelude of Bull found on p. 23 of the second volume of the *Fitzw. V. B.* we have a specimen of exceptional interest, recalling by its grandeur the intonations of the Gabrieli. It is divided into two parts of equal length, and similar in structure. The conclusion differs from the remainder of the piece by its less rapid figuration and its more modulated harmonies.

[50] The *Fitzw. V. B.* does not give the attribution to Byrd, but it is inferred from *Parthenia*.

[51] See *Fitzw. V. B.*, i., pp. 158, 148 ; ii., pp. 22, 23, 248, 259, 274 ; *Parthenia*, p. 16.

Equally interesting is the prelude on p. 22 of vol. ii. Very short, it is divided into two episodes, the first of which consists of a succession of chords with but little figuration, and the second in a play of figurations in which broken chords are prominent. Archaic in its opening, and composed in the Æolian mode, developing in the direction of the modern A minor, it finishes in A major; the last bars have, for the period, quite a new feeling, which anticipates Domenico Scarlatti.

The same character of modernity strikes us in the little prelude on p. 259 of vol. ii. Lastly, *Parthenia* (p. 16) gives us an example in which the figural structure differs almost entirely from the Italianisms of the toccatists, approaching to that which a hundred years later was to become the figuration of the *Well-tempered Clavichord;* that is to say, we can perceive a certain attempt at equilibrium, a sort of anticipatory classicism. The appoggiatura of the final cadence deserves notice for its originality :—

An identical structure appears in the fine prelude by Gibbons to be found on p. 49 of *Parthenia.* In this case also we have to do with a piece which may be looked on as a precursor of the preludes of Bach. The figuration is simple, elegant, and tastefully divided between the extreme parts. Harmonies, sequences, syncopations, sudden skips of the right hand from the middle of the keyboard to the top, all give it an appearance of modernity, coupled with a rare sense of balance and restraint.

Giles Farnaby gives us an example of a prelude (*Fitzw. V. B.*, ii., p. 372) which commences like one of Bach's Inventions in Two Parts, and proceeds in three and then in four parts, to wind up in the style of the toccata. Without being remarkable, this little piece possesses the qualities of grace and playfulness that specially belong to Farnaby. It contains the formidable skip of the left hand which we have already had occasion to notice [52] :—

We notice some similar skips, but less daring, in a prelude by Thomas Oldfield (*Fitzw. V. B.*, i., p. 180). This fact is in itself sufficient to give a comparatively recent date to this piece, by which alone his name has come down to us.

A few words as to the anonymous preludes of the *Fitzw. V. B.* Apart from the one on p. 80 of vol. i., they are nearly all distinguished by progressive elements from which we may infer that they probably date from after the end of the 16th century. At one time we notice a purely virginalistic technique, characterised by the employment of repetitions of notes and the spreading of chords (i., p. 81); at another we have sequential designs predominating (i., p. 85); and lastly, we find again that style which reminds us of J. S. Bach, of which Bull and Gibbons have already furnished us

[52] See p. 149.

with examples (ii., p. 169). The most charming specimen is a very melodious prelude, almost without colorature, and of an exultant and solemn tonality (ii., p. 25); it appears to have been written under the influence of Byrd, whose grace and harmonic charm it recalls.

To sum up, we may say that the virginalistic preludes, taken as a whole, offer us two extreme types: the one archaic, recalling the intonations of the Gabrieli; the other, more modern, which to a certain extent anticipates the preludes of J. S. Bach. Between these two contrasting types there are intermediate species, of which the principal characteristic consists in the adaptation to the archaic style of the new formulas of figuration created by the virginalists.

(6.) THE VARIATION.

A.—IN GENERAL.

The Variation is a form essentially English. The Italians scarcely practised it with any persistence in keyboard music before Frescobaldi; the only example dating from the 16th century which they have left us—the *Pass' e mezzo antico*, by Andrea Gabrieli,[53]—is of so vague a structure that it may, in fact, be looked on as a quite embryonic product of the variation style.[54]

With regard to the Spaniards the situation is quite different. As early as 1536 we see the lutenist Luiz Milan cultivating a type of variation

[53] Reproduced in Torchi, *L'arte musicale in Italia*, vol. iii., p. 71.

[54] On the question of the instrumental variation in general in Italy from the opening of the 17th century, Dr. Hugo Riemann throws fresh light in the second volume of his *Handbuch der Musikgeschichte* (Part ii., § 76, p. 85 ff).

already very characteristic, in his *villancicos* (village songs) for a single voice with accompaniment for the lute. After him there developed, during the 16th century, a whole series of Spanish lutenists, who devoted themselves to the same art without, however, adding any new elements to it.[55] From lute music the variation passed on, with Cabezon, to music for the keyboard.

When speaking of the figured plainsongs of Tallis,[56] we emphasised the importance of Cabezon in the development of keyboard music. We have, however, been compelled from various circumstances to come to the conclusion that as regards the principal methods of figuration adapted to show off the resources of the instrument, the English must be looked on as having the priority over him. One thing, however, remains established in his favour, until proof to the contrary is adduced, and that is that he was the first to write variations on secular songs and on dances for the keyboard. The English, in fact, give us no dated example of this new form earlier than the death of the Spanish organist (1566). If, then, the latter appears to have borrowed from England, during his travels in 1554, certain elements of figuration, it seems in return that the virginalists are indebted to him for the idea of establishing systematic series of variations on secular themes. The application of this idea was destined to become essentially fruitful, for it provided the English with a foundation of discipline which to a certain extent was still wanting in them. In constraining them

---

[55] See *Les luthistes espagnols*, 1902, by Morphy. As to the meaning we attach to " lutenists," see note on p. 82.

[56] See p. 167.

to confine themselves within the comparatively narrow boundaries of a short and concise subject it furnished them with a complete plan, the proportions of which, by their nature restrained, preserved them from falling into excess of development and a loss of proportion. It took them a very little time to perceive that in no other form could they find better opportunities for using their inexhaustible figurative material. This is why they adopted it, and made it not only their favourite form, but also that which has had the largest share in giving a lasting character to their works.

The most ancient virginalistic variations, according to the date assigned to them in the *Fitzw. V. B.*, are those of Philips on a pavan subject (*Fitzw. V. B.*, i., p. 343). They are dated —according to the express statement of the manuscript – 1580; that is to say, fourteen years after the death of Cabezon, and two years after the publication of an important part of his works by his son, Hernando.[57] This varied pavan is far from offering the richness of combinations presented by the virginalistic variations of songs and dances which belong to a more recent period. There is even a certain resemblance between its sober figuration and that of the " varied " dances of Cabezon.

Ten years later, in 1590, we find Byrd's variations, *The Wood's so wild* (*Fitzw. V. B.*, i., p. 263). Here we already notice the intervention of new elements, strange to Cabezon. On the other hand there is a feature common to the two masters, in that, from variation to variation, the subject

[57] *Obras de musica*, 1578.

passes to different parts; this was an archaic manner of variation for which Cabezon showed some predilection.[58]

For the present we will confine ourselves to these two examples, which show well, in their general features, the relationship between the variation as conceived by the Spanish master and that which the English made of it after their first experience of it.

We must not conclude these general considerations without remarking that in reality the question of the rise of the variation is much larger than appears at first sight. One becomes more and more conscious, in retracing the course of musical development, that the variation style was actually in use previous to the 16th century; we are not alluding here to the simple ornamentation of a given melody, which goes back to a very high antiquity, but to much more complex forms, such as those met with in certain polyphonic pieces of the 15th century. If we analyse, for example, a Mass of William Dufay, we are not a little surprised to recognise that the work, viewed as a whole, is nothing but a succession of long variations on the sacred or secular theme that gives it its title; this theme being placed in the tenor and treated sometimes in normal values, sometimes in values augmented or diminished, is found surrounded, at each new appearance, with contrapuntal parts in various combinations. As there is at present a tendency more and more pronounced to admit that the polyphonic works of the 14th and 15th centuries were accompanied by instruments, we

---

[58] *Le Chant du Chevalier (Hisp. Schol. Mus. Sacr.,* viii., p. 3) shows specially characteristic applications of it.

have good right to maintain that the roots of the instrumental variation in truth reach back much further than the 16th century.[59]

We shall treat separately the variation of the secular song and the variation of the dance. This division is forced on us on account of the complex aspects shown by the works which belong to the first category, and of the comparative simplicity on the other hand of those which form the second group.

B.—Variation of Secular Song.

The variation of the secular song is the most important English form which we shall have to study. It is in fact in this field of activity that the virginalists have displayed their inventive ingenuity with the greatest power and originality. It is in this form, too, that they have given us the most interesting works, both from the æsthetic and the technical point of view.

The number of variations of secular songs which they have left us is relatively limited in comparison with their variations of dance tunes. What is still more remarkable is that, in spite of this limitation, the former show much more diversity of combinations than the latter.

We are about to make a general conspectus of these combinations, and we shall make use of diagrams so as to bring out the abstract principle with greater clearness.

[59] The French motets of the 14th century (*Roman de Fauvel* and Guillaume de Machault) already employ regularly the variation on a given tenor (numerous examples in the *Gesch. der Mensuralnotation* of Johannes Wolf, vol. ii. and iii.; see Nos. 5, 7 to 10, and 13 to 16).

1. Firstly, we meet with what may be called the *polyphonic variation.* The melodic subject submitted to variation maintains its simplicity from one end to the other of the piece; from variation to variation it passes from one voice to another, and each time it is surrounded with fresh figural counterpoints. If the subject is represented by an unbroken horizontal line, and the counterpoint by a waved line, the diagram of this type of variation appears as follows:—[60]

1st variation:

superius

altus

tenor

bassus

2nd variation:

altus

3rd variation:

tenor

4th variation:

bassus

This diagram and all those which follow are constructed so as to show in an abstract form the *absolute type* of the kind of variation which they are intended to represent; we shall have occasion to show that in practice this absolute type is almost always departed from. On the other

[60] N.B.—In all the diagrams which follow, the broken line, although always presenting the same appearance in each variation, answers in each case to a different melodic or figural line. For example, in the first diagram the tenor line of the second variation, although represented in the same way as the tenor line of the first, nevertheless supposes a different melodic or figural movement.

hand, with a view to simplification, we assume a harmony of four parts, which constitutes the normal practice, though this strictness is far from being actually observed by the virginalists.

2. The second type is that to which we may give the name of *melodic variation*. The subject, given out in the *superius*, remains in it during the whole course of the piece. At one time it undergoes figuration, at another it is free from it. The other parts in each variation supply figural counterpoints:—

1st variation :	2nd variation :	3rd variation :

The little vertical signs over the unwaved line in the third variation indicate that in this variation the subject itself is subject to a figural embroidery, independent of that made by the other parts.

3. Next we meet with the *harmonic variation*. On a bass which forms the subject and which remains unchanged the composer constructs a series of variations that are entirely confined to the other voices :—

1st variation :	2nd variation :	3rd variation :

4. The fourth type is the *mixed* or *melodico-harmonic variation*. This is the one by far the

most frequently met with, and is, so to speak, the only one which we shall find used in the variation of the dance. Its principle is simple enough, but its applications are at times complex. It may be defined as follows: *bass* and *superius* form in each variation a harmonic and melodic extreme which cannot be exceeded, while in between is elaborated a different figuration in each variation. The actual type of this kind of variation may be represented thus :—

1st variation :   2nd variation :

But in reality we never meet with this rudimentary form ; for in every case it is complicated by the fact that, from variation to variation, the bass and the *superius* alternately undergo figurations which alter their outlines, without, however, doing violence to the principle according to which the two extreme parts form the frame of each variation. It is hardly necessary to say that in this system the subject is placed in the *superius;* the bass is nothing but a permanent harmonic foundation. The following diagram will give a simplified idea of the combination described :—

1st variation :   2nd variation :   3rd variation :

In fact, alternation between the figuration of the *superius* and that of the bass almost always occurs within the variations themselves, taken separately :—

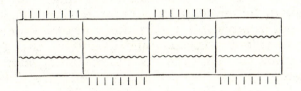

The great majority of virginalistic variations, whether applied to songs or to dances, are constructed according to this last diagram. It is evident that in these conditions the middle parts must suffer some impoverishment of their figuration, which would otherwise fetter and delay the already sufficiently complicated progression of the extreme parts.

This kind of variation is the one most of all representative of the advance in musical development. It has, in fact, lost all touch with the ancient polyphony, and is part and parcel of the new principle of accompanied monody.

One would be equally tempted to grant a progressive character to the purely harmonic variation, which at first sight appears to have affinity with the modern idea of harmony. But in most cases this would be a mistake ; for the subject which, in each variation, forms the foundation of the musical structure is in no respect combined in advance so as to make a harmonic bass. Rather is its function similar to that of the tenor in the ancient polyphonic compositions, or even in certain cases to that of the old popular drone: the upshot of it all being that the harmonic variation inclines rather to the past than to the future.[61]

It is well to bear in mind that, in fact, virginalistic pieces written in the variation style do not always fall very readily into this or that compartment corresponding to this or that type. In other words, the boundaries between the different kinds of variation are often very difficult to define, for the reason that the composers seldom conform to absolute plans as represented in the diagrams, but frequently indulge in the unexpected, and consequently in mixed combina- tions much more complex than those we have gathered together under the fourth type. The following examples are very instructive in this respect. In the variations by Byrd, *The wood's so wild* (1590), we have to do in the main with the polyphonic type; yet certain passages are allied to the mixed kind, *melodico-harmonic*. In the purely melodic variations, *Quodling's Delight*, by G. Farnaby, one of the variations borrows the polyphonic plan. In *Up tails all*, by the same master, we notice leanings towards the harmonic variation, although on the whole this series of variations belongs to the melodic type. It also happens that both melodic and polyphonic elements enter into variations that are purely harmonic; for instance, in *A Galliard Ground* by Inglott. Finally, in the mixed type of melodico-harmonic variation, which is moreover the most stable of all, we now and then find a fitful intervention of a

---

[61] On this subject see chap. xii. of Dr. Naylor's book, *An Elizabethan Virginal Book* (p. 141 ff), which is specially concerned with drone basses.

polyphonic type; thus in *All in a garden greene*, by Byrd, in which the subject passes into the alto in one of the variations; thus again in *Bony sweet Robin* and *Why aske you*, by G. Farnaby. It also often happens in variations of this kind that there is a predominance more or less marked of the harmonic element over the melodic element, or vice versa. Thus in *Barafostus Dreame*, by Tomkins, we discern a strong preponderance of melody; while the variations on the same subject written by an anonymous composer leave the very distinct impression of a harmonic predominance.

A last remark must be made before passing on to the detailed analysis of the different kinds of variations of the song which have been left us by the virginalists. The subject intended for variation is never, or almost never, given by them in its original simple form, devoid of ornaments. From the very outset it already appears in the shape of a variation. It sometimes even happens that the first variation is more complicated than others which follow, and that the subject is more easily recognised in the body of the piece, or at the end, than at the opening.

I.—The Polyphonic Variation.

The examples which the virginalists give us of this first kind of variation show, from the very first, how wrong it would be to suppose that they conform completely to absolutely regular plans of construction. Even Cabezon, devoted as he was to balance, has only written one series of variations in which we can discover an almost complete symmetry in the distribution of the subject between the different parts; the *Diferencias sobre el canto del Cavallero*[62] in which the melody, first stated twice in the *superius*, passes subsequently to the tenor, then to the alto, and finally to the bass.

With the virginalists it is only in one case out of eight that we meet with this comparative regularity of plan—in the variations by Inglott (1554-1621), *The leaves bee greene (Fitzw. V. B.*, ii., p. 381). The subject is at first given out in the bass, then, in a second variation, in the tenor, and in the third in the *superius;* subsequently in three other successive series of three variations we find the same arrangement. The piece ends with a thirteenth variation in which the subject reappears in the bass; the symmetry, absolute up to this point, is then broken at the conclusion. The interest of these variations is purely theoretical. The simplicity of their figuration and their polyphonic character justify us in assigning them to a pretty remote date. Their general turn shows the influence of Byrd.[63]

Of this last master we possess four series of variations which show a leaning to the polyphonic idea. We have already cited *The wood's so wild (Fitzw. V. B.*, i., p. 263) on account of the antiquity of its date—1590. This piece comprises fourteen variations, very irregular in structure, and presenting a mixed aspect at several points. In the first two the subject is in the *superius*, the bass being different in each of them. It passes to the alto in the third, in which we meet again with the bass of the first

---

[62] *Hisp. Schol. Mus. Sacr.*, vol. viii., p. 3.

[63] Byrd himself also wrote a piece with the same title, which is to be found in two manuscripts of the end of the 16th century (No. 1 of the Add. MS. 32377 of the British Museum, and No. 105 of Add. MS. 31390 of the Brit. Mus.; see *A Catal. of the MS. Mus. in the Brit. Mus.*, vol. iii.). This composition, apparently vocal in origin, is there arranged for five viols.

variation, a sort of countrified drone. In the fourth it undergoes a strong figuration, and is distributed between the upper parts; there is the same drone bass. This reappears in the fifth variation, in which the subject passes to the *superius*, and also in the sixth, in which it occupies the tenor. The seventh variation treats it in the *superius* with a new bass. In the eighth it disappears altogether, but we find the drone bass again. The ninth variation brings it back, almost completely disguised, and with a free bass. The variations 10, 11, 12 have a common bass [64] on which are erected counterpoints having no relation with the subject. The latter reappears in the alto in the thirteenth variation, and in the *superius* in the fourteenth. These last two variations have a completely free bass. As we see, the polyphonic element is at several points crowded out by a harmonic element, which appears under the archaic form of the popular drone. This series of variations is impregnated with a country feeling, and leaves behind it a delightful impression of the open air.

A virginalist of a merit no less great than Byrd, but belonging to a more recent generation, Orlando Gibbons, has treated the same melody (*Fitzw. V. B.*, i., p. 144) in nine variations which equally belong to the polyphonic system; this may be concluded with fair confidence from the fact that the subject occupies the tenor in the second variation and the bass in the ninth. In all the other variations it appears in the *superius*, under forms sometimes simple, sometimes figured. In the fifth and the seventh the figuration is such that it amounts to an

---

[64] The same which we have seen treated previously in the form of a drone.

P

almost complete deformation. In the sixth, the first two notes of the song are given out in the bass; the remainder is continued two octaves higher in the *superius*. The bass changes with each variation. In reality, if it were not for the fact that in the two variations the subject passes to other parts than the *superius*, it would be a matter of purely melodic variations.

Gibbons's figuration has a more pronounced character of virtuosity than that of Byrd. In places where it reaches its highest development, the piece assumes a not altogether pleasant scholastic appearance which makes us think of Czerny's studies. Apart from this, the variations have a fine romantic colouring, and show clearly how a musician of Gibbons's scope was able to make himself independent of a predecessor of the strength of Byrd when treating the same subject.[65]

Among the other variations of Byrd which belong to the polyphonic type, we first of all meet with *Walsingham* (*Fitzw. V. B.*, i., p. 267), which dates from 1591 at the latest. This work consists of twenty-two variations, followed by a short postlude in the style of a prelude-toccata. Here, again, we meet with a most complex construction, in which no sort of symmetry is to be found. From the very first variation, the melody is alternately divided between the tenor, where it is undisguised, and the *superius*. In the second it occupies the tenor entirely, where it is still undisguised. The variations 3, 6, 7, 9, 14, 17, and 21 show us the subject in the *superius*, with a bass

[65] The subject of the song *The wood's so wild* was also used by Bull in the version of his *Courante Jewel*, republished by Pauer, p. 53 of his *Old English composers for the Virginals and Harpsichord*.

each time different. Six variations (4, 8, 10, 11, 16, 18) treat it in the tenor, and two (5 and 20) in the bass. Twice (13 and 21) it is met with in the alto, the first time partially undisguised. In the twelfth variation it appears figured, in the *superius*, with the exception of a short passage entrusted to the tenor. In the fifteenth it is divided between the alto and the *superius;* the same in the nineteenth.

The melody *Walsingham*, which has also been treated in variation form by Bull (*Fitzw. V. B.* i., p. 1), has an exquisite legendary charm; the implied modulation from minor to major which gives it its character is full of the unexpected. The variations of Byrd have not, perhaps, the breadth of those of Bull, but they are no less remarkable for the grace of their figuration, and for a general feeling of mystery and sweetness.[66]

A third series of variations by the old master, *The mayden's song* (*Fitzw. V. B.*, ii., p. 67) offers yet another interesting example of polyphonic variations. This piece consists of eight variations. In the first the subject is given to the tenor undisguised, with this peculiarity, that the first phrase of it is given out in unison, and then repeated accompanied by two bass parts in counterpoint. In variations 2 to 6 the melody is in the *superius;* in the seventh it is in the tenor; and

---

[66] The melody *Walsingham*, the original of which must have been earlier than 1538, begins with these words :—

> " As I went to Walsingham
> To the shrine with speed,
> Met I with a jolly palmer
> In a pilgrim's weed."

Walsingham was a celebrated pilgrimage-place in Norfolk; it was suppressed in 1538, at the Reformation. The subject of the song is a love-story such as sometimes happened on the occasion of pilgrimages. (Chappell, *Pop. mus. of the old. time*, p. 121.)

in the eighth it is divided between the alto and the *superius*. A good part of these variations might therefore be classed under the purely melodic type. The work is charming; the delicate and ingenuous theme is surrounded by sweet and suave counterpoints, whose dreamy expression reminds us of Schumann.

Byrd furnishes a last example of variations which may be included in the polyphonic kind; those which he wrote on the lively song, *John come kisse me now* (*Fitzw. V. B.*, i., p. 47). They are somewhat complex in structure, and have the appearance of a transitional style between the polyphonic and the melodico-harmonic type. Of the sixteen variations comprised in the piece, there are ten in which the subject is in the *superius*, with or without figuration; among the latter we find five in which, under a figuration at times somewhat overladen, there is an identical bass. In the tenth variation the melody is shared between the tenor and the *superius*; in the eleventh it is entirely in the tenor, as again in the twelfth, in which the second half is discernible in the bass; in the thirteenth it takes the *superius*, but passes for a moment to the tenor about the middle of the variation; in the fourteenth it is given to the bass, and in the sixteenth to the alto. Sometimes the bass that is common to a certain number of variations reappears, more or less figured, in the six variations in which the subject is not, or not completely, in the *superius*; sometimes it is wholly missing from them.

The figuration of *John come kisse me now* has a different character from that which we have seen used by Byrd in *The wood's so wild*, *Walsingham*, and *The mayden's song.* It shows, by its tendency to virtuosity, a development in which the influence of John Bull and Farnaby may perhaps be discovered.[67]

We have still to speak of two other series of variations which we think should be included in the polyphonic type. These are the *Grounde* of G. Farnaby (*Fitzw. V. B.*, ii., p. 353), and *A grounde* of Tomkins (*Fitzw. V. B.*, ii., p. 87), two works in themselves of only comparative importance, but which nevertheless are of a nature to interest us because they introduce us to a new idea, very important in the history of English music,—*The ground.*

Ground signifies the foundation, the base. This original meaning gradually widened, and ended by being applied to a musical form in which the subject constitutes an unchangeable base to a numerous series of variations. In this sense we might describe as *grounds* a large number of the Masses of the 15th and 16th centuries which consist in a series of variations on a permanent *cantus firmus.* But actually the term *ground* appears originally to have been applied to instrumental music alone, to the exclusion of vocal or vocal-instrumental music. *My Lady Nevell's Booke* contains three examples of *grounds* for the virginal,[68] which so far as we know are the most ancient of which the approximate date is known; in fact, as *Nevell's Booke* was compiled in 1591, they cannot be later than that year.

[67] *John come kisse me now* is a humorous song, celebrated at the end of the 16th and the whole of the 17th centuries (Chappell, *op. cit.*, p. 147). Byrd only treated the first part.

[68] No. 1, *Lady Nevel's grownde;* No. 30, *The second grownde;* No. 35, *Hughe Astons grownde.*

At the end of the 16th and the opening of the 17th centuries the *ground* of the virginalists is most frequently akin to the polyphonic variation in the sense that the *cantus firmus* which forms its foundation passes, from variation to variation, into the different parts. Yet we meet with examples which revert to the purely harmonic type of variation. This last type of *ground*, unusual at the period of which we are treating, becomes little by little the rule in proportion as the device of the continued bass developed. If we examine the clavier works of Dr. Blow, who lived from 1648 to 1708, and was the master of Purcell, we shall discover that in the pieces which he calls *grounds* the persistent motive always occupies the bass, where it appears sometimes simple, sometimes figured.[69]

From the répertoire of the virginalists the term *ground* soon passed into that of the artists of the bow. Thus we find in the celebrated collection of Playford, called *Division Viol*, dating from about 1680, a large number of pieces entitled *Division on a ground*—that is to say, *Variations on a ground*.[70] One of these pieces has this additional

---

[69] See Pauer, *Old English Composers*, &c., pp. 90, 100 and 103. See also p. 143, a *ground* by Purcell, composed according to the same system, but without submitting the fundamental subject to figuration.

[70] See Riemann, *John Playford's Division Viol, and Michel Farinelli's Folies d'Espagne (Die Musik,* x., 24).
Long before the term *ground* was applied to this method of composing for bowed instruments it was in use among the Spanish viol-players. The *Tratado de glosas sobre clausulas y otros generos de puntos en la musica de violones*, published at Rome in 1553 by Diego Ortiz, contains six *ricercadas* entirely composed according to the principle of the harmonic variation. A bass of a certain length having been given, the player of the viol (*i.e.*, the viol da gamba) performs a new melody on each resumption of the said bass. The latter is played and realised on a keyboard instrument (see pp. 56 ff. and xxv. of the preface of the modern re-issue of the *Tratado*, by Max Schneider, Liepmannssohn, Berlin, 1913).

interest that the subject given out in the upper part is actually the melody—completed in the second part—of the song *John come kisse me now*. The bass, called the *ground bass*, remains identical in all the variations, but the melody is entirely lost to sight after the very first variation, embroideries skilfully adapted to the harmonic foundation replacing it during the whole of the remainder of the piece.

Again, the principle of the *ground bass* may be seen in the traditional treatment of two dances, which in truth are allied by their rhythm and internal structure—the chaconne and the passacaglia.[71] The 17th and 18th centuries afford us an incalculable number of chaconnes constructed on a persistent bass, which serves as the foundation of successive series of variations.[72]

Lastly, vocal music with accompaniment of *continuo* does not escape the application of principles analogous to those of the *ground bass*. We find pretty numerous examples among the larger number of the great masters of the 17th and the first half of the 18th centuries.[73]

[71] The *Tratado* of Ortiz (see the *ricercadas*, p. 107 of the modern edition) gives us as early as the middle of the 16th century very characteristic specimens of dances for the bass-viol with clavier accompaniment, in which the system of *ground bass* appropriate to the chaconne and the passacaglia receives a very characteristic application. It is curious that the *bassi ostinati* of these pieces essentially employ, as foundation points, the tonic, dominant, and subdominant (the last predominating over the dominant).

[72] Schumann and Brahms, who willingly adopted ancient forms into which they had the skill to infuse new blood, each well on in the 19th century left an example of the application of the principle of the chaconne: Schumann in his *Impromptu on a theme by Clara Wieck* (for pianoforte, in two-time), and Brahms in the *finale* of his 4th Symphony.

[73] The principle of the persistent bass shows itself in two ways in vocal music: either a bass of a few notes is repeated constantly throughout the whole length of a piece which itself constitutes a definite whole, or else a more or less developed bass forms a basic-point for a series of vocal

Let us return to the *grounds* of Farnaby and Tomkins, which started us on this digression. In that of Farnaby the subject which serves for bass seems to be simply a pretext for figuration. Given out first in the bass, in unison, it is successively variations, each of which corresponds to a clearly-defined division of the text, and which taken apart are complete in themselves. The first case occurs very frequently in the Venetian opera from the time of Monteverde (*Incoronazione di Poppea*) and of Cavalli, especially in that form of air to which the name *lamento* has been given (see *Die Venetianische Oper und die Werke Cavallis und Cestis*, by H. Kretzschmar, in the *Viertelj. für Musikw.*, 1892, p. 44 ff, and *Cavalli* by E. Wellesz in the *Beiheft I.* of the *Denkm. der Tonkunst in Oesterr.*, p. 38). It is to be found also in Purcell (*lamento* of Dido, in *Dido and Æneas*), and still more in his church music (see Riemann, *Handb. der Musik.*, II., iii., p. 48 ff) ; finally, in the cantatas of J. S. Bach (*ib.*, p. 87 ff), &c.

The second case, which answers in every way to the harmonic variation of the virginalists, may also be frequently noticed in the masters of the 17th century. Thus Monteverde wrote, among other things, an *Ave maris stella* (*Psalms* of 1610), the seven strophes of which consist of seven vocal variations on the same bass (Riemann, *Handb.*, II., iii., p. 11). Two hymns by Schütz (in the *Kleine geistliche Concerten* of 1636-39) are constructed in the same manner ; one of them, *Ich hab mein Sach*, with eighteen strophes (Riemann, *Handb.*, II., iii., p. 11). We find, again, two examples of this nature in the *Symphoniae Sacrae* of 1629 of the same master (Riemann, *ib.*, p. 20). A complete composition—a sort of cantata —by Chr. Bernhard (*Letzte-Ehren Nachklang*, 1669), is governed by one and the same bass, the various repeats of which undergo but slight modifications (Riemann, *ib.*, p. 27 ff). The Cantatas of Buxtehude give us numerous specimens of one *continuo* common to several different airs (see *Buxtehude*, by A. Pirro, Paris, Fischbacher, 1913, pp. 188, 191 ff, 197, 204, 216, 301 ff, 328, 356, &c.).

Dr. Hugo Riemann has very properly called attention to the stylistic importance of the principle of the *ostinato*. He makes his study of it one of the principal *leitmotifs* of the whole of that part of his *Handbuch der Musikgeschichte* which treats of the 17th and 18th centuries. See, further, in the *Sammelbände* of the I.M.G., XIII., iv., p. 531, his very interesting article, *Der " Basso ostinato " und die Anfänge der Kantate*. We may also read with advantage on the same subject a study by Einstein, *Die Aria di Ruggiero*, which appeared in the *Sammelbände* of the I.M.G., XIII., iii. The author there speaks of those well-known airs (*Ruggiero, la Romanesca*, &c.) which were used as basses in the 17th century, and which formed the subject of improvised variations in the other parts, whether in music for the voice with accompaniment, or in music purely instrumental (*Forster's Virginal Book* (1624) contains, under No. 33, an anonymous piece entitled *Rogero ;* it would be interesting to know if this composition is built on the theme of which Einstein speaks). We find, again, a few particulars relating to the *ostinato* in the criticism by Einstein of the *Handb.* of Dr. Riemann (II., ii.) which appeared in the *Monthly Journal* of the I.M.G., XIV., iii., p. 71.

taken up in the thirteen variations which follow
by one or other of the four parts; in four variations
by the tenor, in four by the alto, in two by the
superius, and in three by the bass. The more and
more animated figurations which surround it have
rather a scholastic character. The piece ends by
a few bars in the style of a toccata. What is very
curious, as showing the tendency of the virginalists
towards modulation according to the principles of
classical harmony, is that the subject is given out
now on the tonic, now on the dominant (once), and
now on the subdominant (four times).

In the *ground* of Tomkins, the subject, although
very short, has greater melodic importance than in
that of Farnaby, and contrary to what happens in
the latter, it is occasionally treated under a figured
form.[74] The accompanying counterpoints call for
unusual skill on the part of the executant;
variations 22 and 23 in particular contain difficult
passages in rapid thirds for the left hand. As in
the *ground* of Farnaby, the subject is first given
out without accompaniment, but in the *superius*.
The finale is also in the free style of prelude.
Of the forty-four variations, in twenty-six the
cantus firmus is in the *superius*, in fifteen in the
bass, in one in the tenor, and in two it is placed in
the alto. In six cases the melody, given to an
upper part, is imitated by one of the lower parts.
Thus in variations 2, 16, 17, and 38 the *superius* is
imitated by the alto, in variation 37 by the bass;
in variation 14 the tenor is imitated by the bass.
We find ourselves then in face of a work somewhat

[74] Dr. Naylor (*An Eliz. V. B.*, p. 188) remarks on the absolute similarity
of the melodic intervals between this subject and the opening of that of
Up tails all, a melody which G. Farnaby has treated in form of variations
(*Fitzw.*, ii., p. 360). The rhythm alone is different.

complex in structure and more or less mixed in character. Tomkins must have been a virtuoso comparable with John Bull if we may judge from the qualities of dexterity called for in the execution of those of his works which have been preserved to us.

II.—MELODIC VARIATION.

The purely melodic variation is very rare, for the reason that it is too absolutely opposed to the tendency—in full force at the period of the virginalists—to adopt the principle of a harmonic foundation. We shall see further on in our analysis that the absolute type of this kind of variation is met with but very exceptionally.

We must first of all place in this category the best known of all virginalistic pieces, the celebrated *Carman's whistle* of Byrd,[75] the date of which at the very latest goes back to 1591. This composition, founded on a popular song of a very original tune, the *Carman's whistle*,[76] is the one which has most frequently been reproduced in modern notation, either in treatises on musical history or in various collections of clavier music. It is a charming work, breathing of the open air, and of a dreamy though rather monotonous good nature that leaves an impression of grave, sweet, and simple poetry.

The subject is treated in eight variations, in each of which it is given to the *superius;* here and there it undergoes a slight figuration in the shape of

[75] *Fitzw. V. B.*, i., p. 214.

[76] In the 16th and 17th centuries carmen had the reputation of knowing how to whistle with great skill airs of their own invention. The song which served as the foundation of Byrd's variations recounts how a carman consoled a pretty girl who was in sorrow by whistling her an air. (Chappell, *op. cit.*, p. 137 ff).

embroidery. The accompanying counterpoints share the same character of simplicity, and form in each variation a new harmonic foundation. It is virtually only at the opening of the second variation that we are able to discover a few notes in the bass recalling those of the resumption of the first phrase of the subject in the first variation. We may remark also that this first phrase is given out without accompaniment at the opening of the piece.

The variations *The Carman's Whistle* have the peculiarity that they are followed by a sort of conclusion or appendix, in which the master treats an entirely new subject, of a pompous and solemn turn; Saint-Saëns has made use of it in his opera *Henri VIII.*, under the title of *Menuet de la Reine Anne*.

A piece to which we have already made several allusions will now have our attention : the thirty variations by John Bull on the subject *Walsingham* (*Fitzw. V. B.*, i., p. 1), which we have also seen treated by Byrd, under the polyphonic form (*see* p. 214). We have called attention above to the implicit modulatory character of this melody. But while Byrd, a musician more devoted to the past than Bull, does not attempt to avail himself to any extent of this circumstance, Bull takes advantage of it, and gives us, in each of his variations, a remarkable instance of passing from the veiled and undecided A minor into the clear and luminous A major. Yet the means which he adopts to this end are not purely harmonic in essence, for, setting aside the first bar of each variation, Bull modifies the bass in each of them, or gives it a figuration so rich or so broken that it becomes impossible to recognise it; we therefore find ourselves in presence of a variation form almost unrestrictedly of the melodic type.

In the first variation the opening episode of the subject is given out without accompaniment. In the twenty-nine variations that follow, the melody, unchanged, takes the top part; it there appears at one time slightly, at another more or less richly, figured. This figuration gives the master, as do the accompanying counterpoints, the opportunity of utilising, so to speak, the whole arsenal which we have catalogued and described in the previous chapter. That which gives value to these variations is the fact that the virtuosity which they exhibit does no damage to their æsthetic effect; Bull has in fact succeeded in realising a masterly balance between the contents and the form. This work is not dated in the *Fitzw. V. B.*, but it is not assuming too much to suppose that it was written at the very earliest between 1610 and 1615, so progressive is its technique. Let us run through it quickly and notice in passing the principal methods of figuration which we meet with: here, bold rhythmical counterpoints as picturesque as could be desired; there, short imitations of an exquisite grace; further on, curious repetitions of notes, some of which suggest drum beats (var. 28); then numerous forms of broken intervals and of decomposition of chords; pleasant symmetrical figurations of a calm and reposeful grace; pliant and agile arrangements of triplets and sextolets. Along with these technical elements, the happy assemblage of which largely contributes to the charm of the work, we notice a crowd of ingenious details which still further increase its interest, and make it one of the most brilliant gems of the virginalistic répertoire; such, for example, as the poetic cadences *perdendosi*, which wind up several of the variations with the delicious colouring of a dream.

We have still to analyse two pieces of Giles Farnaby, which seem to belong to the purely melodic variation, *Quodlings Delight (Fitzw. V. B.,* ii., p. 19) and *Up tails all (Fitzw. V. B.,* ii., p. 360).

Quodling's Delight is somewhat complex in form. The subject comprises two episodes, A and B. In each variation A and B are successively subjected to a varied *reprise*, which is at one time carried out according to the system of the melodic, at another according to that of the melodico-harmonic variation. The first exposition of the subject, with its various repeats, is expressed

by the scheme $\begin{matrix} A & A^I \\ B & B \end{matrix}$

This arrangement becomes in the sequel the occasion for four variations, the various episodes of which fluctuate constantly between the principle of the melodic and that of the melodico-harmonic variation. The dividing line between these two types is often very difficult to trace on account of the complicated figurations which the bass undergoes.

In the third variation, A is announced in the tenor and taken up again (A^I) in the *superius*. In the fourth, A, which has been given out in the *superius*, is taken up again (A^I) in three successive fragments by the bass, the tenor, and the *superius*. We see with what an almost indefinable type of variation we have to do, by what a slender thread this variation can be looked on as allied to the melodic variation. It may be said in favour of this classification that the melody plays an essential part by the side of which the rôle of the harmonic bass is eclipsed and almost disappears. As a technical detail, let us point out the sudden and unexpected passage of the left hand from the top of the middle to the lowest part of the keyboard. The melody of *Quodling's Delight* gives the impression of a little romantic ballad, full of freshness and simplicity.[77] The variations are elegantly written.

Up tails all is much less complicated in structure than *Quodling's Delight*. It consists of nineteen very short variations on an air which might be called a child's song, so simple and artless is it.[78] Treated in the *superius*, either with or without figuration, it is provided with a bass that is figured in all the variations except the first, which assumes the appearance of a monody sustained by a series of chords, with a few rare passing-notes. Analysis of the bass occasionally reveals the presence, in the different variations, of permanent harmonic elements intended to serve as points of support; whence it follows that these variations may to a certain extent be included in the melodico-harmonic type. Nevertheless, the

[77] According to Chappell, *op. cit.*, pp. 456, 782, and 794, it is a melancholy song, in which a young girl from the North of England, removed to London, gives way to regrets for her native land (*I would I were in my own country*).

[78] Chappell speaks of it, *op. cit.*, p. 196, and although he gives but few details on this melody, we may conclude from the first words of the text that it is a jovial song :

> " Fly, merry news, among the crews
>   That love to hear of jests."

We have already noticed, according to Dr. Naylor (see note, p. 221), the analogy which exists between the opening of *Up tails all* and the subject treated by Tomkins in *A grounde (Fitzw. V. B.*, ii., p. 87).

melody is so preponderant that it seems to us fitter to class it in the melodic kind.

Up tails all is a pure gem by reason of its charm, the unexpected nature of its figural play, and the youthful spontaneity of its inspiration. In it we meet with very interesting forms of figuration, especially in the field of harmony (decomposition of chords and intervals) and rhythm. From the latter point of view some of the last variations should be specially noticed, in which the subject, originally in $\mathbb{C}$, takes a $\frac{6}{4}$ form, or else remains in $\mathbb{C}$ whilst the figuration adopts the rhythm of $\frac{6}{4}$. We find also several variations in two parts only, which are of an extreme lightness and delicacy. Finally, we find instances of the sudden passage of the right hand from the middle to the top, and of the left hand from the middle to the lower part of the keyboard, or from the lower part to the middle.

III.—THE HARMONIC VARIATION.

The harmonic variation, as we have seen, implies an invariably identical bass, upon which is raised an erection of counterpoints, changing from variation to variation. The absolute type of this kind of variation is therefore analogous to the *Ground* for keyed instruments such as it appears in the works of Blow during the second half of the 17th century.[79]

William Byrd gives us four examples of harmonic variations. Actually this figure is reduced to three if we decide that the piece called *Pescodd Time* (*Fitzw. V. B.*, ii., p. 430) is only a replica of *The Hunt's up* (*Fitzw. V. B.*, i., p. 218).

[79] See above, p. 217 ff. We have there explained in detail everything concerning the particulars and details of the *ground* as forming a principle of the harmonic variation.

These last two pieces occur again in *Nevell's Booke* under the title *The Huntes upp;* they are consequently earlier than 1592. They take as their foundation a subject which is reproduced in an always similar form in the bass of each of the variations, generally in a simple shape, but at times under a figured aspect :—

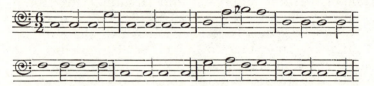

It at once appears, on examining this bass, that its use has coincided with the preoccupation (no doubt unconscious) of making a harmonic progression. The first two bars give the succession tonic, dominant, tonic, in C major. But as at the time of Byrd they did not as yet use in all their strictness the forms of modulation which came into practice a century later, we notice that C major is followed, without transition, by a D minor characterized by its tonic, its dominant, and a passing B♭. We afterwards get back by means of the subdominant F to the original tonic C, and we remain up to the end in the key of C, characterized by its tonic, its dominant, and its subdominant. On this harmonic foundation are raised free counterpoints the combinations of which are modified from variation to variation. At times we find a passing analogy between the melodic part of certain variations and that of certain others, but there is not a sufficiency of precise elements to justify us in regarding it as an example of the melodic variation properly so-called.

Everything in this composition of Byrd's reveals a descriptive intention. It is not a question of the detailed description of a hunt, of which we find examples in other virginalistic pieces, but rather the joyful spirit evoked in the hunters by the beautiful country they are passing through. The open-air feeling is communicated by the monotonous rhythm of the persistent bass, by the special harmonic successions to which this bass gives occasion, and by the effects of imitation and echo.

Pescodd Time has only eleven variations, while *The Hunt's up* has twelve. Except for a few slight differences of detail, the first five in *Pescodd Time* are to be found exactly in the first five of *The Hunt's up*. As to those which follow, we notice the following interchanges:—

The 6th variation of *Pescodd Time* corresponds to the 10th of *The Hunt's up*.

,, 7th	,,	,,	,,	,, 11th	,,
,, 8th	,,	,,	,,	,, 7th	,,
,, 9th	,,	,,	,,	,, 8th	,,
,, 10th	,,	,,	,,	,, 9th	,,

Finally the eleventh and last variation of *Pescodd Time* is a resumption, with simpler figuration, of the ninth variation of the same piece. Thus only variations 6 and 12 of *The Hunt's up* have not been made use of in *Pescodd Time*.[80]

[80] The melodies which Chappell reproduces (*op. cit.*, pp. 60 and 198) as those of the well known popular songs the *Hunt's up* and *Peascodd Time*, are not those which Byrd used. But the texts show us that a feeling for nature pervades them. *The Kinges Hunt is upp* describes a hunt of King Henry VIII. in a clear sunrise smiling in the heavens and lighting up the green grass. Chappell observes that *The Hunt's up* ended by becoming generic, typifying every song referring to the dawn. In *Peascodd Time* the text speaks, among other things, of little boys who look after the cattle in the field, and make themselves a whistle out of a piece of straw.

Q

The two other compositions of Byrd composed according to the system of the harmonic variation are *Treg. Ground* (*Fitzw. V. B.*, i., p. 226)— an abbreviation which the editors of the *Fitzw. V. B.* interpret as meaning *Tregian's Ground*—and *Malt's come downe* (*Fitzw. V. B.*, ii., p. 166).

Tregian's Ground consists of twelve absolute harmonic variations, in which all that is not the bass consists of free counterpoints. The bass is subjected to figuration in a very small number of variations. It conforms to a rhythm analogous to that which we have noticed in *The Hunt's up*. *Tregian's Ground* has not the æsthetic interest of *The Hunt's up*. But the figuration, which especially makes use of short imitations and echo effects, is charming, and gives the work a pleasant and picturesque character.[81]

Malt's come downe carries us back to the field of pastoral music dear to Byrd. Here the bass follows a harmonic progression of quite a modern character, which implies without reserve the key of C major, but with a predilection for the succession tonic, subdominant, tonic, instead of tonic, dominant, tonic :—

Among the nine variations which the piece contains, there are three only in which the bass is adorned with figurations. The other parts are in free counterpoint. In variations 4 and 7 the rhythm of the bass is transferred to the upper

[81] According to a note in Grove's *Dictionary*, the *Treg. ground* of the *Fitzw. V. B.* is identical with *Hughe Astons grounde*, which is No. 35 in *Nevell's Book*. May we conjecture from this that the theme was by Ashton, and that F. Tregian had a special fondness for it?

parts, which are formed into successions of homophonic chords standing above a figured bass. *Malt's come downe* is an exquisite composition, in which all the qualities of Byrd appear, especially the poetical charm of the harmony, in which soft and gentle tones prevail.[82]

Inglott offers an example of harmonic variation mixed with melodic and polyphonic elements, in his *Galliard Ground* (*Fitzw. V. B.*, ii., p. 375). This piece comprises five variations, and follows a somewhat complex plan, which may be compared with that of Farnaby's *Quodling's Delight* (see p. 225). Inglott first of all gives out in the bass an episode A, which at once undergoes a varied repeat, A', in which the accompanying counter-points sustain an integral modification. Then follows an episode B, which is subjected to a repeat B', presented under the same conditions as A'. Thus we have a first variation the scheme of which is :—

A   A'

B   B'

This combination is varied four times in the following part of the piece. In the first two of these four variations the harmonic system is applied without restriction. In the last two the subject passes to the *superius*—all the other parts being free—and undergoes a slight figuration in certain passages of the repeats ; we thus have the intervention of polyphonic and melodic elements.

It remains to quote, as a last example of harmonic variation, a short composition of

---

[82] *Malt's come down* (Chappell, *op. cit.*, p. 74) is a humorous song on beer.

R. Farnaby, *Faine would I wedd* (*Fitzw. V. B.*, ii., p. 263), in which we come across three variations built up in free counterpoints on a bass which appears quite plain in the first and figured in the two others. This little piece charms us by its simple and popular humour.

IV.—The Melodico-Harmonic Variation.

The melodico-harmonic variation became in time the most common kind; in other words, the normal type of virginalistic variation. Although it belongs to the species of accompanied monody, which did not definitely become a musical habit till the opening of the 17th century, we still meet with examples of an earlier date than that period. There is nothing surprising in this if we consider that accompanied monody was already in actual use throughout musical Europe long before the Florentines put forward the theory of it.

In this *genre* Byrd gives us two examples of melodico-harmonic variations which, as they form part of *Nevell's Book*, must be considered as having been written at the very latest in 1591: *All in a garden greene* and *Sellinger's Round*,[83] which are to be found also in the *Fitzw. V. B.*

All in a garden greene (*Fitzw. V. B.*, i., p. 411) develops a pretty, simple subject [84] in six variations, the last of which belongs to the old polyphonic type, for the reason that the melody passes into

---

[83] The date of 1580 given by Pauer (*Old English composers for the virginals and harpsichord*) as that of *Sellinger's Round* is borne out by no serious authority with which we are acquainted. Mr. Barclay Squire is unaware on what grounds Pauer adopted it.

[84] The song, *All in a garden greene*, reproduced by Chappell, *op. cit.*, p. 111, which concerns two faithful lovers, is not that taken by Byrd as the foundation of his variations.

the alto. With the exception of this anomaly, these variations have all the characters of the melodico-harmonic type, including the alternate division of the figuration between the *superius* and the bass. This figuration is of no particular interest; we find few leanings towards novelty in it.

Sellinger's Round (*Fitzw. V. B.*, i., p. 248) is, as indicated by its title, a round, that is to say, a dance. In principle it belongs to the melodico-harmonic variation, insomuch as the greater number of its nine variations are composed according to that type. But frequently grave violence is done to the orthodox plan. Thus in the fifth variation the subject, given to the *superius*, passes suddenly into the alto, where it is soon lost under its figuration[85]; in more than one of the variations the bass becomes almost unrecognisable apart from a few isolated points of support. In this case it is the system of the purely melodic variation which takes the upper hand. The figuration is simple and elegant. It offers a few technical difficulties in the sixth variation, in which passages in rapid thirds have to be executed by the left hand. The subject, in the rhythm of a jig, is extremely characteristic. Byrd has treated it in the pastoral and popular manner which is characteristic of him.[86]

[85] In the ninth variation the subject opens in the alto, but is carried on by the *superius*.

[86] Chappell (*op. cit.*, p. 69 ff) does not know the precise origin of this subject, very popular in England in the 16th and 17th centuries, which also bore the curious title of *The beginning of the world*. According to Dr. Naylor (*An Eliz. V. B.*, p. 53), "Sellinger" should be "Saint-Leger," a place in the south-west of England.

[Saint-Leger is the surname of a well-known English family, generally pronounced "Sellinger."—TR.]

The same master furnishes another example of the *round* treated in the form of song-variation, the *Gipseis Round* (*Fitzw. V. B.*, ii., p. 292). This we may also refer to the melodico-harmonic type, but not without mentioning some important anomalies in it. These consist chiefly in modifications of the melody, and sometimes also of the bass, which reduce these essential elements to a merely shadowy form. We meet also in certain variations (for example, 3 and 6) with fragments of free counterpoints which insert themselves above the melody, and produce the illusion that this has gone into the alto. The subject is like a jig in rhythm. Long fundamental notes, held in the bass, give the effect of the popular drone, imparting to the entire piece a delightfully pastoral colour.[87]

With the variations of Byrd on the song *Fortune* (*Fitzw. V. B.*, i., p. 254), a work the date of which we do not know even approximately, we fall upon a perfected type of the melodico-harmonic variation. The subject is divided into two episodes, A and B, which give occasion for varied repeats in each of the four variations, A[1] and B[1]; it is a plaintive melody which Sweelinck has also developed in variation form, under the German title of *Von der Fortuna werd' ich getrieben* (*Complete works*, i., p. 127).[88]

---

[87] Chappell, *op. cit.*, p. 171, gives some details on the *Gipsie's Round*. When the gipsies played a part in old English plays and had to sing, a special kind of music was usually assigned to them.

[88] S. Scheidt also wrote variations on this song under the title *Fortuna anglica* (*Tablatura nova* of 1624). The melody *Fortune*, the original text of which is a sort of lamentation over the blows of fortune, is one of the most celebrated of the 16th and 17th centuries (see Chappell, *op. cit.*, p. 162).

These variations constitute an attempt to treat the harmonico-melodic variation according to its most normal type, a gradation being effected from the beginning to the end by the use of a more and more animated figuration. Thanks to this piece, we are enabled to form a very clear idea as to the alternation between the figuration of the bass and that of the *superius*. Let us take, for example, episode A, followed by its repeat A¹, in the first variation :—[89]

This passage becomes in the second variation :—

[89] We suppress the inner parts with a view to simplification.

A^{III}

Further on this play of alternation is repeated at narrower intervals; no longer between an episode and its repeat, but within the episode itself.

The opening of episode B of the first variation:—

is transformed as follows in the fourth variation:—

The figuration of the second bar imitates textually that of the first: the bass is taken up by the *superius* without any modification in the melodico-harmonic core.

The *Fortune* variations are not very remarkable from a purely æsthetic point of view. This is not the case with a series of variations of analogous structure and character which Byrd wrote on the exquisite song *O Mistris myne* (*Fitzw. V. B.*, i., p. 258), where the balance obtained by the happy distribution of the figures between the six variations has a most seductive effect. In consequence of the bass being frequently rendered unrecognisable by its figuration, *O Mistris myne* resembles more or less the purely melodic variation: the more so as the melody entrusted to the *superius* receives from variation to variation a very sober figuration, which at no time prevents it being recognisable. The sixth and last variation shows the theme once more in its native simplicity. The conclusion of the piece is thus tinged with a sweet serenity which largely contributes to the charm which it exhales.[90]

In a last series of melodico-harmonic variations by Byrd, *Callino Casturame* (*Fitzw. V. B.*, ii., p. 186), we breathe again that country atmosphere which the old master at all times knows so well how to describe. The melody is of Irish origin. Its true name is *Colleen oge asthore*. Shakespeare alludes to it in his historical drama, *Henry V.* The figuration of *Callino Casturame* in general affects the *superius* with more persistence than the bass; the latter has more or less the character of a persistent drone. The entire work breathes a

---

[90] Chappell, *op. cit.*, p. 209, reproduces, with the words, the melody which Byrd treated. The song is that of the Clown in *Twelfth Night*.

pastoral freshness which is very picturesque. Certain passages remind us of an old bagpipe tune in a tiny village buried in the far-away country.

The Italianising madrigalist, Thomas Morley (born in 1557, died about 1602-3), gives us two series of melodico-harmonic variations : *Goe from my window* (*Fitzw. V. B.*, i., p. 42), and *Nancie* (*Fitzw. V. B.*, i., p. 57).

In the first he treats a very fresh melody—the sequential structure of which is worthy of notice— in seven variations which to some extent approach the purely harmonic type. The bass—simple or figured—remains almost the same in all the variations. As to the melody above, it undergoes such alterations in many passages that one may say there is nothing left of it. Nevertheless, in two variations, the fifth and the seventh, it appears more clearly and perspicuously than in the first, from the fact that it is treated in the *superius* in a succession of homophonic chords ranged on a figured bass. The work has an elegant turn, and betrays Italian influences, especially in the suspensions of the second variation.

The *Fitzw. V. B.* (i., p. 153) contains another series of variations on the same melody, attributed to Munday. In comparing these eight variations with those of Morley, it will be remarked that the first seven are exactly the same as the seven variations of the latter master. Is this an error of attribution or a plagiarism ? And who, in this case, is the real author of the variations ? This it is impossible to decide. In any case the eighth variation of the piece by Munday is not only not to be found in the work attributed to Morley, but, in addition, forms quite a new musical fragment, having no thematic connection with that which precedes it. Here, then, we have that sort of closing postlude which we have already met with in the *Carman's whistle* of Byrd.[91]

The *Nancie* of Morley treats a simple melody, quite popular in structure.[92] Owing to the division of the subject into three episodes, A, B, and C, which eventually give occasion for repeats, this series of variations seems rather complex in structure. Here is the scheme of it :—

1st variation.	2nd variation.		3rd variation.	
A	A^I	A^{II}	A^{III}	A^{IIII}
B	B^I	B^{II}	B^{III}	B^{IIII}
C	C^I	C^{II}	C^{III}	C^{IIII}

The figuration becomes more animated from variation to variation, and affects alternately the melody and the bass, at times transforming them till they become unrecognisable.

John Bull has left us but a limited number of song-variations answering to the melodico-harmonic type; moreover, two of these pieces are nothing but dance-tunes treated in the same way as the variations of secular songs.

The first is specially interesting, for the reason that the motive which is the foundation of it has also been developed by Cabezon, as well as by Sweelinck and his German pupil, Scheidt. It is the *Spanish Paven* to be found at p. 131 of the

[91] The subject of the song, *Goe from my window* (Chappell, *op. cit.*, p. 146), is that of a fair one who, her gallant pleading to be allowed to visit her, repulses him with mockery.

[92] The original song (Chappell, *op. cit.*, p. 149) relates the heroic adventures of a London apprentice, who, having performed prodigies of courage in Turkey, ended by marrying the King's daughter.

second volume of the *Fitzw. V. B.* It comprises eight variations, in which the harmonic principle in great measure overrides the melodic. The melody of the *superius* undergoes, in fact, constant disguises, and is treated with almost absolute freedom. The fourth variation alone gives the melody in a succession of homophonic chords deprived of all figuration except in the bass. Figured or not, the latter remains unchanged in the different variations. The figuration is of great sobriety, and is an argument for the comparative antiquity of the piece, possibly also for some influence, direct or indirect, of Cabezon.

The piece of the Spanish master which develops the same subject is entitled *Pavana italiana*, and belongs to the *Obras* of 1578 (*Hisp. Sch. Mus. Sacr.*, vii., p. 73). Cabezon has written only six variations, to which the nobility of the figural line gives a perfect beauty. The first bars only of the subject treated by him have been borrowed by Bull ; the remainder, with the English master, is simply an almost perfectly free paraphrase. Except for a few points of support in common, the harmonization of Bull is independent of that of Cabezon.

In the *Paduana hispania* which Seiffert publishes in vol. i. of the *Complete works of Sweelinck* (p. 128), we find four variations, the first and third of which are by Sweelinck, the second and fourth by Scheidt.[93] Here, again, the opening of the subject is the same as that found in Cabezon and in Bull. Further on we again find certain points of resemblance between the melody as it is treated

---

[93] According to Seiffert (*Introduction* to vol. i. of the complete works of Sweelinck, p. 13) this combination of variations by Sweelinck and by Scheidt is not the result of rivalry or of concert between the two masters, but really the act of a copyist.

by Sweelinck—Scheidt and the version given by Bull. The harmonization of the Dutch and the German master, apart from a few identical points of support, is independent of that of the Spaniard and of the Englishman. The figuration of the *Paduana hispania* has a much more progressive character than that of the variations by Cabezon and Bull, which is not astonishing in view of the fact that this series of variations is to be found in a manuscript dating probably between 1620 and 1630, and certainly was not composed before 1606, the time when Scheidt became the pupil of Sweelinck.[94]

The variations of Bull have charm and sobriety, and please by their harmonic beauty, but they do not possess the noble gravity of those of Cabezon.

[94] It is curious to notice the contradictory diversity of the titles of these different series of variations. Cabezon says : *Pavana Italiana*. Now, the pavan is supposed to be of Spanish origin ; but by the qualification *Italiana* the master (himself a Spaniard) attributes to it an Italian origin. Bull seems more logical when he says *Spanish Paven*. Again, Sweelinck and Scheidt completely befog our notions of clearness when they say, *Paduana hispania*. The *Paduana* really seems to have been a dance of Italian origin, but Sweelinck and Scheidt apparently add that it came from Spain ! They say, therefore, just the contrary to Cabezon. One fact is absolutely certain. If *pavana* and *paduana* or *padovana* are originally two dances of different source and structure, one being of a binary rhythm and indigenous to Spain, and the other of a ternary rhythm and native to Padova or Padua, in Italy (Boehme, *op. cit.*, i., p. 134), the musicians of the 17th century gave the two names indifferently to one and the same dance (slow and in binary rhythm), thus confounding two ideas primitively independent one of the other.

Chappell (*op. cit.*, p. 240) relates that the subject of the *Spanish Paven* was very popular in England during the reign of Elizabeth and her successor.

In the collection of dance music, *Nobiltà di dame*, by Fabritio Caroso, we find a *Pavaniglia*, the opening of which is absolutely that of the *Spanish Paven*, which also proves the popularity of that dance tune in Italy. *Nobiltà di dame* is a new edition, published in 1605—with new dances—of the *Ballarino* of Caroso, the first edition of which probably appeared in 1577. Oscar Chilesotti has published with Ricordi (*Biblioteca di rarità musicali*) an edition in modern notation of the *Nobiltà* of 1605. (The *Pavaniglia* is to be found at p. 21.)

A second series of melodico-harmonic variations of Bull's is entitled *Les Buffons*, and has been edited by Pauer in his *Old English composers for the virginals and harpsichord* (p. 47).[95] The very short subject is probably of French origin; it is treated in thirteen variations, which represent in complete perfection the melodico-harmonic type, with a sharing of the figuration between the melody and the bass. The very tonal character of the piece, and the numerous spreadings of chords which occur in the figuration, argue in favour of a comparatively recent origin. The conclusion, in toccata style, forming a postlude, having no connection with what has gone before, should be noticed; *Les Buffons* has the qualities of elegant, clear, and joyous virtuosity.

After Bull, Munday. In addition to his variations *Goe from my window* (already noticed, at p. 125), this master gives us one piece of the first order, in which he treats a delightful air, *Robin* (*Fitzw. V. B.*, i., p. 66), the soothing Siciliano rhythm of which delights us by its tenderness and freshness. The three variations which this charming musician has written on this melody have no special technical point worthy of notice. The figuration, simple and ingenious, shows off the subject admirably. The work, short and concise as it is, is delicately treated, and finely chiselled.

[95] Mr. Barclay-Squire informs the author that this piece is taken from MS. 23623 of the British Museum. We find in the *Oude en nieuwe Hollantse Boeren Lieties en Contredansen*, published at the beginning of the 18th century by Roger, at Amsterdam, a piece entitled *De Boufon*, the first two bars of which are absolutely identical with the melody of the first two bars of the *superius* of the *Bouffons* by Bull (see *Uitgave X. der Vereiniging voor Noord-Niderlands Muzikgeschiedenis*). Again, the *Luytboek* of Thysius, a century earlier than the work just cited, contains a piece, *Boter op de pensen*, in which the melodic line is almost identical with that of *De Boufon*.

G. Farnaby has written, under the fuller title of *Bony sweet Robin* (*Fitzw. V. B.*, ii., p. 77), a series of five variations on this same melody.[96] In principle these variations belong to the melodico-harmonic type, but we see the intrusion of certain polyphonic elements into them. Thus in the fifth variation a fragment of the subject passes straight over to the alto from the bass, whilst the left hand, by means of crossing, plays a counterpoint in the *superius*. Towards the end of the piece the final episode of the melody is treated entirely in the tenor. Lastly, we find in this composition sudden skips of the left hand from the middle to the lower part of the keyboard.

The *Daphne* of Farnaby (*Fitzw. V. B.*, ii., p. 12) is interesting from its novelty, as evidenced in various ways by its rhythmic, figural, and harmonic daring. The plan diverges from the usually very simple scheme of the song-variation; and it is rather difficult at first sight to separate the essential elements of it, so irregular is its design. The following diagram will serve to describe it :—

1st part.
{
A A^I
B
C, with *finale* resembling that of A.
B^i
C^I
}

2nd part.
{
A^{II} + *coda*-cadence.
2nd part of C, varied and put in the tenor.
B^{II} (subject in the alto).
C^{II} (,, ,, tenor).
B^{III} (,, ,, ,,).
C^{III} (,, ,, ,,).
}

[96] Of the original only the first words, *My Robin is to the greenwood gone*, **are** known (Chappell, *op. cit.*, p. 234).

It is evident what an anomalous structure we have here.[97] It is not astonishing that in these conditions it becomes somewhat difficult to decide in which group of variations this piece should be classed. It is by only a slender thread that it can be attached to the melodico-harmonic variation, even allowing that various polyphonic elements are to be met with in it. The figuration of *Daphne* is of great richness. We find in it a crowd of details which show that Farnaby set himself to make use of all the resources offered by the keyboard and by the novel figures which the virginalists had created for him : subtle rhythmic formulas, symmetrical figurations, &c., &c., and, running through all these, harmonic turns full of originality.

Pawles wharfe, by G. Farnaby (*Fitzw. V. B.*, ii., p. 17), is an exquisite piece, the *Stimmung* of which makes us think sometimes of Mozart, sometimes of Schumann. The plan is somewhat irregular. It may be represented as follows :—

1st
variation.

$\begin{cases} \text{A} & \text{A}^\text{I} \\ \text{B} & \text{B}^\text{I} \end{cases}$ (B opens differently from A, but has the same conclusion.)

2nd
variation.

$\begin{cases} \text{A}^\text{II} & \text{A}^\text{III} \\ \text{B}^\text{II} & \text{B}^\text{III} \end{cases}$ (the first part of the subject is in the tenor, the second in the *superius*) B$^\text{IIII}$ (same remark.)

Apart from the polyphonic element found in B$^\text{III}$ and B$^\text{IIII}$, this little piece falls without

[97] This structure resembles to a certain extent that of the dance variation. The song (Chappell, *op. cit.*, p. 338), the first words of which are *When Daphne did from Phœbus fly*, recounts the legend of Daphne pursued by Apollo, and metamorphosed into a laurel by Diana. Farnaby has followed pretty faithfully the episodes A and B of the version given by Chappell, but has taken certain liberties with C.

reservation into the category of melodico-harmonic variations. A sudden skip of the left hand from the lower part of the keyboard to the middle is to be noted.[98]

Put up thy dagger Jemy, by the same Farnaby (*Fitzw. V. B.*, ii., p. 72), also belongs to the melodico-harmonic kind, but with a decided predominance of the melody. This is always perfectly recognisable, even where it is much figured, while the bass is at times so distorted that it is almost impossible to discover it (see particularly variations 5, 7, and in part 6). The figuration has a remarkably modern character; the end of the fourth variation, with its broken chords and intervals, is specially remarkable in this respect. The subject on which Farnaby has based these variations, which are refined even to affectation, has no trace of the tragic, in spite of the title of the piece; on the contrary, it is a pleasing melody, of a popular and dancing character.

In *Wooddy-Cock* (*Fitzw. V. B.*, ii., p. 138) Farnaby develops in six variations a subject ravishing in its freshness and its rhythm.[99]

The plan is $\left.\begin{array}{l} A\ A' \\ B\ B' \end{array}\right\}$ varied six times, with a fairly even division of the figuration between the melody and the bass. Both from the expressive and the technical points of view this piece shows a highly developed character. The first part of variation 5, with its rapid and animated thirds in

---

[98] See Chappell, *op. cit.*, p. 130. Paul's Wharf was a public place where people came to draw water, near St. Paul's Cathedral. Chappell gives the melody, but not the words of *Paul's Wharf*.

[99] Chappell, *op. cit.*, p. 793, terms it an "*English country dance*."

R

the middle of the keyboard, is of rare charm, and unique in the whole of virginalistic literature. The second part of this variation, with the subject brought out in augmentation on counterpoints in triplets, requires a somewhat unusual virtuosity if it is to be performed at the right pace.

Rosasolis of Farnaby (*Fitzw. V. B.*, p. 148) exhibits the master in his most gracious light, and almost like a miniaturist, so much ease and delicacy does it show — under the form of melodico-harmonic variation with divided figuration— in its development of the delightfully childish subject which forms the base of the composition.[100]

In *Loth to depart* (*Fitzw. V. B.*, ii., p. 317) Farnaby gives us another example of melodico-harmonic song-variation. In six variations that are delightful for their qualities of ease and unexpectedness, he develops a melody composed of two episodes A and B, B opening exactly in the same way as A, but finishing with a different cadence.[101]

Tell mee, Daphne, of the same master (*Fitzw. V. B.*, ii., p. 446) treats, in three very delicate variations, a pretty subject, which according to Chappell (*op. cit.*, p. 158) has also been used by Byrd, with the title *Go no more a rushing*.

There is also a whole series of variations by Farnaby which from their titles seem to be variations of songs, but which we have not hesitated to group among the dance-variations on account of their special plan, which has more affinity with the latter than with the former.

[100] John Bull also treated this subject under the title *Rose a solis* (Add. MS. 23623 of the British Museum).

[101] According to Chappell (*op. cit.*, p. 173) a *Loth*, or *Loath to depart*, is a kind of song expressive of regret at parting from friends.

Before passing on to the consideration of the dance-variation, we must again point out a few examples of the melodico-harmonic song-variation which we find in the *Fitzw. V. B.*: first of all, *Barafostus Dreame* (*Fitzw. V. B.*, ii., p. 94), the author of which was a virginalist of the later generation, Thomas Tomkins. His variations on this fine subject, of noble and solemn feeling,[102] are more interesting from their character of progressive virtuosity than from the expressive treatment of the melody. This is, in fact, more or less smothered under a too rich and too heavy figural dress. On analysis we notice a certain preponderance of the melodic over the harmonic element, the latter being often rendered unrecognisable by the figuration. The piece ends with a *Coda* independent of the subject. As a technical detail worthy of notice, we may point out the sudden skip of the left hand from the middle to the lower part, and inversely (var. 3 and 5); in variation 5 it appears under a form so far not met with in Farnaby, and aiming apparently at an effect of special sonority :—[103]

The anonymous author to whom we are indebted for another varied version of *Barafostus Dreame* (*Fitzw. V. B.*, i., p. 72) has not perhaps the virtuosity of Tomkins, but his treatment of the subject, in four variations, is more sober and more

[102] *Barafostus* or *Bara Faustus* or *Barrow Foster's Dream*, is, according to Chappell (*op. cit.*, p. 240), a song in praise of love. According to Dr. Naylor (*An Eliz. V. B.*, p. 83) *Dreame* may be *Dreme*, a word which means "song."

[103] We have already pointed out this bold way of writing in our study of forms of figuration (see p. 150).

appropriate in expression. Contrary to what we notice with Tomkins, the harmonic element has the predominance over the melodic. At the opening of the third variation the melody is in the tenor : it is taken up a bar and a-half later by the *superius*. The figuration is very simple, and shows no special feature except a decomposed fifth (end of the second variation), which perhaps points to a somewhat ancient origin.[104]

Finally, Richard Farnaby is the author of a series of variations, *Hanskin*, which from several points of view have a mixed character. Placed by their structure and by their subject (which is that of a dance) halfway between the song-variation and that of the dance, they belong in part to the melodico-harmonic variation and partly to the polyphonic. The melody is that of a dance well known at the end of the 16th and beginning of the 17th centuries, the *Courante Hansken*, which Boehme reproduces in his *Geschichte des Tanzes in Deutschland* (ii., p. 45), from the lute book of Thysius.[105] *Hanskin* is divided into five variations, which pursue the following scheme :—

$$A \quad A^{1}$$
$$B \quad B^{1}$$

In A[1] as well as in B and B[1] of the third variation the melody is in the tenor. Almost everywhere else the plan is that of the melodico-harmonic variation. The work is third-rate. The figuration, which makes frequent use of repeated notes, is dry and clumsy; Richard Farnaby did not inherit the charming genius of his father.

[104] Dr. Naylor (*An Eliz. V. B.*, p. 83) propounds a hypothesis that the anonymous author of *Barafostus Dreame* may really have been Byrd.

[105] According to Chappell (*op. cit.*, p. 73), *Hanskin* was the equivalent of *Hankin* or *Hannikin*, which was the Christian name of a clown.

C.—Dance Variations.

The dance variation is the musical form which was cultivated by the virginalists with the greatest delight. The different collections of virginal music which have come down to us contain a very considerable number of them in comparison with the variations of the song and other musical forms. We shall see, when analysing them, that the dance variations are far from presenting the multiplicity of appearance which we find in the variations of secular songs. We shall show, however, that they offer elements of no less interest, on account of the care which the virginalists took to achieve the maximum of perfection and refinement within this narrow circle of form.

A few preliminary observations become necessary before taking up the study of the various dances which the English masters of the clavier submitted to variations.

1. It often happens that virginalistic dances are met with which, at first sight, do not seem capable of classification under the term " variation." Actually they are composed of two or three episodes, A, B or A, B, C, which may give occasion for textual repeats, but not for variations properly so-called. If, however, these pieces can be included in the category of the variation, it is because these episodes, such as they are, constitute adaptations for the virginal of pre-existing dance tunes; the latter are borrowed from popular music, or from individual music, monodic or polyphonic, and their treatment for the keyboard must consequently be looked on as a form of variation, of the same kind as the

first giving-out of a subject of a secular song at the opening of a series of variations.[106]

2. If, in the variations of the song, we have shown that there exists, side by side with the melodico-harmonic type, a considerable number of variations belonging to the polyphonic, melodic, or harmonic kind; if again we have noted, even within the limits of the melodico-harmonic variation of the song, certain anomalies in virtue of which the latter often appears to moderate the strictness of its principles, on the other hand it must be remarked that in the domain of the dance variation the pure melodico-harmonic type, with the alternate shifting of the figuration between the *superius* and the bass, predominates almost absolutely. There are exceptions, as for example the *Galliard to the Quadran Pavan* of Bull (*Fitzw. V. B.*, i., p. 117), in which we find ourselves face to face with the purely harmonic type, or the *Why ask you* of Farnaby (*Fitzw. V. B.*, ii., p. 462), in which polyphonic elements intervene; but they are extremely rare. We shall see also that the balance between the melodic and the harmonic element is not always very well maintained, and that it is almost always in this case the harmonic element that prevails. The predominance of the melodico-harmonic type in the dance variation is the result of that tendency towards the feeling for harmony which is one of the characteristics of the period of the virginalists. The dance, which is essentially popular in its origin, lends itself admirably to harmonic treatment, and in fact the greater part of those which the English masters have treated in the form of melodico-harmonic variations are

[106] See p. 211.

nothing else than accompanied melodies, submitted to figurations and various colorature. The allemandes and courantes of the *Fitzw. V. B.*, which are distinguished for the most part by the freedom of their rhythm, and by melodic turns completely foreign to the tonal indecision of the Church modes, nearly all have, as a necessary consequence, basses very definite in character, which show by their movement stronger and stronger connections with the music of the end of the 16th and the opening of the 17th centuries—with that which was to become, a hundred years later, classical harmony.

The virginalists have treated the following dance-forms :—

1. *Pavans and galliards.*
2. *Allemandes.*
3. *Courantes.*
4. *Jigs.*
5. *Various dances : voltes, rondes, marches, toyes, spagnolettas, morescas.*
6. Dances *sine nomine.*

Under this last title we group those pieces which, although bearing titles leading us to believe that they are variations of a song, are in fact simply dance variations.

I.—Pavans and Galliards.

If we join these two dances under one and the same title it is because in practice they are most frequently connected together.

The pavan, according to Boehme,[107] is a dance of a grave and majestic character, which was

[107] *Geschichte des Tanzes in Deutschland*, i., p. 134.

much in honour in the 16th and 17th centuries. It was of Spanish origin, and derived its name from the Spanish *pavone*—the peacock, *par excellence* the bird of majesty. It was in a slow $\frac{4}{4}$ time or in $\frac{4}{2}$ (₵) *alla breve.* Here are the first bars of a pavane (*Pavaniglia*), published in 1605, in a collection of the ballet master Fabritio Caroso :—[108]

The galliarde[109] is an ancient Italian dance of a joyful character, much liked and cultivated in Italy, in France, in Spain, in Germany, and in England in the 16th and 17th centuries. Its name comes from the Italian *gagliardo*, answering to the French *gaillard* in the sense of "joyous, lively, brisk." Its rhythm is in $\frac{3}{2}$ or $\frac{3}{4}$. The first beat of each bar should be strongly marked; the first note of the second bar takes two beats, or is dotted :—

By way of example here are the first bars of a galliard given by Thoinot Arbeau in his *Orchésographie* of 1588 :—

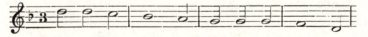

Originally the pace of the galliard was moderately animated, but in time it became

---

[108] It is the opening of the subject of the *Spanish Paven*, treated by Bull under the form of a variation of a song (see p. 239 and the Note, p. 241).

[109] Boehme (*op. cit.*, vol. i., p. 128). We find in Chappell (*op. cit.*, pp. 155-157) information on the pavan and the galliard which agrees with that of Boehme.

quicker and quicker, so that at the period of Thoinot Arbeau it had become very rapid.

When we look through the collections of instrumental music of the 16th century in which dances alone are to be found, we frequently notice the connection which existed between the pavans and the galliards; a pavan was followed by its galliard, and the latter was simply the pavan itself, but treated in such a manner that its binary rhythm was transformed into a ternary rhythm. Thus in the ten books of *Danceries*, published at Paris by Attaignant towards the middle of the 16th century, we find numerous examples of pavans followed by their galliards.[110] This rhythmical transformation, a rudimentary form of the variation, was carried out in the following manner :—

Episode A of a *pavane d'Angleterre* by Gervaise, taken from Attaignant's books of *Danceries :—*

This episode is thus transformed in the galliard which follows :—[111]

[110] See the reprint in modern notation of a selection of these *Danceries* in Part 23 of the *Maîtres musiciens de la Renaissance française* (Expert).

[111] It is the German principle of the *Tanz* followed by the *Nachtanz*. It is of very ancient origin. Boehme (*op. cit.*, vol. ii., No. 8) gives an instance of it dating from the 14th century,—a *Minnelied* in dance form, of Salzburg by origin, entitled *Das Kühhorn*, taken from the *Spörlsliederhandschrift*. In the first part the melodic subject takes this form :—

The virginalists seem to have had a special fondness for pavans and galliards. Of all the dances treated in the form of variations, it was the one which was most affected. Against a total of sixty-eight pavans and galliards to be found in the *Fitzw. V. B.* and *Parthenia,* we can only find twenty-three allemands, eighteen courantes, five jigs, &c. Moreover, pavans and galliards are treated at greater length and with more ingenuity than the other dances. Whilst the latter always preserve something of their popular origin, the former essentially represent the type of the more stylistic dance.

The number of sixty-eight [112] which we have given as the sum of the pavans and galliards which have

In the second it is transformed as follows :—

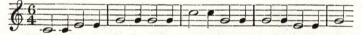

We find, as early as the lute tablatures published in 1508 by Petrucci at Venice, pavans followed by a *Saltarello* and by a third dance (*Piva*), which are nothing but rhythmical transformations (₵ becoming ¾ and ⅜) of the pavan which precedes them. (See *Zur Geschichte der Suite* by T. Norlind, *Sämmelbande* of the S. I. M., VII., ii., and Riemann, *Handb. der Musikgesch.,* II., ii., p. 168). The *Pavana alla venetiana* of J. A. Dalza (Petrucci, 1508) followed by its *Saltarello* and its *Piva*, of which Oswald Körte publishes the melody in his *Laute und Lautenmusik bis zur Mitte des 16. Jahrhunderts* (Breitkopf & Härtel, Leipzig, 1901), does not give a very characteristic example of this rhythmical transformation of a single melody ; it is scarcely possible to trace any thematic analogy except between the opening of the *Saltarello* and that of the *Piva*, which in addition are both in ⅜.

The principle of the rhythmic transformation of a dance subject was maintained till well into the 18th century. (See *Sämmelbande* of the I. M. G., XII. iv., art. by Tobias Norlind, *Zur Geschichte der polnischen Tänze*, p. 513.)

[112] This number comprises neither the *Spanish Paven* of Bull (*Fitzw. V. B.*, ii., p. 131) nor the *Galliard ground* of Inglott (ii., p. 375), which we have reckoned among the variations of secular songs. It refers to the pavans and galliards of the *Fitzw. V. B.* and *Parthenia*, as well as the galliard *Victoria* republished by Mme. Farrenc in the *Trésor des pianistes*. We have also included in this number a little programme piece by G. Farnaby, *His Rest*, on account of its sub-title, which classes it among the galliards.

come under our notice includes the single pavans (twenty), the single galliards (twenty), the pavans followed by galliards (twenty-two), and six more complex groups which may be thus classed:—

Four of them belong to the class " pavan followed by a galliard." The first two—we find them in Richardson (*Fitzw. V. B.*, i., p. 27 and p. 87) consist of :—

1. A varied pavan ;
2. A piece called *Variatio*, which is nothing but a repeat of the complete varied pavan, with more complicated and more rapid figurations ;
3. A galliard varied ;
4. A *Variatio* of the galliard.

The third group consists of a *Quadran Pavan* by Bull, which is followed by a repeat entitled *Variation of the Quadran pavan*, and of a *Galliard to the Quadran Pavan* (*Fitzw. V. B.*, i., p. 99). Bull gives us afterwards a pavan to which are joined two galliards (*Fitzw. V. B.*, i., p. 124), with this peculiarity, that the second does not immediately follow the first in the manuscript, but is separated from it by a large number of other works. We only learn of the connection by an express note in the *Fitzw. V. B.* (i., p. 177).

Lastly, Bull is also the author of two simpler groups, consisting of a galliard followed by a *Variatio* (*Fitzw. V. B.*, i., p. 170, and ii., p. 242; *Pipers Galliard*).

A somewhat large number of pavans and galliards are accompanied by special qualifications which it is worth while to attempt to classify :—

1. There are some to which is coupled the name of another dance. Thus the *Passamezzo Pavana*

and *Galiarda Passamezzo* of Bull (*Fitzw. V. B.*, i., p. 203), and of Philips (i., p. 299).

2. We afterwards come across galliards and pavans the titles of which have a qualification added which shows their origin. Thus we find, for example, the expression *Pavana lachrymae* or *Lachrymae Pavana:* this refers to a celebrated subject borrowed in turn by Byrd (*Fitzw. V. B.*, ii., p. 42), Farnaby (ii., p. 472), and Morley (ii., p. 173)[113] from the lutenist John Dowland.[114] Two other pieces designated by the name of the well-known subject which forms their foundation, are the *Pipers Galliard* of Bull (*Fitzw. V. B.*, ii., p. 242), and the *Pipers paven* of Peerson (ii., p. 238).[115]

3. Other pavans and galliards bear in their titles, or at the end of the piece the name of the musician from whom the subject was borrowed. Thus for

[113] The qualification *lachrymae* is not added to the title of Morley's pavan, but the subject is the same as that treated by Byrd and Farnaby.

[114] This subject is taken from the *Second Book of Songs or Ayres*, 1600. It reappears in 1605 in a second collection by Dowland, *Lachrymae or Seven Teares, figured in 7 passionate Pavans, set forth for the lute, viols or violins, in 5 parts*. The first of these seven pavans is that to which the name of *Lachrymae* has remained specially attached. The theme of *Lachrymae* has also been treated, under the form of variations for the clavier and under the title of *Paduana Lagrima*, by Melchior Schildt (d. in 1667), a German pupil of Sweelinck. (This piece is republished in the *Monatsh. für Musikg.* of 1888, p. 35 ff).

Oscar Chilesotti informs us of the existence of a version for three lutes of the *Lachrimae* by F. (*sic*) Dooland, to be found in the *Novus Partus* of J. B. Besard (1617).

[115] See details on the avatars of this subject in an article by Kurt Fischer : *G. Voigtländer. Ein Dichter und Musiker des 17. Jahrhunderts*, in the *Sammelbände* of the I. M. G., XII., i., p. 50 ff. *Piper* is the general term given to players of instruments of the type of the flute or hautboy. On the pipes and pipers of the British Isles see Dr. Grattan Flood, *The Story of the Bagpipe* (Walter Scott Publishing Co., London, 1911). According to Dr. Naylor (*An Eliz. V. B.*, p. 25) the term has in this case another sense : the *Piper's Galliard* of Bull is actually an instrumental adaptation of *Captain Piper's Galliard*, a madrigal by Dowland on the words *If my complaint could passions move*, which appeared in the collection *Lachrymae* of 1605 spoken of in the preceding note.

example the *Rosseter's galliard* of Farnaby (*Fitzw. V. B.*, ii., p. 450); Philip Rosseter was a lutenist who formed one of the group of royal musicians from 1604-05 to 1623.[116] Elsewhere in the *Fitzw. V. B.* (ii., p. 47) we find a galliard by Byrd[117] the final chord of which is followed by the words, *James Harding, sett foorth by William Byrd :* James Harding or Harden was a member of the English Chapel Royal at the beginning of the 17th century.[118]

The *Pavana Delight* of Byrd (*Fitzw. V. B.*, ii., p. 436) bears the final indication, *Edward Jhonson sett by Will. Byrd;* there is the same indication for the galliard which follows. Lastly, a pavan by Farnaby (*Fitzw. V. B.*, i., p. 141) finishes with the words, *Rob. Jhonson sett by Giles Farnabie.*

4. A certain number of the titles of pavans and galliards have proper names attached which apparently are those of persons to whom the pieces were dedicated. Thus we find among the works of Byrd a *Lady Montegle's Pavan* (*Fitzw. V. B.*, ii., p. 483), a *Pavan S (ir) Wm. Petre* (*Parthenia*, p. 2), two *Galiardo Mrs. Mary Brownlo* (*Parthenia*, pp. 10 and 14), a *Pavana The Earle of Salisbury* (*Parthenia*, p. 13), a *Sir Jhon Grayes Galliard* (*Fitzw. V. B.*, ii., p. 258). Of Bull we have a *Lord Lumley's Paven* and a *Galiarda to my Lord Lumley's Paven* (*Fitzw. V. B.*, i., p. 149 and i., p. 54); of Gibbons, *The Lord of Salisbury his Pavin* (*Parthenia*, p. 42). It may also be supposed that in certain cases they

[116] See the *Lists of the King's Musicians,* in the *Musical Antiquary* of April, 1911, to January, 1912, inclusive.

[117] The one forming part of the *Pavana lachrymae.*

[118] See Nagel, *Annalen,* pp. 36 and 40. A James Harden, flautist, is mentioned as a stranger (*alien*) in a list of persons forming part of the *Queen's Household* in 1591 (see *Publications of the Huguenot Society,* X., ii., p. 427. Aberdeen, 1902). Is this the person from whom Byrd borrowed the subject?

were variations on a subject of which the person mentioned in the title was particularly fond.

5. Other pavans and galliards have qualifications which refer to their expressive contents or to their technical character. In the first case they belong to programme music; this is so with the *Pavana dolorosa* and the *Galiarda dolorosa* of Philips (*Fitzw. V. B.*, i., p. 321) and with the *Hunting galliard* of Tomkins (*Fitzw. V. B.*, ii., p. 100). To the second category belong the *Pavana chromatica* of Tisdall (*Fitzw. V. B.*, ii., p. 278)[119] and the *Pavana Canon Two parts in one* of Byrd (*Fitzw. V. B.*, ii., p. 427).

6. In the last place, accompanying the titles of pavans and galliards we meet with the names of persons and things and sometimes also abbreviations or initials the precise meaning of which is generally indeterminable. Of Byrd we have the *Pavana Bray* (*Fitzw. V. B.*, i., p. 361), the *Pavana Delight*[120] (*Fitzw. V. B.*, ii., p. 436), the *Quadran Pavan* (ii., p. 103)[121], the *Pavana Fant(asia ?)* (ii., p. 398), and the *Pavana Ph. Tr.* (Tregian?) (i., p. 367). Of Bull there exists also a *Quadran Pavan* (*Fitzw. V. B.*, i., p. 99), and in addition a *Pavana* and a *Galiardo St. Thomas wake* (*Parthenia*, p. 17). Philips wrote a *Pavana Pagget* (*Fitzw. V. B.*, i., p. 291), and Tisdall the *Pavana Clement Cotto* (*Fitzw. V. B.*,

[119] This pavan bears as second title, *Mrs. Katherin Tregians Paven.* No doubt it was dedicated to this lady, or was her favourite piece.

[120] There exists a *Pavyn de Lyght* by Rich. Machyn in the lute book of Thysius, but the melody is different from that of Byrd (see Land, *op. cit.*, No. 329, p. 300). Richard Machin was, according to Pirro (*Heinrich Schütz*, Paris, Alcan, 1913, p. 12), chief of one of the numerous troupes of comedian-musicians that traversed Germany towards the end of the 16th and the beginning of the 17th centuries.

[121] We shall return to the probable meaning of this expression when we analyse this piece.

ii., p. 306). By Farnaby we find *Walter Erle's Paven* (*Fitzw. V. B.*, ii., p. 336), the *Farmer's Paven*[122] (*Fitzw. V. B.*, ii., p. 465), and the *Flatt Paven* (*Fitzw. V. B.*, ii., p. 453). Finally, among the anonymous works there are a *Pavana MS.* (*Fitzw. V. B.*, i., p. 68) and *Nowel's Galliard* (*Fitzw. V. B.*, ii., p. 369).[123]

Having thus given the purely outward details of the pavans and galliards of the *Fitzw. V. B.*, it is desirable to examine their inner essential characteristics.

The first of these which should attract our attention is that referring to the thematic relationship existing between pavans and galliards where these are connected. Analysis shows that the galliard borrows elements from the pavan which precedes it, in a little less than four-fifths of the examples. Most frequently these elements are very trifling, and in certain cases there is even a doubt as to whether there have really been borrowings; when these exist, they consist of scarcely perceptible fragments of the upper melody, or of the bass of the opening of the pavan.

The cases in which the principle of thematic relationship is applied in full strictness become under these conditions extremely rare. In truth we have only lighted upon three : the *Pavana-galiarda Delight* of Byrd (*Fitzw. V. B.*, ii., p. 436), the *Pavana-galiarda dolorosa* of Philips (i., p. 321), and the *Pavana-galiardo St. Thomas wake* of Bull (*Parthenia*, p. 19).

[122] Possibly the madrigalist John Farmer, whose activity covered the confines of the 16th and 17th centuries.

[123] Does this mean *Galliarde of Noël ?* or is *Nowel* a person ? This latter suggestion is very probable : the melody *Nancie*, varied by Morley in the *Fitzw. V. B.*, has for another sub-title *Sir Eduward* (or *Edward*) *Nouwel's* (or *Noel's*) *Delight.*

In all the other cases we notice more or less important restrictions.[124] Let us take, for example, a *Pavan* by Morley (*Fitzw. V. B.*, ii., p. 209) which, following the most classic plan reserved for this kind of dance, is divided into three episodes, A, B, C. The galliard which follows consists of three identical episodes, A, B, C: A and B borrow the whole of their material from A and B of the pavan; C on the other hand is entirely independent.[125] In the *Quadran Paven* of Bull (*Fitzw. V. B.*, i., p. 99) the episodes A and B of which the pavan is composed have a harmonic foundation which, such as it is, is to be found again in A and B of the galliard but without the rhythm; but it would be vain to seek for any melodic affinity between these two dances. Beyond these pieces by Morley and Bull, we still find a certain number of pavans and galliards between which some harmonic or melodic connections may be discovered; vague as they are they suffice, however, to recall the old principle of thematic dependence.[126]

[124] Dr. Naylor (*An Eliz. V. B.*, p. 21) remarks that according to Morley the most correct galliards were those which took their melody and harmony from the pavans to which they belonged. The collection of twelve instrumental Pavans and Galliards of the Dutchman Cornelis Schuyt (1611) is an example—contemporaneous with the *Fitzw. V. B.*—of the absolute observance of this rule. (See the article by Max Seiffert on *Cornelis Schuyt* in the *Tÿdschrift der Vereeniging voor Noord-Nederlands Musikgeschiedenis*, v., p. 252.)

[125] The episode C of the pavan is exactly identical, except as regards the key, with a pavan by Farnaby (*Fitzw. V. B.* ii., p. 459), where also it acts as third episode.

[126] We find, in the *Fitzw. V. B.* (ii., p. 242) a *Pipers galliard* by Bull, which immediately follows a *Pipers Paven* by Peerson (ii., p. 238). The sub-title *Pipers* shows a community of origin, and there is a certain melodic resemblance between the opening of the episode A of the galliard and that of the same episode of the pavan. There is also an agreement of key between the two dances. But is the galliard a piece composed by Bull expressly to form a succession to the pavan of Peerson? Or is it the compiler of the *Fitzw. V. B.* who has brought together these two pieces on account of their kinship? This cannot be decided.

In the cases where this has no existence, there is only a single bond between the two dances, that of tonality. Here we find ourselves face to face with an important principle, which forms the foundation of the *suite de clavier* of the 17th century; that musical form consists, in fact, of a succession of dance pieces which have nothing in common but the bond of tonality.[127]

A few words as to the method of variation adopted by the virginalists in their pavans and galliards. We have already had occasion to remark [128] that in the great majority of their dance variations the English masters made use of the melodico-harmonic procedure. What is true in a general way of the body of varied dances remains equally true of the pavans and galliards. It is interesting to mention, on this point, that the *Fitzw. V. B.* contains two pieces, a pavan followed by a galliard, by Byrd (*Fitzw. V. B.*, ii., p. 204), and a pavan by Philips (*Fitzw. V. B.*, i., p. 343), the precise or approximate dates of which are of a nature to give us an idea of the period in which this essentially evolutionary practice came into use for the first time. The pavan of Philips is dated 1580 and bears on the margin the inscription *The first one Philips made*. The pavan followed by a galliard of Byrd is accompanied by the remark, *The first that ever hee made*. As Byrd was about forty years of age in 1580, it is not rash to suppose that this piece is contemporary with that of

---

[127] We find also *suites de clavier* in which, in addition to a common tonality, we notice a certain thematic relationship between the pieces of which they are composed. We may cite, from recollection, the *Suites* of Froberger and those of Johann Caspar Ferdinand Fischer.

[128] See p. 250.

S

Philips.[129] Let us remark, finally, that these two pieces are probably anterior to the most ancient melodico-harmonic song-variations which we have met with in our preceding investigations.[130] Both are arranged according to the most usual plan for pavans and galliards, namely, A A¹, B B¹, C C¹. Their figuration is very simple. In the piece by Philips it consists almost wholly of embroideries; in addition, in the episode C C¹, which is a sort of plainsong in long notes sustained in the *superius*, the accompanying counterpoints consist of little detached figures (*hoketus*).

The pavan and galliard of Byrd offer by way of figurations only embroideries, decomposed fifths, and a little rhythmic figure ♩. ♪ ♪. ♪ at the end of episode A. They are far from possessing the plastic qualities to be found in the other pavans and galliards of Byrd, which date from a more recent period. Their tonality alone, which more or less resembles our modern C minor, carries us away by its strangeness.

By preference let us dwell on the pavan of Philips, which is simpler and of a more sober beauty. The subjects of it are so characteristic in their natural simplicity that Sweelinck took them up later and made on them [131] a series of variations

---

[129] Byrd and Philips are not the first to have written pavans and galliards for the virginal in England. The MS. *Royal Appendix 58* of the British Museum, which dates from the opening of the 16th century, contains two pavans and two galliards (see above an addition concerning this MS.). *Mulliner's Book*, compiled about the middle of the 16th century, contains, as No. 113, *A Pavyon* by Newman. (See a *Catal. of the MS. music in the Brit. Mus.*, vol iii., p. 77.)

[130] *All in a garden greene* and *Sellingers Round*, by Byrd. We have supposed that these two series of variations date from 1591 at the latest. (See p. 232.)

[131] See *Œuvres complètes de Sweelinck*, vol. i., p. 107. Mr. Barclay Squire notices further (Grove, *Dictionary*, art. Philips) that this pavan of Philips occurs again in *Morley's Consort Lessons* of 1599, and also in tablature, in the *New Citharin Lessons* of Thomas Robinson (1609).

under the title of *Pavana Philippi*. The piece of Sweelinck is in dimensions double that of Philips, and is developed according to the following plan :—

$$A \ A^I \quad B \ B^I \quad C \ C^I$$

$$A^{II} \quad A^{III} \quad B^{II} \quad B^{III} \quad C^{II} \quad C^{III}$$

The figuration of the great Dutch organist is richer than that of his English predecessor ; it is also more delicate, and adopts, although sparingly, new forms of figuration, such as the breaking of intervals and chords (in C^{II}). The way in which Sweelinck adopts the *hoketus* used in C and C^I of Philips's pavan, and develops it by figuring it in the most ingenious way in C, C^I, C^{II}, and C^{III}, shows the fertility of invention and the exquisite taste of the Amsterdam master. These variations of course date from a long time after those of Philips. At the period in which the latter were composed, in 1580, Sweelinck was only eighteen years of age, and as yet could not possibly have had any intercourse with the English virginalists.

It remains for us to point out what are the exceptions to the principle of the harmonico-melodic variation to be met with in the pavans and galliards of the English virginalists. Hardly any of these exceptions are absolute, and they may be reduced, with rare exceptions, to a predominance of the harmonic element over the melodic. Let us quote a few characteristic examples : in the *Pavana lachrymae* of Morley (*Fitzw. V. B.*, ii., p. 173) the bass undergoes no figuration ; for that very reason it acquires a greater prominence than the *superius*, the somewhat complicated figuration of which does not, however, modify the principal features of the melody. The *Pipers Paven* of Peerson (*Fitzw. V. B.*, ii., p. 238) is an example of harmonic predominance: the bass of it is figured in several passages, without this doing any violence to its general contour; the melody on the other hand is at times completely altered by the figuration. Lastly, the galliard of the *Quadran Pavan* of Bull (*Fitzw. V. B.*, i., p. 117) is an example of a purely harmonic variation, in which the bass remains untouched throughout all its figurations, whilst the melody is modified from variation to variation.

There are cases in which the very plan of the pavans and galliards forbids the direct application of the melodico-harmonic idea. Thus in the *Passamezzo Pavana* (*Fitzw. V. B.*, i., p. 299),[132] and the *Galiarda passamezzo* (*Fitzw. V. B.*, i., p. 306), of Philips, in which we find a succession of episodes, A, B, C, D, &c., independent of each other and offering no opportunity for variation. The two pieces by Byrd bearing the same title (*Fitzw. V. B.*, i., pp. 203 and 209) are formed on an entirely different plan; they both develop a single episode, A, in a certain number of variations. Analysis shows, especially in the galliard, a fairly strong harmonic predominance, the melody undergoing much more important modifications than the bass.[133]

* * * * * *

It is now desirable to arrange the pavans and galliards of the *Fitzw. V. B.* and of *Parthenia* according to the plan on which they were written.

[132] This piece is dated 1592.

[133] In view of their form, we might have included these two pieces of Byrd with the song variation, for the same reason as the *Spanish Paven* by Bull.

The most frequent plan is the following :—

A A¹ B B¹ C C¹

which means that the dance treated in variation form comprises three episodes, A, B, and C, of equal length, which are alternately followed by a varied version A¹, B¹, C¹. It must not be lost sight of that A, B, and C, are already themselves varied forms of the original subject.

It cannot be said that this plan is inspired by the usual plan of the non-artistic pavans and galliards. If we examine in Boehme's *Geschichte des Tanzes in Deutschland* the various examples of pavans and galliards which he gives, we notice that it is the plan A, B which predominates.[134] We find the division A, B, C in regular use only in galliards for several instruments by German composers of the early part of the 17th century—Haussmann, Demantius, Staden, Möller and Melchior Franck,[135] and in a part of the pieces which they call sometimes *Pavane*, sometimes *Paduana* or *Paduan*.[136]

If it were permissible to generalize from a pretty widely extended series we might come to the conclusion that the division into three equal episodes occurs by preference in the more elaborate style of dances, which seems to show a preoccupation

[134] See Boehme, *op. cit.*, ii., pp. 45 ff, 51, 58.

[135] See Boehme, *op. cit.*, ii., p. 92 ff.

[136] See Boehme, *op. cit.*, ii., p. 87 ff. On the German pavans and galliards of the beginning of the 17th century, see also Riemann, *Handb. der Musikg.*, II., ii., § 78, p. 168 ff. In this paragraph, devoted to the *Origin of the Suite*, Riemann speaks, among other things, of the influence which the English musicians may have had over the Germans in the domain of elaborated dance music ; he also considers the question (p. 178 ff) of the thematic relations existing between the series of dances forming the " Suite."

with a certain formal balance on the part of the musicians. In fact, this division, whether improved or not by the addition of the variations A¹, B¹, C¹, gives occasion for pieces the general proportions of which satisfy the taste and the ear by their harmonious character.

A.—Pavans followed by Galliards, Written according to the Normal Plan:

A A¹. B B¹. C C¹.

The pavans thus arranged amount to nineteen in the *Fitzw. V. B.* and *Parthenia.*[137] Among the nine for which we are indebted to Byrd, all are not of the first order. Several of them indeed are of secondary value and show but little interest on analysis. We shall be content to dwell on two of them which deserve to be placed above the others,

[137] Here is the enumeration of them : 1. *Pavana lachrymae* followed by a galliard on a subject of Harding, by Byrd (*Fitzw. V. B.*, ii., pp. 42 and 47) ; 2. *Pavan (the first that ever hee made) and galliard* by Byrd (ii., pp. 200 and 202) ; 3. *Pavan and galliard* by Byrd (ii., pp. 384 and 387) ; 4. *Pavan and galliard* by Byrd (ii., pp. 389 and 392) ; 5. *Pav. fant. and galliard* by Byrd (ii., pp. 398 and 400) ; 6. *Pavana Delight and galliard* (subject by E. Johnson) by Byrd (ii., pp. 436 and 440) ; 7. *Pavana S. Wm. Petre and Galiardo* by Byrd (*Parthenia*, pp. 2 and 6) ; 8. *Pavana (lachrymae) and Galiarda* by Morley (*Fitzw. V. B.*, ii., pp. 173 and 177) ; 9. *Pavana and Variatio, galliard and Variatio*, by Richardson (i., pp. 27, 29, 32, 34) ; 10. *Pavana and Variatio, galliard and Variatio* by Richardson (i., pp. 87, 90, 93, 95) ; 11. *Pavana Pagget and Galiarda* by Philips (i., pp. 291 and 296) ; 12. *Pavana and Galiarda dolorosa* by Philips (i., pp. 321 and 327, dated 1593) ; 13. *Pavana of my Lord Lumley and galliard to my Lord Lumley's Pavan* by Bull (i., pp. 149 and 54) ; 14. *Pavan* followed by two *galliards* by Bull (i., pp. 124, 129, 177) ; 15. *Pavan and galliard* by Bull (ii., pp. 121 and 125) ; 16. *Pavan and galliard* by Bull (*Parthenia*, pp. 23 and 28); 17. *Pavan and galliard* by Warrock (*Fitzw. V. B.*, i., pp. 384 and 388) ; 18. *Pavana Bray and galliard* by Byrd (i., pp. 361 and 365) ; 19. *Pavana Ph. Tr. and galliard* by Byrd (i., pp. 367 and 371).— In all nineteen pavans followed by galliards, of which nine are by Byrd, one by Morley, two by Richardson, two by Philips, four by Bull, and one by Warrock.

the *Pavana-galiarda Delight* (*Fitzw. V. B.*, ii., pp. 436 and 440), and the *Pavana-galiarda S. Wm. Petre* (*Parthenia*, pp. 2 and 6).[138]

The *Pavana Delight* is constructed on a subject by Edward Johnson. It is more remarkable for the beauty and refinement of its details than for its figuration, which is very simple and hardly gets beyond embroidery. There should be noticed, at the opening of episode B, a short chromatic advance of the bass, F, F sharp, G. The galliard possesses the same character of noble simplicity as the pavan.

The *Pavana S. Wm. Petre* and its galliard (*Parthenia*, pp. 2 and 6) also give no room for many remarks, and impress chiefly by their æsthetic value. Beyond a few rhythmical outlines of an instrumental character (B of the pavan) their figuration is sobriety itself.

Morley gives us a version of the *Pavana lachrymae*, the figural treatment of which is tinged with Italian feeling; the secondary value of the work justifies us in not dwelling on it. It is otherwise with the two pavans and galliards of Richardson, each of which comprises, as we have already seen,[139] supplementary variations which provide them with a sort of "double." The following scheme will make this combination clear:

Pavan :—   Galliard :—

A A^I B B^I C C^I.   A A^I B B^I C C^I.

Its *variatio* :—   Its *variatio* :—

A^{II} A^{III} B^{II} B^{III} C^{II} C^{III} A^{II} A^{III} B^{II} B^{III} C^{II} C^{III}

[138] The *Pavana Bray* by Byrd and its galliard (*Fitzw. V. B.*, i., pp. 361 and 365) are also worthy of mention on account of the exquisite freshness of the melody and the refinement with which it is treated.

[139] See p. 255.

These two groups of pieces are of special interest on account of the exceptional modernity of their figuration. The matter is the more remarkable in that the author, who seems to have been a dilettante rather than a professional musician, was born and died before John Bull.[140] That which is not surprising in Tomkins, who survived till 1656, astonishes us in a much older master, and the surprise becomes greater still when it is ascertained by analysis that this "amateur" is not only a virtuoso of the stamp of Bull, but also a musician of taste who has the power of giving life and charm to his colorature, and does not simply use them as a proof of his learning and of the skill of his fingers.

Let us begin with the first of these two groups (*Fitzw. V. B.*, i., p. 27 ff). In the *Variatio* of the pavan (A''') we find those sudden skips of the left hand from the medium to the lower part of the keyboard, of which Farnaby has already furnished us with so many examples; further, we find interesting forms of broken intervals (final cadence of A'') or of broken chords (B''' and the final cadence of C'''). The galliard gives us systematic successions of parallel fifths (see the bass at the beginning of C), and its *Variatio* has one or two instances of sudden skips in the left hand from the lower register to the medium (B''').

It is especially in the second group (*Fitzw. V. B.*, i., p. 87 ff) that Richardson astonishes and charms by the variety and unexpectedness of his figuration. Certain final

[140] John Bull lived from about 1562 to 1628; Richardson from about 1558 to 1618.

cadences of the pavan (A A^I, C, and C^I) have an appearance of extreme novelty, and delight by their character, at once sprightly and airy. The *Variatio* of the pavan introduces no new surprise, but delights by the art with which the musician has succeeded in exhausting all the possibilities of variation of which the subject was susceptible. The final cadence of C^{III} has inflections which make us think of Schubert.

At first sight the galliard hardly seems to belong to the pavan, for the double reason that the two dances have no thematic relationship, and that the galliard begins with a flat in the key, while the pavan has none. But a more attentive examination shows that this difference is only apparent. In fact the pavan, which opened in a sort of G major, develops little by little into other keys which require a flat in the key; the latter appears after the episode B and in the *Variatio*, after the middle of A. Lastly, pavan and galliard both end on the chord of G major.

The galliard, like the pavan, has a figuration of the greatest ingenuity. Specially to be noticed, in B^I, is the way in which the melody seems to be pieced out in the *superius* by means of cross-times, partly detached, which stand out from the other parts (p. 94, bars 4 and 5). In the *Variatio* of the galliard we find, as a most remarkable form of figuration (in C^{II}), decompositions of chords the systematic character of which foreshadows the " Alberti bass " of the 18th century.

After the pavans and galliards of Richardson we meet with those of Philips: the *Pavana Pagget* and its galliard, and the *Pavana dolorosa* and its galliard. The *Pavana Pagget* (*Fitzw. V. B.*, i., p. 291), a noble and melancholy work, written in a key which makes us think of C minor, recalls Spanish gravity; it has this peculiarity, that the episode C is larger than A and B, and is divided really into two subordinate episodes, *a* and *b*. Its figuration is smooth and delicate. Specially are to be remarked the effects of thirds in A¹, the delightful triplets of B¹, and the syncopations which give to C so tender a feeling. The galliard reminds us of Cabezon by the sobriety of its figuration.

The *Pavana dolorosa* (*Fitzw. V. B.*, i., p. 321) possesses the same qualities as the *Pavana Pagget*.[141] The episode C contains a passage in which is developed, by means of figural accompaniments, the ascending chromatic tetrachord, A, B flat, B natural, C, C sharp, D, the presence of which in a piece supposed to express grief is significant.

Of Bull we have four pavan-galliards constructed according to the usual type. Three of them are noticeable on various grounds. In a sober style and free from all virtuosity—a somewhat rare case with Bull—we find a pavan followed by a galliard in *Parthenia* (pp. 23 and 28). The figuration of it is very simple, and shows no characteristic details

---

[141] According to Mr. Barclay Squire (Grove, *Dictionary*, art. Philips), the letters *Treg* which are added to the title of the *Pavana dolorosa* in the Cambridge MS. probably indicate that this pavan was originally written by the elder Tregian, who was in prison at the date indicated (1593) as that of the composition. The MS. 191 of the Berlin library also contains the *Pavana dolorosa*, but followed only by the name of Philips. However, the index adds " *composta in prigione* " ; we may no doubt conclude from this that Tregian wrote this pavan in prison, and that it was subsequently the subject of an arrangement on the part of Philips.

beyond a few repetitions of notes in C¹ of the pavan.[142]

The *Pavana of my Lord Lumley* (*Fitzw. V. B.*, i., p. 149) and the *Galliard to my Lord Lumley's Pavan* (i., p. 54) are written in a rather unusually clear key, which nearly corresponds with our G major. We notice in the pavan a number of rapid passages, lively successions of thirds for the left hand, and pleasing effects of decomposition of intervals and of chords. The galliard, the thematic material of which is independent of that of the pavan, offers hardly any traces of actual virtuosity, but effects of detached syncopations (B¹), and most interesting forms of decomposition of chords (final cadence).

In a last pavan (*Fitzw. V. B.*, i., p. 124) followed by two galliards (i., pp. 129 and 177) Bull again shows in several details how varied was his art. The pavan makes use of many forms of figuration, of a progressive and specially instrumental

---

[142] In B of the pavan the following faulty passage (Rimbault and Pauer)—

has been corrected in the following way by Mme. Farrenc :—

character : rhythmic designs, little sequential figures in demisemiquavers, syncopation, decomposition of chords, repetition of notes, &c. The greater part of the cadences are made by means of decomposition of chords which produce the effect of distance. The piece is also very interesting to study from the point of view of modulation. The first galliard uses, at least in A and B, the material of the pavan, but abbreviated. The figuration is simpler than that of the pavan; and this is a remark which may be applied in a general way to all galliards compared with the pavans which precede them. The reason is obvious : in spite of stylisation, the virginalists were bent on preserving in the two dances the movement properly belonging to them—a slow movement for the pavan, a more lively movement for the galliard. Now it is plain that a piece written in slow movement lends itself better to a complicated figuration than a piece composed in quick rhythm.

Bull's second galliard borrows from the pavan the material of episode A alone. Its figuration is somewhat sober, and presents no peculiarities. In a passage of C^I we notice the brisk jump of the left hand from the middle to the lower part, and from the lower part to the middle, of the keyboard.

A last pavan-galliard belonging to the normal type A A^I, B B^I, C C^I, was written by Warrock (*Fitzw. V. B.*, i., pp. 384 and 388). This group of dances is written in a tonality of a somewhat exceptional character, which strongly approaches our modern B flat. The thematic material is curious and gives to the two pieces, especially to the galliard, an extremely original appearance. The pavan suffers a little from an excess of figuration, but the galliard has great character and offers interesting peculiarities, among others the two bare fifths (one in the right hand, the other in the left) with which B and B¹ open. On hearing this piece we are struck by the singular mixture of solemnity and fancy. Certain passages (end of B¹) make one think of the French lutenists of the beginning of the 17th century.

B.—Pavan-Galliards Written on an Unusual Plan.

The pavan-galliards which do not conform to the usual plan A A¹, B B¹, C C¹, may be grouped in three categories :—

(1.) Types in which the habitual plan is maintained in principle, but undergoes more or less pronounced modifications ;

(2.) Types resembling the varied song ;

(3.) Types diverging from the first two.

(1.) Eight groups of pavans and galliards may be arranged in the first category. In a single case—a not very remarkable piece by Byrd (*Fitzw. V. B.*, ii., pp. 200 and 202)—we notice that some addition has been made to the usual plan ; it is a coda D of eight bars in the free prelude style, at the conclusion of the galliard. In the seven other cases there has been a retrenchment of one or another of the elements forming the normal plan.

In a pavan of Morley, followed by its galliard (*Fitzw. V. B.*, ii., pp. 209 and 213), the episode C of the pavan does not give occasion for variations. The scheme is therefore :—

Pavan :   A A' B B' C
Galliard : A A' B B' C C' [143]

The figuration of these pieces exhibits quite an Italian tendency.

Byrd (*Fitzw. V. B.*, ii., pp. 226 and 228) and Gibbons (*Parthenia*, pp. 42 and 44 ; *Fitzw. V. B.*, ii., p. 479, for the pavan only) each gives us an example of a pavan followed by a galliard, in which the pavan consists only of A, B, C, whilst the galliard comprises the usual elements, A A', B B', C C'. The pavan of Byrd is a masterpiece of melodic, contrapuntal and harmonic refinement ; the figuration is of extreme simplicity.

The pavan by Gibbons is that of " The Lord of Salisbury." Like its galliard, it is remarkable for its pathetic style and the boldness of its harmonies. It offers, in C, remarkable sequences, a practice which seems to have been usual with Gibbons. The galliard has interesting spreadings of intervals or chords (B') as well as repetitions of notes (B').

We find subsequently pavans and galliards in which the episode C has been suppressed. This is the case in the pavan-galliard, *The Earle of Salisbury*, by Byrd (*Parthenia*, pp. 13 and 14). The variation element is here reduced to its most simple expression ; the episodes A and B of which it is composed merely

[143] The episode C of the pavan is identical, except in key, with the episode C of a pavan by Farnaby (*Fitzw. V. B.* ii., p. 456). The CC' of the galliard by Morley is absolutely independent, from a thematic point of view, of the C of the pavan.

give place to unvaried repeats. There is variation only with regard to the original subject. The treatment of the subject has been carried out by Byrd in a style of sobriety imprinted with a noble melancholy.

In the *Quadran Pavan* by Bull (*Fitzw. V. B.*, i., p. 99), followed by its *Variatio* (i., p. 107), and its galliard (i., p. 117), we come across a more complicated construction, although it is erected on the same foundation, A B. Here is the scheme:—

Pavan: A A^I B B^I A^{II} A^{III} B^{II} B^{III}

Variatio: *id.*

Galliard: A A^I B B^I A^{II} A^{III} B^{II} B^{III}
A^{IIII} A^{IIIII} B^{IIII} B^{IIIII}

This group of dances, very important on account of its dimensions, since by itself it occupies twenty-five pages in the modern edition of the *Fitzw. V. B.*, is specially interesting from its figuration, the exceptional complexity of which helps to make very difficult the reconstruction of the plan of which the above scheme has given some idea; the melody and bass are in fact so transformed or deformed by the figural work that it is often almost impossible to recognise them. Rhythmic designs, counterpoints in thirds or sixths,—ticklish in execution,—effects of echo, brisk skips of the right hand from the middle to the top, sequences, decomposition of chords or intervals, charming passages of virtuosity written for two parts only, syncopations of all sorts: these are the most characteristic elements of detail of these three pieces, which, as a whole, undoubtedly leave an impression of prolixity, but in certain passages astonish by their modernism, and charm

by a *Stimmung* which makes one think sometimes
of Haydn, sometimes of Schubert. The name of
Quadran Pavan comes probably, according to
Chappell (*op. cit.*, p. 104) from the fact that this
pavan was danced by four persons.

We also owe a *Quadran Pavan*, followed by its
galliard, to W. Byrd (*Fitzw. V. B.*, ii., pp. 103 and
111). It develops the same subject as that by
Bull, as far as it is possible to recognise any
definite melody under the constantly changing
figuration which rules in this piece. The plan of
Byrd is exactly the same as that of Bull, but the
variations are at times so free that it is still more
difficult to discover it. The figural material is far
from being so rich as that of Bull; with the
exception of a few rhythmic inventions it contains
nothing worthy of special note.

After the *Quadran Pavan* and galliard of Bull
and of Byrd we again meet with a *Pavane
St. Thomas Wake* (*Parthenia*, p. 17) by the first of
these masters, followed by a galliard *St. Thomas
Wake* (*Parthenia*, p. 19 and *Fitzw. V. B.*, i., p. 131),
the plan of which recalls, but in a much more
concise form, that of the *Quadran Pavan*. The
pavan consists of the elements A, B, varied
according to the scheme:—

$$A \; A^{I} \;\; B \; B^{I} \;\; A^{II} \;\; A^{II} \;\; B^{II} \;\; B^{III}$$

The galliard varies the group A A^{I} B B^{I} four
times. The variations belong to the melodico-
harmonic type, but with a marked predominance of
the melody, which is only slightly ornamented,
while the bass is subjected to very flowery
figuration. The work is charming, especially the
pavan, which is characterised by simplicity and

a fine balance of proportions. The subject is delightful for its freedom and abandon.

(2.) *Pavans-galliards resembling the varied song.* We have already, in our previous investigations (see p. 239) met with a *Spanish Paven* by Bull (*Fitzw. V. B.*, ii., p. 131) which consisted of a single episode A varied a certain number of times; on account of this circumstance we classed it among the variations of secular songs. We might have done the same for the *Passamezzo Pavana* of Byrd and its galliard (*Fitzw. V. B.*, i., pp. 203 and 209), which also are content to vary a single episode A.

The *passamezzo* or *passemezzo* is, according to Boehme (*op. cit.*, i., p. 136), a dance of a calm and tranquil character. It flourished in Italy in the 16th century. Its name was derived from the fact that it required only about half as many steps as a lively dance like the galliard. The time of the passamezzo is binary. This dance is generally followed by a " post-dance "[144] in three-time, which bears the name of *Saltarello*.[145] Boehme gives two examples of *Passamezzo*, one of which is followed by a galliard (p. 51) and the other by a *saltarello* (p. 79). Here is the opening of the first:—

[144] This is a literal translation of the German term *Nachtanz* used in the 16th and 17th centuries.

[145] This term appears to be very ancient. We already find it under the form *Salterello* in MS. 29987 of the British Museum, which contains Italian pieces of the 14th century : it is applied to four pieces for a single voice, divided each into several parts (see J. Wolf, *Gesch. der Mensuralnot.*, i., p. 273). Mr. Hughes-Hughes (*Catalogue of the MS. Music in the Brit. Mus.*) thinks the *Saltarelli*, as well as various other pieces in the MS. 29987, may possibly be organ music (vol. iii., p. 77).

T

which is transformed as follows in the galliard :—

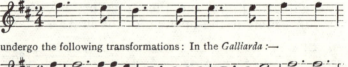

It is apparent from this that the *passamezzo* followed by the *galliard* or the *saltarello* is in point of fact equivalent, on account of the identity of measure and movement, to the pavan followed by the galliard.[146]

The *Passamezzo Pavana* of Byrd is formed, therefore, of a single episode A submitted to six variations. The galliard consists of eight variations; it has strong melodic and specially harmonic affinities with the pavan. The variations, especially those of the galliard, have a character rather harmonic than melodic; they are in general very free, and often disguise the elements to which they are applied. The last four variations of the galliard

---

[146] Certain collections of simple dance music give interesting examples of successions of dances in various rhythms in which it is possible to specify the actual rhythmical shades which distinguish these dances from each other. See for example the collection *Nobiltà di Dame*, of which we have already had occasion to speak (see p. 241, Note 94).

The first bars of a *balletto* in two-time (p. 29) :—

undergo the following transformations : In the *Galliarda* :—

in the *Saltarello* :—

In the elaborated *Balli d'arpicordo* of Giov. Picchi we find a *Pass' e mezo* varied, followed by its *saltarello* also varied (modern edition by Chilesotti, *Bibl. di rarità musicali*, Ricordi, Milan, p. 9).

are particularly interesting. In the seventh we find a marked rhythm, and short imitations which remind one of certain passages of the *Vivace* of the seventh symphony of Beethoven.

(3.) We notice, lastly, among the irregular types of pavans followed by galliards, an isolated example which approaches in its structure a musical form of which we shall have to take notice later—the *Medley*. The examples of *Medley* which are to be met with in the *Fitzw. V. B.* consist of successions of episodes of about equal length, each of which treats a different motive.

Under this category we may range a group of dances by Peter Philips, dated 1592, which bear the titles of *Passamezzo Pavana* (*Fitzw. V. B.*, i., p. 299) and *Galiarda passamezzo* (i., p. 306). As we see, this title is the same as that of the piece which we have just analysed; but while Byrd varies a single episode A a certain number of times, the composition of Philips presents the following scheme :—

Pavan: A, B, C, D, E, F, G (7 motives).

Galliard: A, B, C, D, E, F, G, H, I (*saltarella*), J (10 motives).

The thematic material of the piece by Philips is entirely foreign to that of the work by Byrd. Moreover, the melodic and harmonic elements of the galliard of Philips have no connection with those of his pavan, apart from a few vague fragments of the bass. Besides, when we examine the pavan and the galliard separately, we cannot help perceiving that among the various fragments which make up each of them there is sometimes an appearance of melodic and still more of harmonic community. It is even possible that the starting-point of the composer may have been the notion of melodico-harmonic variation, with a predominance of the harmonic element. But he used it with such liberty that we may well look on these fragments as independent of each other.[147]

The pavan-galliard *passamezzo* of Philips is remarkable for its melodic richness and the perfectly Italian charm of its *Stimmung*. We discern the influence of the madrigal, with its technical and æsthetic peculiarities. There is, however, in the pavan (episode C or 3) an element purely instrumental; a persistent bass in the form of a sequence:—[148]

[147] Hugo Riemann, in his *Handb. der Musikg.* (II., ii., p. 103), gives interesting details about the *passamezzo*. He remarks that after the last quarter of the 16th century this dance often served as the foundation for compositions laid out in a very free style of variation. We have already implied this in referring (p. 201) to the *Pass 'e mezo antico* by A. Gabrieli, which is earlier than 1587.

[148] This *ostinato* recalls that of a fantasy by Bull, which we have met in the course of our previous investigations (see p. 194). It hints at the chaconne subject which Bach uses as the persistent bass in his chorale prelude *In dir ist Freude* :—

The bass contour employed as *ostinato* by Philips is very often used in the final cadences of vocal or instrumental pieces belonging to the early times of the *stile nuovo* (numerous examples in Riemann, *Handb. der Musikg.* II., ii.); see among others, p. 103, the bass of a fragment of a *passamezzo* by Biagio Marini, in which this design appears eight times (four times in the major, four times in the minor) with all the marks of an *ostinato*. The latter differs however from that of Philips in that it does not of itself constitute the bass, but is completed by means of short passages of transition of a free character. See above (p. 217) what we have said of the *ostinato* in general, in speaking of the *ground* and the *ground bass*.

Moreover, there are in E (or 5), in the bass, interesting decompositions of chords, mingled with rhythmic elements. In the last episode (G or 7) we find an application of the double-chorus style of the Venetians.

The galliard has charming rhythmical designs (C or 3), and curious syncopations (G or 7). The episode I (or 9) bears the significant sub-title of *saltarella*, which proves that the master was well acquainted with the relations which, in Italy, united the *saltarello* to the *passamezzo*.

C.—ISOLATED PAVANS COMPOSED ON THE NORMAL PLAN A A¹, B B¹, C C¹.

Twelve isolated pavans are composed in agreement with the ordinary scheme A A¹, B B¹, C C¹.[149] Byrd in the first place gives us a pavan bearing the sub-title *Canon, Two parts in one* (*Fitzw. V. B.*, ii., p. 427). In this piece the two upper parts form a strict canon between them. The mechanism of this canon is in places very difficult to decipher, at least in the doubly varied episodes A¹, B¹, C¹, on account of the complications of the figuration. Without being of the first order, this pavan is curious from its character, at once harsh and smooth, which reminds one of Monteverde, and by its final cadences, vague and poetic in feeling. We find again a cadence of this kind in the

[149] 1. *Pavana, Canon, Two parts in one* by Byrd (*Fitzw. V. B.*, ii., p. 427); 2. *Lady Montegle's Paven* by Byrd (ii., p. 483); 3. *Pavana* dated 1580, by Philips (i., p. 343); 4. *Walter Erles Paven* by Farnaby (ii., p. 336); 5. *Flatt Paven* by Farnaby (ii., p. 453); 6. *Pavana* by Farnaby (ii., p. 456); 7. *Farmer's Pavan* by Farnaby (ii., p. 465); 8. *Lachrymae Pavan* by Farnaby (ii., p. 472); 9. *Piper's Paven* by Peerson (ii., p. 238); 10. *Pavana* by Tomkins (ii., p. 51); 11. *Pavana chromatica* by Tisdall (ii., p. 278); 12. *Pavana* by Bull (i., p. 62).

episode A¹ of *Lady Montegle's Paven,* by Byrd (*Fitzw. V. B.,* ii., p. 483), a piece also of secondary interest, but containing charming details.

If we examine the whole of the isolated pavans of Farnaby constructed on the usual type, we shall be more or less deceived by their somewhat laboured character, which results, in spite of their originality, in their seldom giving complete satisfaction. The interest is too much concentrated on the details of the harmony, which is often very daring, and of the figuration, which at times approaches the fantastic.

In *Walter Erles Paven* (*Fitzw. V. B.,* ii., p. 336) we meet, in addition to abrupt skips of the right hand from the middle to the top of the keyboard, little devices of counterpoint of charming ingenuity. The *Flatt Paven* (*Fitzw. V. B.,* ii., p. 453) has curious harmonies and very original figural designs. Another pavan (*Fitzw. V. B.,* ii., p. 456) is encumbered with a figuration the fantastic conduct of which verges on singularity.[150] In the same way, the *Farmer's Paven* (*Fitzw. V. B.,* ii., p. 465) and the *Lachrymae Paven* (ii., p. 472) interest in detail rather than as a whole. In the second there are curious sequences and repetitions of notes.

The *Piper's Paven* of Peerson (*Fitzw. V. B.,* ii., p. 238) is of an exquisite poetic feeling. The figuration is of a refined taste; the greater part of the cadences are of an airy limpidity. Syncopations and little rhythmic formulas contribute very happily in varying this ravishing composition. In C¹ there is a rhythmical design the sprightly

---

[150] The episode C of this pavan is found again, note for note, but in another key, at the end of a pavan by Morley (*Fitzw. V. B.,* ii., p. 209). We have already pointed out this detail at p. 260, Note 125.

lightness of which makes us think of the *scherzi* of the French school of the present day.[151]

A *Pavan* of Tomkins (*Fitzw. V. B.*, ii., p. 51) is distinguished by the too prominent character of its figuration, and the singularity which at times is the result. In the episode C, C¹ an important passage should be noticed in which the musician brings in, in different parts and in different degrees of the musical scale, the descending chromatic tetrachord: A, G sharp, G natural, F sharp, F natural, E (further on, E, D sharp, D natural, C sharp, C natural, B).

Further on we meet with a *Pavana chromatica* by Tisdall, bearing the sub-title *Mrs. Katherin Tregians Paven* (*Fitzw. V. B.*, ii., p. 278). It is only occasionally that it presents us with what we to-day call " chromatic progressions." In reality, at that period the term "chromatic" was applied equally to the seldom-used dissonant alterations, as to melodic progressions by successive semitones.[152] Thus, examining Tisdall's pavan in detail, we notice the comparatively frequent use of D sharp, an alteration rare at that period. The key of the movement remains in suspense between E major and minor in one part, and between B major and minor in another, with inner modulations answering to tonalities less encumbered with sharps.

[151]

[152] In his essay *Die Anfänge der Chromatik, &c.* (Breitkopf & Härtel, Leipzig, 1902), Theodor Kroger touches incidentally on the chromaticism of the virginalists.

Melodic progressions by successive semitones are often met with in the lutenists of the first half of the 16th century, but seldom extend beyond the interval of a third (Körte, *op. cit.*, p. 82 ff).

Finally, Bull gives us an isolated pavan arranged according to the typical plan (*Fitzw. V. B.*, i., p. 62). This somewhat insignificant piece presents characteristic examples of repeated notes.

D.—Isolated Pavans Composed According to an Unusual Plan.

The five isolated pavans written on an irregular scheme are :—

(1.) A pavan by Byrd (*Fitzw. V. B.*, ii., p. 294), the plan of which is A A', B B', C : a mediocre work, the coloratura of which is somewhat formal and mechanical.

(2, 3, 4.) Three pavans following the scheme A, B, C :—

    a. A pavan by G. Farnaby on a subject by R. Johnson (*Fitzw. V. B.*, i., p. 141) ;

    b. A pavan by Tisdall (*ib.*, ii., p. 307) ;

    c. A pavan by the same, with sub-title *Clement Cotto* (*ib.*, ii., p. 306).

The pavan of Farnaby is remarkable from every point of view. Its harmonic design is disconcerting from its boldness. Among other things a chromatic passage (A, B flat, B natural, C natural, C sharp, D) must be noticed. The expressive character of the work is of a pathetic subjectivity in the style of Monteverde.

The first pavan of Tisdall is distinguished by its harmonic audacities, but the second, *Clement Cotto*, has in addition an æsthetic value of the first rank ; its open fifths, its retardations, and its appoggiaturas give it a very special colouring.

(5.) Finally, an anonymous pavan, bearing the initials M. S. (*Fitzw. V. B.*, i., p. 68), is constructed according to the plan A A¹, B B¹. It is worthy of notice on account of its fine carriage and its modernising air.

E.—Isolated Galliards Written According to the Normal Plan A A¹, B B¹, C C¹.

Thirteen isolated galliards conform to the plan A A¹, B B¹, C C¹.[153]

The three galliards of Byrd which fall under this category teach us very little that is new. The one which Mme. Farrenc reproduces in the *Trésor des Pianistes*, under the title of *Victoria*[154] is of secondary importance; the one to be found at p. 198 of the second volume of the *Fitzw. V. B.* is more valuable on account of the character of its melody than of the treatment of it. Lastly, the *Galiarda Mrs. Mary Brownlo*, to be found in *Parthenia*, is somewhat exceptional for Byrd in that it adopts a series of rhythmical and sequential figurations very progressive in character, such as we do not observe generally in the dance variations of this master.

The two galliards followed by a varied double by John Bull (*Fitzw. V. B.*, i., p. 170 and ii., p. 242) are remarkable for their figuration. The

[153] 1. *Galiarda* by Byrd (*Fitzw. V. B.*, ii., p. 198) ; 2. *Galiarda Mrs. Mary Brownlo* by Byrd (*Parthenia*, p. 10) ; 3. *Victoria* by Byrd (Farrenc, vol. ii. of the *Trésor des Pianistes*) ; 4. *Galliard* and *Variatio* by Bull (*Fitz. B. V.*, i., pp. 170 and 173) ; 5. *Pipers Galliard* and *Variatio* by Bull (ii., pp. 242 and 244) ; 6. *Galiarda* by Bull (ii., p. 251) ; 7. *Galiardo* by Bull (*Parthenia*, p. 30) ; 8. *Galiarda* by Farnaby (*Fitzw. V. B.*, ii., p. 419) ; 9. *Rosseter's Galiard* by Farnaby (ii., p. 450) ; 10. *Galiardo* by Gibbons (*Parthenia*, p. 35) ; 11. *Galiarda* by Tisdall (*Fitzw. V. B.*, ii., p. 486) ; 12. *Galiarda*, anonymous (i., p. 77) ; 13. *Nowel's Galiard*, anonymous (ii., p. 369).

[154] Is this perhaps the *Galliarde for the Victorie* of *Nevell's Book* ?

thematic material of the first has a very modern air; certain passages, notably C, remind one of Haydn; in the *Variatio* there are abrupt skips of the left hand from the medium to the lower part and vice versâ; as to figuration, curious repetitions of notes, sequences, and decompositions of chords. In the second (*Pipers Galliard*) there is an abuse of virtuosity, particularly in the double.

Another galliard by Bull (*Fitzw. V. B.*, ii., p. 251) shows, in its episode C C¹, effects of echo and of syncopation. Lastly, the galliard by the same master to be found in *Parthenia* (p. 30) is by exception written in a sober manner; the figuration is very simple, and very happily appropriate to the subjects submitted to variation.

The two galliards by G. Farnaby (*Fitzw. V. B.*, ii., pp. 419 and 450) are beyond comparison, as much on account of their harmonies as of their figuration. The first is of an exquisite delicacy; the second (*Rosseter's Galiard*) has charming figural details, especially in B¹ and C¹: Farnaby, an inexhaustible melodist, succeeds in some way in creating new melodies simply by the manner in which he figures his subjects.

Gibbons (*Parthenia*, p. 35) gives us a very special type of galliard, which, while retaining the ternary rhythm, nevertheless takes the movement of a solemn march, calling up the impression of an imposing cortège of princes and high dignitaries. The figuration of this piece, at times very animated, has a character of brilliant virtuosity which accentuates its pompous colouring.

Tisdall's galliard (*Fitzw. V. B.*, ii., p. 486) is an original composition, full of unexpected and charming details, especially in its episode C, in which we meet with repetitions of notes possessing a melodic value.

Lastly, two anonymous galliards (*Fitzw. V. B.*, i., p. 77 and ii., p. 369) are interesting, the first from its evolutionary character, which is shown by its repetitions of notes and sequences, the second —*Nowel's galiard*—by its thoroughly popular simplicity.

F.—Isolated Galliards Written According to an Abnormal Plan.

The eight galliards of the *Fitzw. V. B.* and *Parthenia* which do not follow the plan A A¹, B B¹, C C¹ may be grouped in the following manner :—

(1.) Four of them conform to the plan A, B, C. The first, which is by Byrd (*Fitzw. V. B.*, ii., p. 259)—it is entitled *Sir John Grayes Galiard*, and has only the initials of the musician, " W. B."—is composed in the popular manner, and avoids all subtlety of figuration. The second is by Oystermayre (*Fitzw. V. B.*, ii., p. 405), and offers no detail worthy of remark.[155] The third is by

---

[155] As we have already seen (see p. 56) Oystermayre was a musician of whom nothing is known. The hypothesis of Dr. Naylor (*An Eliz. V. B.*, p. 22) according to which Jehan Oystermayre may have been the same as a certain Jerome Ostermayer, organist at Cronstadt (Transylvania), is inadmissible, for the reason that the latter died in 1561, and the technique of the galliard of the *Fitzw. V. B.* makes it impossible for it to have been written before the extreme end of the 16th century.

R. Oppel (*Beiträge zur Gesch. der Ansbacher-Königsberger Hof-Kapelle unter Riccius: Sammelbände* of the I. M. G., XII. i., p. 11) speaks of a Vice-Kapellmeister at the Court of Anspach, named Endres (Andreas?) Ostermayer, who was in office about 1592. Pirro (*Heinrich Schütz*, pp. 14 and 40) refers to an Andreas Ostermeyer—probably the same as the precedent—who was deputy of the Kapellmeister of the Landgrave Maurice of Hesse Cassel, at the beginning of the 17th century (about 1613). Is there identity between this musician and the Oystermayre of the *Fitzw. V. B.*? It is scarcely probable, in view of the difference of Christian name.

Farnaby (*Fitzw. V. B.*, ii., p. 261). It is intended according to its title, *His rest*, to represent the master in a reposeful state; it forms part of a series of works belonging to descriptive music. We shall return to it under that head. Its rhythm,—a sort of ⁶⁄₈ with dotted notes,—reminds us more of a jig than of a galliard, but this has not prevented the compiler of the *Fitzw. V. B.* from qualifying it as a galliard. The fourth is the second galliard *Mrs. Mary Brownlo* (*Parthenia*, p. 14) by Byrd, a simple and charming work, in which each of the three episodes A, B, C is repeated textually, if we may trust the modern edition by Rimbault.

(2.) The type A B is represented by a galliard by Philips (*Fitzw. V. B.*, i., p. 351) of no great interest.

(3.) The type A A¹ B B¹ is found in two galliards by Bull (*Fitzw. V. B.*, i., p. 70; ii., p. 249; and *Parthenia*, p. 33), and in the *Hunting galliard* of Tomkins (*Fitzw. V. B.*, ii., p. 100). The first galliard of Bull has this interest, that its figuration contributes in great part, by its special rhythm, to accentuate the general rhythm of the piece. This figuration consists largely of spreading of intervals and chords.

The second galliard of Bull has a very modern character, thanks to its repetition of notes and its decomposition of chords. Lastly, the *Hunting galliard* of Tomkins gives a specimen of the music of this master in which the ingenuity of the virtuoso is found in just equilibrium with the expressive feeling for melody and rhythm. Sequences, spreadings of intervals and chords, sudden skips of the left hand from the bottom to the middle, &c., are here employed in the most brilliant manner, and give the piece an animated character from which we may perhaps deduce a programmatic intention.

II.—ALLEMANDES.

According to Boehme (*op. cit.*, i., p. 122) the allemande is, as its name indicates, of German origin. The organ and lute tablatures of the 16th century call it *Deutscher Dantz*, or *Ein guter deutscher Tantz*: in these it appears in binary measure, always followed by its *Nachtanz* or rhythmical transformation into ternary measure. In France, where the allemande was introduced in the course of the last third of the 16th century, the *Nachtanz* did not survive; and all the allemandes we meet with in the French collections are written in binary measure. Here is the opening phrase of an allemande which Boehme (vol. ii., p. 42) takes from the *Harmonie universelle* of Father Mersenne (1636) :—

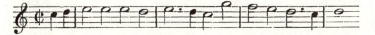

One of the characteristics of this dance consists, as may be seen from this example, in the employment of an anacrusis, *i.e.*, the commencement at the end of a bar. The music of allemandes is generally major, and expresses by preference a feeling of repose and contentment. The allemande in four-time is nothing else but the old slow German dance of the Middle Ages; it is opposed by its character to the dances in ternary rhythm, the movement of which is more rapid (*Springtänze*). Adopted as it stood by the composers of the 17th century and part of the 18th, it forms the introductory piece of their suites for the clavier. At the period of Mozart and Schubert we often meet in Germany with dances for the orchestra, or for the clavier, which bear the name of *Deutsche* (allemande). These dances, which have the three-time rhythm of waltzes, are entirely different from the archaic allemande, which in fact passed out of use in the course of the second half of the 18th century.

Boehme finally remarks that in the time of Shakespeare the allemande was well known in England; it was there looked on as a slow dance, with binary rhythm, exactly as on the Continent. Let us remark, however, that the principle of the anacrusis is applied in only a very small number of allemandes in the *Fitzw. V. B.*

This kind of dance is represented by twenty-three examples in the Cambridge manuscript. One of them (by Byrd) is followed by a double or *Variatio* (*Monsieur's Alman, Fitzw. V. B.*, i., pp. 234 and 238). They are generally designated by the English terms *alman, almain, almand.* We also find the Italian form *allemanda.*

As to other external particulars which distinguish these allemandes, let us point out that a few have their titles accompanied by a qualification which denotes sometimes a person (*Monsieur's Alman* and *Queen's Alman* of Byrd, *The Duke of Brunswicks Alman* of Bull), at other times an object the meaning of which is not very obvious (*Meridian Alman* of G. Farnaby; *Dalling Alman* by an anonymous composer). An allemande of Farnaby

(*Fitzw. V. B.*, ii., p. 160) borrows its subject from another musician, Robert Johnson.

If we examine the internal structure of the allemandes of the *Fitzw. V. B.*, we notice that they are essentially governed by the principle of the melodico-harmonic variation. But it frequently happens that there is a predominance of the harmonic factor, in that the bass, less figured than the melody, constitutes by this very fact a more characteristic element of permanence than the *superius*. This is notably the case in all the allemandes of Byrd—of which there are five— and in the single ones of Bull and Peerson. This preponderance of the bass, the square rhythm of the latter, and the method of its development, have the result that in some cases the allemandes of the *Fitzw. V. B.* possess a harmonic character which one would look for in vain in the pavans and galliards. They also have much more in common with the unsophisticated popular art. This absence of stylisation is noticeable also in the figuration, which only rarely gives rise to those extreme refinements which we notice in the variations of the song and in the pavans and galliards.

The plan A A^1 B B^1 C C^1, which answers to the most usual structure of the pavans and galliards, is also met with in the allemandes, but not in the majority of them. In fact, out of twenty-three allemandes, five only are constructed according to this scheme.[156] One of these, by Byrd (*Fitzw. V. B.*, ii., p. 182) is a charming example of

[156] 1. *Alman* by Byrd (*Fitzw. V. B.*, ii., p. 182) ; 2. *Meridian Alman* by Farnaby (ii., p. 477) ; 3. *Allemanda* by Marchant (ii., p. 253) ; 4. *Allemanda*, anonymous (ii., p. 424) ; 5. *Dalling Alman*, anonymous (ii., p. 470).

quite popular gaiety. This gaiety is pushed even
to fooling and vulgarity in the *Meridian Alman*
of Farnaby (*Fitzw. V. B.*, ii., p. 477), in which the
repetitions of notes by nature partly figural, partly
purely melodic, produce a most humorous effect.
Repetitions of notes also give to the anonymous
Dalling Alman (*Fitzw. V. B.*, ii., p. 470) a
noticeably popular character, but without the
vulgarity of the *Meridian Alman.*

We afterwards meet with two anonymous
allemandes which conform to the type A B C,[157]
each of the episodes eventually giving occasion for
textual repeats. These two pieces are interesting,
the first from its popular feeling, which recalls
certain Netherlandish songs of the period, the
second (*Fitzw. V. B.*, ii., p. 312) by the very
modern freedom of its tonality—we find D sharps
in it—and by its interesting figural syncopations.

All the other allemandes of the *Fitzw. V. B.*
(sixteen out of twenty-three) conform to the plan
A B. Sometimes this scheme appears in its
complete simplicity, sometimes complicated with
variations.

Seven allemandes contain only unvaried episodes
A B.[158] Some have a purely popular cast, others
show an appearance of stylisation. Among the
latter let us cite Farnaby's allemande on a
subject by Robert Johnson (*Fitzw. V. B.*, ii.,
p. 160), a work graceful and full of charm, in
which we come across the characteristic procedure
of the repetition of notes ; and the two allemandes

---

[157] 1. *Alman* anonymous (*Fitzw. V. B.*, i., p. 65) ; 2. *Id.* (ii., p. 312).

[158] 1. *Alman* by Hooper (*Fitzw. V. B.*, ii., p. 309) ; 2. *Alman* (subject
by R. Johnson) by Farnaby (ii., p. 160) ; 3 and 4. Two *Almans* by
R. Johnson (ii., pp. 158 and 159) ; 5, 6, 7, three anonymous allemandes
(ii., pp. 266, 375).

of R. Johnson (*Fitzw. V. B.*, ii., pp. 158 and 159), which immediately follow each other in the manuscript. The second of them has this peculiarity, that its episode B is merely a variation of the same episode in the first.

The second of the three anonymous allemandes (*Fitzw. V. B.*, ii., p. 266) has a specifically English feeling, with a comic element represented by the dancing rhythm produced by the dotted notes; for the meaning of this little piece one thinks involuntarily of an essentially Britannic personage, the clown. The *Alman* of Hooper (*Fitzw. V. B.*, ii., p. 309) is written in the almost pure A major.

The most simple alteration to which the scheme A B gives rise is A A¹ B B¹. Five allemandes of the *Fitzw. V. B.* conform to it.[159] One of these, that of the *Duke of Brunswick*, by Bull (ii., p. 146),[160] is of extreme originality, both in its melody and its figuration, in which the author multiplies the repetition of notes and the spreading of chords and intervals. The one by Peerson (i., p. 359) interests by its numerous melodic and figural sequences, and that of Tisdall (ii., p. 276) by the very modern character of its figuration. In the anonymous *Alman* of vol. i., p. 75, we find again that more or less "clownish" feeling which we have already met with.

Then comes the variant A A¹ B B¹ A¹¹ A¹¹¹ B¹¹ B¹¹¹.[161] The three cases of this given by the *Fitzw. V. B.* have no detail worthy of notice.

[159] 1. *Alman* by Byrd (*Fitzw. V. B.*, i., p. 245); 2. *The Duke of Brunswicks Alman* by Bull (ii., p. 146); 3. *Alman* by Peerson (i., p. 359); 4. *Almand* by Tisdall (ii., p. 276); 5. *Alman*, anonymous (i., p. 75).

[160] The plan of it presents a slight anomaly, as B¹ is followed by a third variation B¹¹.

[161] 1. *Monsieurs Alman* by Byrd (*Fitzw. V. B.*, i., p. 234); 2. *Alman* by Byrd (ii., p. 196); 3. *Alman* by Morley (ii., p. 171).

U

Finally, we have two allemandes in which the scheme becomes still more complicated, as follows :—

A A' B B' A" A''' B" B''' A'''' A''''' B'''' B'''''

These are the *double* of *Monsieurs Alman*, by Byrd (i., p. 238)—a piece of somewhat secondary interest, if we except the curious persistent syncopations[162] —and the *Queens Alman* of the same master (ii., p. 217), a charming composition, the joyous and elegant figuration of which remind one of the sprightly technique of the lutenists.[163]

III.—COURANTES.

After the pavans, galliards, and allemandes it is the courantes which are represented by the greatest number of examples in the *Fitzw. V. B.* and the other collections of virginal music which we have examined. We find eighteen dances of this kind.

The courante (*corrente* in Italian) is, according to Boehme (*op. cit.*, p. 127), an old French dance of moderate quickness, written in $\frac{3}{2}$ or $\frac{3}{4}$ time. It was never a popular dance: from the 16th to the 18th centuries it was, on the contrary, practised by preference in aristocratic circles. It has a special character of tenderness and joyful aspiration. It was danced slowly, in a graceful manner, and with a thousand refinements of detail; in the 16th century it was even a little pantomime rather than an actual dance.

---

[162] The subject of *Monsieurs Alman* is without doubt of French origin. "Monsieur" was at the Court of France the title of the eldest brother of the King. The lute book of Thysius contains an *Allemande Monsieur* the thematic material of which has nothing in common with that of *Monsieurs Alman* of Byrd. (See Land, *op. cit.*, No. 311, p. 281.)

[163] The *Quyns Almand* of the lute book of Thysius (Land, *op. cit.*, No. 318, p. 285) does not resemble that of Byrd.

The clavier suite of the 17th century and of the first half of the 18th adopted it as one of its essential elements; there it immediately followed the allemande and preceded the saraband.

Here are the first bars of a courante taken from the *Harmonie Universelle* of Mersenne (Boehme, ii., p. 44) :—

&c.

The courantes of the *Fitzw. V. B.* are notated in a different manner as regards the barring: the above example would have the following appearance if we applied to it the rhythmic signs most frequently used by the compiler of the manuscript:—

&c.

But the rhythmic effect remains the same if we interpret each bar, as we should, as composed actually of two bars, each of three-time.[164]

[164] There are cases in which the value of the notes is double; thus in the anonymous *Coranto*, vol. ii., p. 308 :—

Or again, we find a $\frac{12}{4}$, comprising in reality four bars in three-time (*Corranto* by Byrd, *Fitzw. V. B.*, ii., p. 359) :—

Mr. Barclay Squire informs us that in the modern edition of the *Fitzw. V. B.*, which we have followed, the bars have always been placed strictly in the same place as in the manuscript.

Our observations refer, not only to the fifteen courantes of the *Fitzw. V. B.*, but also to three other dances of this nature, one by Gibbons and two by Crofurd, reproduced by Mme. Farrenc in vol. ii. of her *Trésor des Pianistes.*

All the courantes of the *Fitzw. V. B.* except one, *Dr. Bull's Juell*, are designated by their Italian name, *Corranto* or *Coranto*. This fact, taken in connection with the circumstance that twelve courantes are anonymous, and that several of them have a decidedly Italian melodic character, is of a nature to make us believe that at least some of them may well be the work of Italian musicians.

On the other hand, although the courante was in principle an aristocratic dance, those of the *Fitzw. V. B.* present a character of simplicity much greater than that of the allemandes; and without our being able to say that they are more popular, they are characterized possibly still more than the latter by their comparative absence of stylisation.

In the cases in which the episodes composing the courante are subject to variation, the latter is conducted essentially according to the melodico-harmonic principle.

The majority of the courantes which we have been able to analyse are based on the plan A B, either in its complete simplicity, or with modifications.[165]

Among the simple types we meet with pieces which are of special interest from their variety and

[165] 1. *Corranto* by Hooper (*Fitzw. V. B.*, ii., p. 312) ; 2. *Corranto* anonymous (ii., p. 267) ; 3. *Id.* (ii., p. 267) ; 4. *Id.* (ii., p. 268) ; 5. *Coranto* anonymous (ii., p. 308) ; 6. *Corranto* anonymous (ii., p. 310) ; 7. *Corráto* anonymous (ii., p. 310) ; 8. *Corranto Lady Riche* anonymous (ii., p. 414) ; *Courante* by Gibbons (Farrenc, vol. ii.) ; a second *Courante* by Crofurd (*ib.*).

the charm of their melodic invention. This is the case, for example, in the *Corranto* by Hooper (*Fitzw. V. B.*, ii., p. 312), and in the greater part of the anonymous courantes. We have pointed out above the Italian character of several of the latter; it thus happens that the two courantes of vol. ii., p. 310, of the *Fitzw. V. B.* have melodic turns strongly analogous to those employed by Frescobaldi in his courantes in the collection published by Borbone, at Rome, in 1637.[166] The harmonies are certainly heavier, and the working of the counterpoint has not the masterly concision which we find in the great organist of Ferrara, but the feeling is the same. Thus we also meet in the courante of p. 308 of vol. ii. with melodic designs of a truly Italian character. The fragment:—

is found again almost note for note in a *Serenata* by Stradella (air: *Ragion sempre addita*) which dates from at least fifty years later.[167]

On the other hand the courantes of Gibbons and Crofurd, republished by Mme. Farrenc, have rather a French feeling, which already more or less suggests Chambonnières, the precursor of the Couperins; their agile technique, which has

---

[166] See a few examples in modern notation in Torchi, *L'Arte musicale in Italia*, vol. iii., p. 207 ff.

[167] Modern edition in the *Arie Antiche* of Parisotti, vol. ii., p. 50. Handel used this subject in one of the choruses in *Israel in Egypt*. We find also this same melodic and rhythmic progression in a composition by Buxtehude (see *Buxtehude*, by A. Pirro, p. 376, first musical quotation).

The courante in which this subject is used is curious also on account of the rhythmic contradiction—a refinement rare in this kind of piece—which there is between the bass and the other parts in episode B.

affinities with that of the lute, accentuates still more this resemblance.[168]

The *Coranto Lady Riche* (*Fitzw. V. B.*, ii., p. 414) is an exquisite example of the courante of the type A B.[169] The romantic turn of the melody and the grace of the accompanying counterpoint give a very favourable idea of the manner in which these virginalists knew how to treat this kind of dance.[170]

After the quite simple type A B we come across its variants. Crofurd, in the first place, gives us a charming courante in the French style, arranged according to the scheme A A¹ B B¹. The same plan was followed by Byrd in the original courante (*Fitzw. V. B.*, ii., p. 305), in which he has turned into ternary rhythm the well-known subject of the song-pavan, *Belle qui tiens ma vie* (see Boehme, *op. cit.*, ii., p. 58).

An anonymous composer is the author of a courante (*Fitzw. V. B.*, ii., p. 266) in which we find the abnormal scheme A, B B¹, where the melodic development is in great part conducted by means of sequences.

By Byrd we have (*Fitzw. V. B.*, ii., p. 359) a courante in which A is twice as long as B, and is

---

[168] Let us remark, as regards the French influence, that *Forster's V. B.* contains three courantes by Byrd (Nos. 2, 3, 4) entitled *French Coranto*.

[169] We find in the lute book of Thysius (Land, *op. cit.*, No. 370, p. 334), a *Lady Rich hir gaillard* by John Douland. Lady Riche was the Penelope Devereux for whom Sir Philip Sydney composed his sonnets *Astrophel and Stella*.

[170] One or two more remarks referring to the courantes treated according to the type A B : the second courante of vol. ii., p. 267, is almost a textual reproduction of another piece in the *Fitzw. V. B.* entitled *A Toye* (ii., p. 260). The courante of p. 268 has, thanks to its strongly marked rhythm, a very popular character. The bass is partly formed by an *ostinato* drone in open fifths, which also contributes to emphasise the popular side.

itself divided into two sub-episodes *a* and *b*. The complete plan is :—

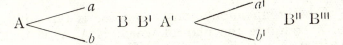

$$A < \begin{matrix} a \\ b \end{matrix} \quad B \; B^I \; A^I \quad < \begin{matrix} a^I \\ b^I \end{matrix} \quad B^{II} \; B^{III}$$

A curious piece in which sequences play a great part.

The scheme A B C is rarer than A B. We find it in two anonymous courantes (*Fitzw. V. B.*, ii., pp. 309 and 311) the first of which reminds us of Frescobaldi.[171] The second is entirely English in character : the syncopations at the end of episode A remind us of those in the *Carman's Whistle* of Byrd.

John Bull gives us an example of a courante in which we find again virtually the usual plan of the pavans and galliards : *Dr. Bull's Juell* (*Fitzw. V. B.*, ii., p. 128), a charming work in virtue of the fresh and popular character of its subjects and the refined manner in which they have been treated by the master. The scheme is A A^I B B^I C C^I C^{II}. There exists another version of this piece, bearing the title of *Courante Jewel*, which Pauer published in his *Old English Composers for the Virginals and Harpsichord*, p. 52.[172] The difference between the two versions consists simply in the introduction, between C^I and C^{II}, of a new variation, which is at the same time a real surprise ; in fact, by means of an insignificant change in the original bass of episode C, Bull has succeeded in placing, in the *superius* of that variation, the well-known song

[171] This piece is reproduced a second time in the *Fitzw. V. B.*, ii., p. 414.

[172] Mr. Barclay Squire tells us that this piece is taken from MS. 23623 of the British Museum.

The Wood's so wild, which we have seen treated in song-variation form by Byrd and Gibbons (see p. 212 & ff).

Finally, an anonymous composer is the author of a courante the plan of which is A A¹ B B¹ C (*Fitzw. V. B.*, ii., p. 415). The episode C is in reality a sort of final *coda*. This piece, of a more or less elaborate character, possesses an exquisite melodic grace; it has some interesting repetitions of notes.

IV.—Jigs.

After the pavans and galliards, the allemandes and the courantes, the virginalists also practised various forms of dances, but in a much more limited number. The *jigg* is the one best represented in the *Fitzw. V. B.*, where we find five examples of this dance. This small number may appear strange in view of the fact that when speaking of the jig we can scarcely separate the word from its implied qualification, "English."

Boehme (*op. cit.*, i., p. 130) describes the jig as a dance of a joyful character, of a lively movement, and always written in $\frac{6}{8}$ or in $\frac{12}{8}$, or even in a $\frac{4}{4}$ consisting of twelve crotchets in triplets. Badly informed, he assumes that we do not find examples in notation before the middle of the 17th century, but that from that time it spread rapidly in England, Scotland, France, and Italy, where it soon became an integral part of the instrumental suites and of the violin concertos, a custom which prevailed well into the early part of the 18th century. The works of the virginalists are sufficient to contradict the statement that no jigs are found in notation before 1650. What probably led Boehme into error is the fact that the special treatises of the 16th century and the opening of the 17th (*Orchésographie* of Thoinot Arbeau, 1588, and *Terpsichore* of Prætorius (1612) do not breathe a word about this dance. In the 19th century the jig was still a popular dance among sailors in Great Britain and Ireland.[173] The historians of music of the 17th century (Mattheson, Walther) generally consider it as being of English origin.

Boheme gives, as an example of the jig, a piece taken from two choreographic collections of the beginning of the 18th century (*op. cit.*, ii., p. 48). Here are the first bars :—

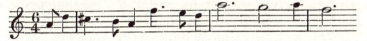

Among the jigs of the *Fitzw. V. B.* there are three in which the rhythm is analogous with that of this example : *A Gigg* of Byrd (*Fitzw. V. B.*, ii., p. 237), *A gigge, Dr. Bull's myselfe* (*Fitzw. V. B.*, ii., p. 257), and *A gigge* by Bull (*Fitzw. V. B.*, ii., p. 258).

The first and the third are noted in $\frac{6}{4}$, the second in $\frac{12}{4}$; it is only necessary to diminish by half the absolute value of the notes to obtain the equivalent of the $\frac{6}{8}$ or $\frac{12}{8}$ of the classical jig of the end of the 17th century and during the 18th.

When we compare these three pieces with the courantes which we have already analysed, we see

---

[173] According to Boehme (*Gesch. des Tanzes in Deutschl.*), who wrote in 1886. In *Popular music of the olden time* (p. 495), a work earlier than that of Boehme, Chappell remarks that the jig is scarcely now cultivated except in Ireland.

that there is, from all points of view, an obvious identity between these two dances. Yet it is scarcely probable that they could be actually confounded in the minds of the virginalists, the more so as one is a slow dance, the other quick. It is therefore very probable that if the courantes transcribed in $\frac{6}{4}$ or in $\frac{12}{4}$ ought to have each bar interpreted as if it consisted of two or four bars of three-time, the jigs ought on the contrary to have the advantage of a more animated pace, and consequently to have each of their bars in $\frac{6}{4}$ or $\frac{12}{4}$ counted in two- or four-time.

The jig by Byrd follows the plan A B. It is of an exquisite charm, that comes from its freshness and the playfulness of its melody. It is the same with the second jig by Bull (*Fitzw. V. B.*, ii., p. 258), in which we come across, in addition, those rhythmical refinements to which we have already had occasion to direct attention (see p. 71).

The first jig by Bull bears the sub-title *Dr. Bull's myselfe*, which doubtless implies that the subject was invented by Bull himself. The plan is A A¹ B C; this piece does not possess the charm of the two preceding.

Was it as a witty reply to Byrd that Richard Farnaby entitled the jig for which we are indebted to him *Nobody's gigge* (*Fitzw. V. B.*, ii., p. 162)? It may be; but in any case we notice here a curious anomaly: this jig is in fact composed according to a binary rhythm, which shuts out entirely the employment of triplets and of those cheerful dotted notes which characterize the jig of the first type. Were there really two sorts of jigs? We may suppose so, since the *Fitzw. V. B.*

supplies this semblance of proof.[174] The piece by R. Farnaby is written on the plan A A^{I} B B^{I} A^{II} A^{III} B^{II} B^{III}, and according to the type of melodico-harmonic variation. It is not wanting in character. Of little interest from the harmonic point of view —the key is a pure C major, in which we find, as all there is in the way of alteration, two F sharps in the space of four pages—it presents agreeable embroideries, a distant echo of those of the father of the author, the charming Giles Farnaby.

Bull gives us another piece, *The King's Hunt* (*Fitzw. V. B.*, ii., p. 116), which a certain number of modern transcribers call the *King's Hunting Jigg*, in virtue of a tradition of the origin of which we are ignorant. This composition presents the same rhythm as the jig by R. Farnaby; it follows the plan A A^{I} B B^{I} A^{II} A^{III} B^{II} B^{III} A^{IIII} A^{IIIII} B^{IIII} B^{IIIII}. The variations are laid out according to the melodico-harmonic type. We shall have occasion to return to *The King's Hunt* in the chapter on descriptive music; it is in fact obvious, seeing the manner in which Bull has varied his subject, that he was desirous of evoking the animation of the hunt in full cry.[175]

[174] The Lute Book of Thysius gives an example of a jig of English origin (*Cobbler's Jig*) written in ₵ (see Land, *op. cit.*, No. 66, p. 75). In the *Partitas* of Kuhnau there is also an isolated example of a jig in strictly binary measure (see Partie 1 of the *Neue Klavier Übung*, p. 37 of the complete works of Kuhnau for the clavier in the *Denkm. der Deutsch. Tonk.*, I., iv.). J. S. Bach also gives us in his *Partitas* two examples of jigs in binary measure (1st and 6th of the *Partitas*); but in the first the persistent accompaniment of triplets has the result that the rhythm of C may also be interpreted as a ternary rhythm in $^{12}_{8}$.

[175] The popular melody in $^{9}_{8}$, *The King's Jig*, reproduced by Chappell, *op. cit.*, p. 496, has no connection with that of the *King's Hunting Jigg* by Bull.

V.—Various Dance Forms.

The dances other than pavans, galliards, allemandes, courantes and jigs are too few to allow us to give to each a separate heading.

(1.) The first which we shall examine are those which bear the title of *Toye*. There are five of them in the *Fitzw. V. B.* Nowhere but in England do we meet with the word *Toye* as the name of a dance. Again, no work on the dance defines the *Toye* as being any definite dance. A certain anonymous courante of the *Fitzw. V. B.* (ii., p. 267) is, with the exception of a few trifling details, the reproduction of another piece in the same collection entitled a *Toye* (ii., p. 260). As the word *Toye* means a plaything, pastime, we may come to the conclusion from these various circumstances that the title of *Toye*, applied to a certain number of pieces in the *Fitzw. V. B.*, does not constitute the specific designation of any well-defined dance, but rather a general qualification given to pieces of a playful character, composed in the style of one or other of the dances current in the time of the virginalists.

Another fact tends to confirm this hypothesis; it is that among the five *Toyes* of the *Fitzw. V. B.* three are in ternary rhythm ($\frac{6}{4}$, $\frac{6}{2}$, or $\frac{12}{4}$, each bar permitting a subdivision into two or four bars of three-time each), and two with the rhythm of ₵. In spite of these essential differences of rhythm, these five pieces have a common character of playfulness and of agreeable and mocking simplicity which justifies the denomination of *Toye*.

In addition to the *Toye* courante to which we have just alluded—a piece as graceful as it is short[176]—we find a *Toye* by Bull, entitled *The Duchesse of Brunswick's Toy* (*Fitzw. V. B.*, ii., p. 412), a worthy pendant to his allemande of the Duke of Brunswick. The plan is A A¹ B B¹.

We find the same plan again in the *Toye* by Farnaby (*Fitzw. V.B.*,ii.,p.421). It is in ₵, with very piquant melodic designs, and curious figurations, such as syncopations and breakings of chords and intervals. The same scheme exists in an anonymous *Toye* (*Fitzw. V. B.*, ii., p. 413), also in ₵. Finally, an anonymous *Toye* (*Fitzw. V.B.*, ii., p. 418) follows the same plan, but is augmented by a *coda* C; further, it is in ternary rhythm.[177]

(2.) After the *Toyes*, we find *Voltes*. These, the name of which designates specifically a well-known dance, amount to two only in the celebrated manuscript. Both are by Byrd, and bear the Italian title *La Volta* (*Fitzw. V. B.*, ii., pp. 180 and 188). Boehme (i., p. 140) attributes definitely an Italian origin to the *Volte*. From Italy this dance overran France and Germany, where it enjoyed great vogue in the 16th and 17th centuries. It is nothing but a variety of the galliard, from which it borrows the ternary rhythm. From a choreographic point of view it seems more or less to have resembled the modern German waltz, like which it turned round (*volta* comes from *voltare* = to turn). Here is the opening of a *Volte* taken by Boehme (*op. cit.*, ii., p. 56) from the *Terpsichore* of Prætorius (1612) :—

---

[176] Plan : A B.

[177] Where there is a variation in the *Toyes* it is the melodico-harmonic principle that is used.

The two *Voltes* by Byrd are among the most exquisite dance pieces in the *Fitzw. V. B.* They are of a pronounced Italian colour. The first (ii., p. 180) adopts the plan A A¹ B B¹ A¹¹ A¹¹¹ B¹¹ B¹¹¹.[178] The opening of the episode A bears a singular resemblance to the refrain of an *Italiana* of the 16th century, published by Chilesotti (No. 2 of the *Canzonette del secolo XVI. a voce sola.* Ricordi, Milan)[179] :—

This *Volte* is transcribed sometimes in $\frac{12}{4}$, sometimes in $\frac{6}{4}$, in the modern edition of the *Fitzw. V. B.* Each bar ought to be interpreted as if it comprised respectively four or two beats of three-time each. The figuration, simple and elegant, is allied to the melodico-harmonic idea of variation.

The second *Volte* by Byrd borrows its subject from the Italianising Morley. Its plan, A A¹ B B¹ A¹¹ B¹¹ B¹¹¹, is irregular. The figuration is very restrained,—a little more animated at the end of the piece than in the previous *Volte*.

[178] We find the same piece again, under the unrecognisable title of *Levalto*, in *Forster's Book.* It also occurs in the Lute Book of Thysius, where it is called *Volte*, and is followed by a second part, in the minor, of the same length as the first and also composed of two episodes A B (see Land, *op. cit.*, No. 380, p. 338).

[179] The original of this *Italiana* occurs in an Italian lute book of the 16th century which Chilesotti published in 1890 with Breitkopf & Härtel, reproducing the original in facsimile.

(3.) Byrd afterwards gives us two examples of pieces called *Rounds*, which evidently means the old dance in a ring which is called *Ronde* in French. We have already met with these two rounds in the course of our previous investigations; in fact, for the reason that they consist of a single episode A, varied a certain number of times, we classed them among the song variations (see p. 233 : *Sellinger's Round*,[180] *Gipseis Round*). We return to them simply to remark that their rhythm is a $\frac{6}{8}$ with dotted notes, analogous to that of the jig.

4. After the rounds we find in the *Fitzw. V. B.* two examples of a dance bearing the name of *Spagnioletta*. Without giving precise information on the subject, Boehme (*op. cit.*, ii., p. 125) reproduces from the *Terpsichore* of Prætorius a piece called *Espagnolette*, of which this is the opening :—

This, as we see, is a dance in ternary rhythm. The dotted notes are not an essential characteristic, for we find them appearing only exceptionally in the continuation of the piece.

The two espagnolettes of the *Fitzw. V. B.*—both are by Giles Farnaby—have each a different rhythm: the *Old Spagnoletta* (ii., p. 471) is in $\frac{6}{4}$; the other, *Spagnioletta* (i., p. 199), is in ₵.

The melody of the *Old Spagnoletta* borrows the opening of its episode A from the espagnolette given by Prætorius.[181]   The plan is A A¹ B¹ C C¹.

---

[180] *Sellinger's Round* is found again in the Lute Book of Thysius (Land, *op. cit.*, No. 389, p. 351) under the title of *Brande* |branle| *d'Angleterre*.

[181] We find again the same subject, under the title *L'Espagnolette*, in the Lute Book of Thysius (Land, *op. cit.*, No. 440, p. 390).

The variations are melodico-harmonic. The whole is delicious for its charm and languor. According to Prætorius the melody of the espagnolette came originally from the Netherlands, which were then, at least as regards the southern part, the Spanish Netherlands.

The other *Spagnioletta* has quite a different turn, not only on account of its binary rhythm, but also on account of the bright and piquant quality of its subjects. The plan is A A^I B B^I A^{II} A^{III} B^{II} B^{III}; the variations are melodico-harmonic. The figuration, very modern although very simple, in a marked degree adopts the repetition of notes—of which it makes a curious use—and the decomposition of chords.

It follows from what has preceded, that according to all probability the espagnolette was not a real dance, but that certain dance pieces of Spanish or Belgo-Spanish origin bore that name, which served simply to recall their source.

(5.) We may again include in the category "dance" the single march which the *Fitzw. V. B.* contains—*The Earle of Oxfords march* (ii., p. 402) by Byrd. It follows the exceptional plan A B A^I B^I, and conforms, but in a very free manner, to the principle of the melodico-harmonic variation. Its true place, as we shall see further on, is among descriptive music.[182]

(6.) A dance which we are surprised to find represented by a single example only in the *Fitzw. V. B.* (*The King's Morisco*, ii., p. 373) is the *Moresca* or *Morisca*. This was, in fact, one of the most popular dances throughout Western Europe

---

[182] *The Earle of Oxfords March* occurs in the Lute Book of Thysius, under the title *La Marche* (Land, *op. cit.*, No. 445, p. 393).

during the whole of the 16th and the opening of the 17th centuries ; according to Boehme (*op. cit.*, i., pp. 132 and 135) it was really of Moorish origin. From Arabic Spain it must have penetrated into England as early as the 14th century, to spread rapidly over the whole of Europe. Its English name is *Morris dance*. It soon came into favour in the British Isles, where the young people adopted it to celebrate yearly the return of May. Choreographically speaking, it is a warlike dance, which appears to have had the intention of perpetuating the memory of the struggles of the Christian West against the Mussulman East. The music is in rhythm a quick $\frac{3}{8}$. When the opera was invented at the beginning of the 17th century, it became the custom to introduce a *Moresca* as the final dance. This is noticeably the case in the *Orfeo* of Monteverde.

According to Nagel, the *Mauriska* was, from 1510, the dance most in vogue at the English Court.[183] It is therefore somewhat singular that the virginalists have not left us a greater number of them.

[183] W. Nagel, *Annalen*, p. 6. See also in Chappell, *op. cit.*, pp. 48 and 49, an account of the private expenses of King Henry VII., from which it appears that on January 2, 1494, he paid £2 sterling *for playing of the Mourice Daunce*, and on September 30, 1501, £1 6s. 8d. *to theym that daunced the mer' daunce*. This popularity existed also in the Netherlands. Thus we gather from the municipal accounts of the town of Malines that the *Moryssche dansen* were danced in that town as early as the year 1509 (Van Aerde, *Ménestrels communaux et instrumentistes divers établis ou de passage à Malines, de 1311 à 1790;* Godenne, Malines, 1911).

[*Morris*, from the Flemish *Moriske*, is the received derivation, and has the sanction of the *New English Dictionary*. But this has been rejected by Messrs. Cecil J. Sharp and H. C. Macilwaine on account of the very wide distribution of the Morris throughout the Continent of Europe, " always associated with certain strange customs . . . which must be looked on as the survival of some primitive religious ceremonies." Blacking the face was one of the traditions of the Morris Dance, and with our forefathers every swarth man was a Moor or Blackamoor. See their *Morris Book*, Part I, revised edition, London, Novello & Co., Ltd.—Tr.]

X

Boehme (*op. cit.*, p. 49) gives an example of a *Moresque* taken from Mersenne. It begins thus :—

The single *Moresca* of the *Fitzw. V. B.* is noticeable for two peculiarities. In the first place its plan is that of the *Medley :* it consists, in fact, of six successive episodes A, B, C, D, E, F, each absolutely different from the others; and further, the first five episodes are in binary rhythm. They have therefore no connexion with the *Moresque* as we have defined it above. Only the rhythm of the final episode F—a $\frac{12}{4}$ divisible into four measures of three-time each—corresponds exactly with that of Mersenne's example. *The King's Morisco* is a charming composition, very simple and with more or less of a popular turn.[18]

VI.—Dances without Titles.

Lastly, it remains for us to examine, in the domain of dance variations, the pieces which we have included under the general rubric of nameless dances.[185] With the exception of one which bears the title of *Daunce* (*Fitzw. V. B.*, ii., p. 268), and another (*Fitzw. V. B.*, ii., p. 274) which has no title whatever, these pieces are all designated by an appellation which would make us suppose, at first sight, that they are varied songs. In more than one case this is certainly so, in the sense that the subject submitted to variation is really a

[184] Chappell gives detailed particulars on the Morris Dance as it was performed in England (*op. cit.*, p. 130 ff).

[185] See p. 251, for the meaning of this expression.

popular song; there is, however, this peculiarity in the species, that the melodies which form the base of these compositions are treated not as variations of the song, but according to the general plan characteristic of the dance variation. We have previously met with dance subjects developed as song variations, following the arrangements A A¹ A¹¹ A¹¹¹, &c: here the case is reversed, and we find ourselves face to face with schemes, such as for example A A¹ B B¹, which suppose the division of the melody into distinct episodes, giving occasion alternately to variations.

The *Daunce* and the piece without title to which we have just alluded are anonymous. The *Daunce* is composed of two distinct episodes, A and B, the first in binary measure, the second in ternary; one might call it a very short allemande, followed by a volte hardly any longer. Its style is homophonic and popular. The piece without title seems to be a sort of courante divided into two episodes, A and B, the second of which, more figured than the first, contains pretty effects of sequences and of the decomposition of chords.

The initial plan—that is to say, looked at in its most simple form—of the dances without name, is :—

A ;

A B ;

or A B C.

In fact we do not notice on a single occasion the plan A in its pure simplicity, but, rather, augmented by a variation A¹, and that in the unique case of an anonymous piece, *Martin sayd to his man* (*Fitzw. V. B.*, ii., p. 275), the melody of which, in the rhythm of a courante, is taken from an old popular song of the 16th century.[186]

The plan A B is only met with once, actually, in *The Irish Ho-Hoane* (*Fitzw. V. B.*, i., p. 87), an anonymous piece the title of which seems to be a corruption of *The Irish Och-one*, " Och one " being the form of lamentation of the Irish. The episode B is double the length of A. The melody, in the rhythm of a slow courante, has an air of wild and sombre grandeur; it is harmonized almost entirely note against note, with numerous parallel fifths.[187]

In four cases the plan A B is developed according to the formula A A¹ B B¹. The first case is that of *Tower Hill*, by G. Farnaby (*Fitzw. V. B.*, ii., p. 371), a charming little piece in the rhythm of an allemande, the opening of the two episodes of which, A and B, curiously recalls the dance in the first Scene of the *Hänsel and Gretel* of Humperdinck. Then comes *Mal Sims*, by the same composer (*Fitzw. V. B.*, ii., p. 447). According to Chappell (*op. cit.*, i., p. 177 and ii., p. 789) this is an old English dance without words, the origin of which goes back without doubt to the ancient bards who played the harp in the Middle Ages.[188] The binary rhythm and the more or less pompous character of the melody remind one of the pavan. The variations are of exquisite delicacy. A third piece by Farnaby, laid out according to the same scheme, *The New Sa-Hoo* (*Fitzw. V. B.*, ii., p. 161), is specially interesting on

---

[186] Chappell, *op. cit.*, p. 76; Song *Who 's the fool now?*

[187] We have already drawn attention to these fifths: see p. 118.

[188] This piece was very popular at the time of the virginalists. We find it in a large number of instrumental collections of the period. (Chappell, *op. cit.*, p. 177.)

account of the extraordinary vogue of its subject, not only at the time of the virginalists and in England, but also well into the 19th century and on the Continent ; Gevaert used it as the principal element of his cantata *Van Artevelde.* Sweelinck wrote some interesting variations for the clavier on this melody (complete works, vol. i., p. 115, under the title *Est-ce Mars ?*)[189] Van Duyse, in his great work on the Netherlandish song, devotes an important notice to the origin and successive appearances of this subject (p. 1139 ff), which was, according to him, of French origin. The rhythm is obviously that of a pavan.

The last piece which follows the plan A A¹ B B¹ is *Muscadin,* by an anonymous composer (*Fitzw. V. B.,* i., p. 74). The subject which serves as its foundation presents more or less the character of an allemande. It has also been treated by Farnaby in a greater number of variations according to the scheme A A¹ B B¹ A" A'" B" B'" (*Fitzw. V. B.,* ii., p. 481). The master has put into the figuration all the sportiveness of which he was capable, thanks mainly to some charming play of sequences. Byrd follows an identical plan in *The Ghost* (*Fitzw. V. B.,* ii., p. 193). The rhythm is that of the allemande. The figuration is very simple, and at times charming, but scarcely progressive in character. *Parthenia* (p. 47) gives in the *Queen's Command* by Gibbons a piece the subject of which is that of a courante or a jig. The figuration, which is very animated, reconciles virtuosity with taste ; in A'" we

---

[189] Scheidt, the principal German pupil of Sweelinck, wrote variations on the same subject, under the title of *Cantio gallica* (*Tabulatura nova* of 1624).

find a descending scale of nearly three octaves, given to the left hand. Lastly, the plan $A\ A^I$ $B\ B^I\ A^{II}\ A^{III}\ B^{II}\ B^{III}$ has been followed in *Why aske you*, by an anonymous composer (*Fitzw. V. B.*, ii., p. 192). It is a very short piece, the rhythm of which is that of a slow allemande.

The same subject has been taken up again by Farnaby, according to the more complex scheme $A\ A^I\ B\ B^I\ A^{II}\ A^{III}\ B^{II}\ B^{III}\ A^{IIII}\ A^{IIIII}\ B^{IIIII}\ B^{IIIIII}$ (*Fitzw. V. B.*, ii., p. 462). In spite of the ingenuity of the figures, this piece is not one of the master's best. *Rowland*, by Byrd (*Fitzw. V. B.*, ii., p. 190), is constructed on the same plan.[190] The subject is that of Lord Willoughby's March (Chappell, *op. cit.*, pp. 114, 115, 770). This English captain, conqueror of the Spaniards in Flanders, was so greatly appreciated by his compatriots that they composed a ballad in his honour and adapted it to the melody of which Byrd availed himself to make his variations. These present no technical detail worthy of remark, but they have that charm of lightness and melodic ease so often met with in the old virginalist.

The plan A B C is met with in two anonymous pieces, *The Irishe Dumpe* (*Fitzw. V. B.*, ii., p. 236) and *Can shee* (*Fitzw. V. B.*, ii., p. 256). *The Irishe Dumpe* is an Irish popular song.[191] *Dumpe* signifies "grief," "sorrow." The *Irishe Dumpe* means, then, Irish melancholy. The rhythm is that of a very slow jig. The piece in the *Fitzw. V. B.* consists of a simple harmonization of the melody, according to the resources of the period, with frequent open fifths in the bass, in the

---

[190] The piece by Byrd is found again in *Nevell's Book* and in *Forster's Book*, under the title *Lord Willobie's Welcome Home*.
[191] Chappell, *op. cit.*, p. 793.

manner of the popular drone ; it has accent and character. *Can shee* is a very original. In episode C the melody, partly given to the alto, suggests a fragment of the song *The Wood's so wild*, which was used for variations by Byrd and Gibbons ; there is even so great resemblance in the succession of intervals and in the rhythm that it would scarcely be rash to recognise a case of borrowing. The rhythm, which is somewhat capricious, approaches that of a courante.

The ordinary plan of pavans and galliards, A A¹ B B¹ C C¹, occurs again in an anonymous piece *Watkins Ale* (*Fitzw. V. B.*, ii. p. 236), and in a composition by Tomkins, *Worster Braules* (*Fitzw. V. B.*, ii., p. 269). *Watkins Ale* is founded on a charming melody in the rhythm of a galliard, concerning a young girl who wished to marry.[192] *Worster Braules* is of a much more elaborate nature, and the figuration is of extreme interest on account of its modern character, so well adapted to the instrument. The rhythm is that of a pavan.[193] The *ensemble* of the work has the charm of an exquisite product of the goldsmith's skill.

We come across the plan A A¹ B B¹ C C¹ A¹¹ A¹¹¹ B¹¹ B¹¹¹ C¹¹ C¹¹¹ in a series of anonymous variations entitled *Pakington's Pownde* (*Fitzw. V. B.*, ii., p. 234). The melody, the rhythm of which may be compared with that of a courante, and its colour with that of a romantic ballad, is taken from a popular song much in vogue on the confines of

---

[192] Chappell, *op. cit.*, p. 136.

[193] According to Chappell, *op. cit.*, pp. 77, 626, 768, *braule* is the English equivalent of *branle*, a French dance which was most usually in binary rhythm (see examples in Boehme, *op. cit.*, vol. ii., pp. 42 and 43). But does the unusually pompous rhythm of *Worster Braules* show any similarity to that dance which was of an essentially popular and joyful character, although of a comparatively moderate movement?

the 16th and 17th centuries (see Chappell, *op. cit.*, i., p. 123). It got its name probably from Sir John Packington, surnamed Lusty Packington, who was celebrated for having one day bet £3,000 that he would swim the Thames from Westminster to Greenwich; Queen Elizabeth, however, would not allow him to run the risk of the adventure. The variations in the *Fitzw. V. B.* show a musician of skill and much taste.[194]

Lastly, Byrd gives us in *Wolseys Wilde* (*Fitzw. V. B.*, ii., p. 184), a plan identical with that of the preceding piece, the only difference being that the episode A does not have a variation A^{III}. The scheme is therefore A A^I B B^I C C^I A^{II} B^{II} B^{III} C^{II} C^{III}. The variations are pleasing, but teach us nothing fresh. The episode C seems borrowed from the second part of the *Carman's Whistle*.

All the variations which have occupied us under the heading *Dances without Titles* belong to the melodico-harmonic type, with the exception of a few passages of *Why aske you*, by Farnaby (A^{IIII} A^{IIIII} and B^{IIII}), in which the passing of the melody into the tenor brings in a polyphonic element.

VII.—Scholastic Pieces.

We have already spoken of scholastic pieces, when we were studying the figured plainsong.[195]

---

[194] The melody of *Packington's Pownde* occurs again—singularly modified from an orthographic point of view—as *Pacce tous pon*, in the Lute Book of Thysius (see Land, *op. cit.*, No. 74, p. 84). We also find it under the title *Peckingstons Pond* in the *Friesche Lusthof* of Starter (1621). See *Uitgave X.* of the *Vereen. voor Noord-Ned. Muzickg.* It reappears again, as late as 1728, in the *Beggar's Opera* by Gay and Pepusch (see No. 43 of the modern edition by G. Calmus, Liepmannssohn, Berlin, 1912).

[195] See above: p. 170, *In nomine* by Blitheman; *Miserere* in three parts by Byrd; *In nomine, Gloria tibi, Christe redemptor, Fantasia upon a plain song*, by Bull; *Veni*, anonymous; p. 171; plain-song variations: *Salvator Mundi* and *Miserere*, by Bull.

Those which we are now about to analyse
cannot be included in any of the musical
forms hitherto considered; it is for this reason
that it is necessary to assign to them a special
heading.

We have to consider first of all a very short
piece of a single line, anonymous and without any
title (*Fitzw. V. B.*, ii., p. 12), which consists of a
simple exercise of counterpoint note against note, a
very unusual thing with the virginalists. It might
be called a fragment of plainsong harmonized in
three parts, in a stiff and clumsy fashion.

We dwell no longer on this insignificant piece,
and pass on to two scholastic pieces for which we
are indebted to Byrd. The first is entitled *Ut, re,
mi, fa, sol, la* (*Fitzw. V. B.*, i., p. 395), and consists
of a long exercise of counterpoint on the scale of
solmisation, up and down, used as a *cantus firmus*:—

As long as we are not well informed as to what
" solmisation," that is to say the solfeggio, was in
the 16th century, we may well be astonished to
see the names *Ut re mi fa sol la* given to the notes
which we in the present day call *Sol la si do re mi*.
It becomes quite intelligible as soon as it is
known that before the 17th century the vocable
si did not exist. All the notes which one had
to sol-fa had therefore to be designated by
means of the six syllables *Ut re mi fa sol la*,
according to the system of *mutations* invented
in the 11th century by the school of Guido
d'Arezzo. The essential principle of this system
is that in a succession of notes the position of

the semitone was always to be expressed by the syllables *mi fa*.[196] From this it results that our modern *Sol la si do re mi* had to read, in the ancient solfeggio, *Ut re mi fa sol la ;* it is the same for all the transpositions of this fragment of the scale. Byrd moreover furnishes us with precise examples in this regard. The fragment of the scale of *sol* which forms his *cantus firmus*[197] is subject in the course of the piece to various modulations. It appears seventeen times in all : eight times in G, four times in C, twice in D, once in A, once in F, and once in B flat. The position of the semitone being always the same in each of these transpositions, the latter are *sol-fa-ed* uniformly *Ut re mi fa sol la.*

It is needless to say that such a *cantus firmus*, having in itself no melodic value, is in reality simply a pretext for contrapuntal developments, as varied and as ingenious as possible. The general impression, as in the greater part of the figured plainsongs constructed in the same manner, is one of monotony and constraint, in spite of the charming details which Byrd has lavished on his figuration, and of the harmonic suavity by which many passages are distinguished. The seventh and eighth returns of the subject give occasion for some charming dancing figures. The rhythm of $\frac{6}{4}$ which takes the place of the ₵ in the thirteenth to the sixteenth re-entries inclusive, breaks the monotony but imperfectly. Lastly, the syncopated counterpoints of the seventeenth re-entry produce a curious effect of *perdendosi.*

[196] See on this subject *Studies in the technique of 16th century music*, by Wooldridge, in the *Musical Antiquary* of January, 1912, especially p. 90.

[197] Its first appearance is preceded by a short prelude, based on the same fragment of the scale, but modified rhythmically.

It would be possible, in short, to regard a work of this kind as belonging to the variation *genre*, with this peculiarity, that the subject modulates in more than one half of the work. The *cantus firmus* is most frequently treated in the *superius*, but as it is partially treated also in other parts, these variations belong rather to the polyphonic-melodic system.

The second scholastic piece by Byrd, entitled *Ut, mi, re (Fitzw. V. B.,* i., p. 401), has the same character as the preceding, and simply develops the same *cantus firmus*, complicated, however, by a figuration which gives it the appearance of a staircase, and by a rhythm which breaks its regularity :—

Yet this rhythm is regularised again in most of the re-entries which follow the first two. *Ut, mi, re* indicates the way in which the first three notes of the subject are *sol-fa-ed*. This is treated eleven times in G, once in C, and once in D.[198] The result is a harmonic monotony still greater than in the previous piece. The tenth and eleventh re-entries adopt the measure of $\frac{6}{4}$. The counterpoints and the figuration have not even the transitory charm met with in the first scholastic piece by Byrd.

---

[198] The *cantus firmus* is most frequently in the *superius*, but now and then it passes to one or other of the remaining parts.

Bull also gives us two compositions of a scholastic nature. They both have the title *Ut, re, mi, fa, sol, la.*[199] The less interesting (*Fitzw. V. B.*, ii., p. 281) comprises twenty-three re-entries of the fragment of the scale of G, ascending and descending :—

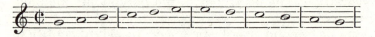

Throughout the piece the *cantus firmus* is subjected to no transposition. The accompanying counterpoints have a perfectly symmetrical character. Up to the eighth entry, exclusive, there is but a single part of counterpoint, the figuration of which gradually becomes more animated. From the eighth to the twelfth variation, inclusive, the writing is in three parts; certain counterpoints in rapid thirds and sixths for the left hand are of great difficulty of execution. From the beginning of the writing in three parts the *cantus firmus*, as if by design, yields to the ternary rhythm. The last eleven re-entries consist of writing in four parts; the rhythm becomes more complicated as well as the figuration, but no less scholastic. Many fragments are treated as a harmonization of the subject by means of homophonic chords, with the bass figured. In the variations 18 to 20 we notice a repetition of the

[199] According to Sir Hubert Parry (*Oxford Hist. of Music*, vol. iii., p. 90) the subject *Ut, re, mi, fa, sol, la* was in as universal use as the motive of *L'omme armé* in the Masses of the 15th and 16th centuries. This author rightly looks upon these scholastic fantasies on the scale of solmisation as a sort of intermediary form between the fugue and the variation. During the first half of the 16th century compositions based on the subject *Ut, re, mi, fa, sol, la* were frequently used for the teaching of solfeggio (see Schering, *Die Notenbeispiele in Glarean's Dodekachordon, Sammelbände* of the I. M. G., XIII., iv., p. 571 ff).

notes of the *cantus firmus* similar to that which we observed in certain figured plainsongs :—

The *cantus firmus* occupies the *superius* throughout. This series of variations on the scale of solmisation has no real æsthetic value. Its composition has only an instructive aim in view. It forms a collection of technical exercises intended to loosen the fingers of virginalistic pupils, and to make them attain to the maximum of virtuosity necessary for the performance of the greatest difficulties to be found in virginalistic productions.

Altogether different is the other *Ut, re, mi, fa, sol, la* of Bull (*Fitzw. V. B.*, i., p. 183). Here it is no longer a matter either of virtuosity or of making the fingers flexible. While the preceding piece is characterized by a complete absence of systematic modulations, the one which we are now occupied with is on the contrary a veritable study of modulation.

The subject which we find developed in it throughout is the hexachord which we have already met with in the other pieces with the same title. Its first appearance takes place under the form of a fragment of the scale in G :—

The general impression produced by the combination of this *cantus firmus* with its counterpoints is that of C major rather than G major.

In fact we find once only an F sharp, whilst F natural appears three times : again, the final G acts as a fifth in the tonic chord of C major. In reality this identification with C major is only an approximation, for the succession of chords to which the contrapuntal tissue can be reduced is in no respect constructed according to the rules which are calculated to bring the key into the greatest prominence. The principle which looks on chords of the tonic, dominant, and subdominant as the essential agents of tonality is scarcely observed, the reason being that the church modes were still far from having lost their command in the days of Bull.

If successions of modulations take place in modern harmony according to the principle of the neighbouring key, situated at the fifth, or the relative minor key, at the major sixth—in the piece by Bull this is not at all the case. Thus the second re-entry of the subject is made not at the fifth, but at the major second, or, if we prefer to express it so, at the double fifth :—

The rarity of G sharp in the accompanying counterpoints prevents us detecting in this case a key corresponding exactly to our A major. Moreover, we are not quite in D major, on account of the persistent connections with the church modes.

The following transposition is made afresh at the major second :—

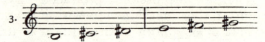

An A sharp used in one of the counterpoint parts creates for a moment an impression of B major, but the presence of several A naturals makes this feeling soon disappear.

From the hexachord beginning on B natural, Bull passes at once into that beginning on D flat. Really this is again a transposition to the major second, but the C sharp which should be the normal starting point is looked on enharmonically as a D flat:—

Attention must be drawn to the interest which this enharmonic transformation presents, and the use—comparatively rare for the period—of D flat and G flat.[200] The contrapuntal development is made by means of alterations which are those of the modern scale of D flat major; and we experience here, more than elsewhere, the feeling of the major mode. This impression ceases towards the end in consequence of the intervention of a

[200] The theorists on chromaticism in Italy used them in their demonstrations as early as the first half of the 16th century. See Riemann, *Handb. der Musikg.* II., No. 1, p. 377 ff, especially the piece by Willaert, *Quidnam ebrietas* (p. 379). We may even go still further back ; according to Wolf (*Geschichte der Mensuralnot.*, i., pp. 117 and 118), Prosdoscimus de Beldemandis, who lived at Padua about the opening of the 15th century, already recognised theoretically the following chromatic sounds : F sharp, G sharp, A sharp, C sharp, D sharp, G flat, A flat, B flat, D flat, E flat. But the practice of the same period made use only of B flat, E flat, F sharp, C sharp, G sharp, and altogether exceptionally A flat. (Wolf, *op. cit.*, i., p. 356.)

On the other hand it must be added that the lutenists, who were not troubled by the restrictive rules of vocal music and of the traditional notation, and who had not to pay attention to the limits imposed by unequal temperament of the keyboard instruments, preceded the virginalists in the use of exceptional modifications. From the first half of the 16th century we find them making use of A sharp (Dalza, 1508), of D flat (Attaignant, 1529), of E sharp, and even of F double sharp (Neusiedler, 1535-36) (see Körte, *op. cit.*, pp. 85, 87 ff, 135).

C flat, the effect of which is to lower a semitone the note which otherwise might be looked on as the leading C natural of the scale of D flat.

The next re-entry of the subject carries us once again a major second higher :—

The D flats which intervene in the accompanying counterpoints prevent us recognising in this episode a real E flat major, and the succession of chords prevents our regarding it as a pure A flat major. Let us point out the passing use of a C flat, from which results an inflexion which makes us think of the modern minor.

The sixth entry of the *cantus firmus* takes place in F natural :—

Here again charged with alterations (E flat, A flat) that are necessary for the management of the transition, the counterpoints of the opening of this episode form an obstacle to our regarding it as in the modern F major. But these alterations gradually disappear, the end of the episode leaving this time an impression of a pure F major.

After the seventh entry, the subject, which up to that time had occupied the *superius*, passes into the bass and begins with an A flat, that is to say, a minor third higher than the preceding hexachord. This anomaly is in order to avoid falling again upon the initial hexachord in G : —

We shall no longer, from this point, enter into analytical details as to the similarities which may be found between the various transpositions of the subject and the tonalities of modern harmony; from that point of view the remainder of the piece behaves absolutely in the same way as in the passages which we have analysed up to now. We shall be content to follow out the inventory of the successive entries of the subject. After the entry in A flat we have one in B flat :—

Then in C :—

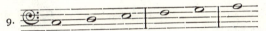

From this point sharps are substituted for flats in the alterations which the accompanying counterpoints undergo.

Next we have :—

The succeeding hexachord opens in the bass, but ends by taking the place of the tenor :—

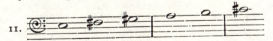

The next entry belongs entirely to the tenor :—

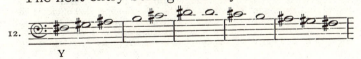

Y

The last note of the descending hexachord gives rise to an extremely abrupt modulation :—

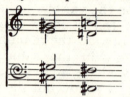

Let us pause a moment here : the twelve entries of the subject which we have been noticing have up to now been made on the various steps of a complete chromatic scale :—

The accompanying counterpoints make use of all the alterations employed nowadays, which have come into current practice since the *Well-tempered Clavichord* of Bach,—excepting E sharp, B sharp, F flat, the double-sharps and the double-flats. Here we have a considerable gain, by which the virginalists have partly profited in their works, where modulations play a most important part, and certain alterations are used with remarkable boldness.[201]

[201] An article in the *Musical Antiquary* of January, 1912 (*An Oxford Book of Fancies*, by Dr. Walker), informs us that Bull was the head of a school in this matter, and that several among the fancies which the author analyses are based on the hexachord treated in the manner of Bull. An example for which Alfonso Ferrabosco the younger is answerable, reproduced by Dr. Walker, is of considerable interest. The hexachord serving for *cantus firmus* has for successive starting-points no longer, as with Bull, notes distant a tone from each other but a semitone :—

The number of hexachords brought into play (8) is less than in the case of Bull, but the modulations are none the less of incredible boldness; they give occasion for the use of F flat and E sharp, which we do not find in Bull. The piece, written in four parts, sounds singularly well, and the modulations are made in an easier fashion than in the *Ut, re, mi, fa, sol, la* of Bull.

The abrupt modulation to which we have alluded above brings us back to the hexachord in G of the opening of the piece. This thirteenth entry might have brought the piece to an end by means of a happily-contrived cadence. But Bull finds that this is not sufficient, and inflicts on us, before winding up, four other entries based on the same hexachord. The final chord is a tonic chord of G, but as the bars which precede it contain F naturals only, it gives the impression of C major finishing on the dominant, or more exactly, of a myxolydian church scale without the leading F sharp.

The last five re-entries of the hexachord (the first is made in the tenor, the four others in the *superius*) give rise to little inner modulations in which we notice especially the intervention of passing-tones which suggest our modern A minor or E minor. Elsewhere Bull endeavours to vary his effects by means of rather curious rhythmical complications (entries 14 and 15).

To say that this composition presents any actual important æsthetic interest would be going rather too far. In fact, one is much too conscious of the effort made for the resolution of a difficult problem. Certain over-abrupt modulations are really painful in effect, and leave an impression of clumsiness and want of skill. But a scholastic piece of this nature none the less contains in the germ a crowd of technical and expressive possibilities which we shall find expand in the most brilliant manner in the period when modulation became a musical element governed by clearly established principles. We may already form an estimate from certain passages in the *Ut, re, mi, fa, sol, la* of Bull as to the future opposition of the major and the minor;

we may also judge, from the transition between the eighth and the ninth entries of the hexachord, of the singularly graduated shades of light created by the passage from a key filled with flats to one filled with sharps. No doubt the Italian "chromatists," such as Marenzio, the Prince of Venosa, and Monteverde, gave many an example in their madrigals of the result of certain more or less abrupt alterations, and their work is in that particular a lively demonstration of the expressive value of modulations. But with them these modulations were invariably called for by a poetic text, while in the piece by Bull they occur in the domain of pure music, and thus acquire an incalculable theoretic value.

Another interesting point of view is that of the impossibility of executing the *Ut, re, mi, fa, sol, la* of Bull on a keyboard instrument the temperament of which does not conform to the equal temperament definitively laid down by J. S. Bach about a hundred years later. In fact, as soon as a piece included other alterations than B flat, E flat, A flat, F sharp, C sharp, and G sharp, it was impossible to play it on a harpsichord or clavichord tuned according to the rules of unequal temperament in use in the 16th and the opening of the 17th centuries, without false intonations resulting. Bull must therefore have tuned his clavier according to the principles of equal temperament to enable him to perform his *Ut, re, mi, fa, sol, la* without forfeiting truth of sound.[202]

[202] Messrs. Fuller Maitland and Barclay Squire have already drawn attention to this fact in their introduction to the modern edition of the *Fitzw. V. B.* (pp. xviii. and xix.).

On the question of the temperament of stringed and keyboard instruments at this distant time, see Kinkeldey, *op. cit.*, Chap. iii.

VIII.—Forms of Various Kinds.

Under this head we propose to study the *Mask* and the *Medley*. The latter may be looked on as a true "musical form"; the Mask is rather a "genre" capable of including forms of more or less variety.

It may be supposed that the *Masks* which we meet with in the *Fitzw. V. B.*, which are all by G. Farnaby, are simply scenic music composed for that class of piece, so much in favour in the reigns of James I. and Charles I., which bore the name of *Masque*. The "Masque" was the forerunner of the opera. It was a dramatic entertainment, the subject of which was usually allegorical or mythological, in which were found in combination poetry, music instrumental and vocal, *mise en scène*, dancing, complicated "machines," splendid costumes and scenery. It was executed at Court or in the mansions of the aristocracy, and the actors were generally persons of high rank. The most celebrated author of masques is Ben Jonson; Milton also composed one (*Comus*, 1634).

Among the musicians who collaborated in these *divertissements*, Orlando Gibbons and the brothers Lawes may be cited.[203]

It is not unlikely that virginal music was employed in the Masques of the early 17th century. At the meeting of the 29th April, 1911,

[203] See Grove, *Dictionary of Music*.

Nagel (*Annalen*, p. 5) carries back the origin of Masques to the 14th century and gives some interesting details on the evolution of that kind of dramatic entertainment, up to the period of its greatest splendour, which is that of Shakespeare and the virginalists.

Paul Reyher has written a book on English Masques (*Les Masques anglais, études sur les ballets et la vie de Cour en Angleterre, 1512–1640*), (Hachette, Paris, 1909). A short chapter (p. 424 ff.) is devoted to the music of the Masques.

of the Paris Section of the International Society of Music, a piece of lute music entitled *Intrada Anglicana*, which formed part of *Lord Zouche's Mask*, was performed. It may be presumed that where the lute was made use of, the virginal might equally have served the same purpose. Now, we actually find in the *Fitzw. V. B.* (ii., p. 350) a piece by Farnaby with the title *The L. Zouches Maske*, an abbreviation which in their index the editors of the celebrated collection have translated as *The Lady Zouches Maske*. This piece was therefore probably intended as an integral part of one of these entertainments, the popularity of which was so great during the reign of James I.[204] The plan of this composition is that of a dance varied according to the melodico-harmonic principle. The rhythm is that of an allemande. But in the scheme which serves as the foundation of the grouping of the elements of the variation there is something exceptional :—

1. $A \overset{a}{\underset{b}{\diagdown}}$ $A^I \overset{a^I}{\underset{b^{I\prime}}{\diagdown}}$ B, b^{II} from A, B^I, b^{III} from A, B^{II}, b^{IIII} from A.

2. $A^{II} \overset{a^{II}}{\underset{b^5}{\diagdown}}$ $A^{III} \overset{a^{III}}{\underset{b^6}{\diagdown}}$, B^{III}, b^7 from A, B^{IIII}, b^8 from A.

We notice, in the succession of these various episodes, the application of the popular principle of the refrain; in fact A is divided into two sub-episodes *a* and *b*, the second of which reappears

---

[204] The Addl. MS. 36526A in the Brit. Mus., which contains the separate parts of pieces by anonymous English musicians, includes, under No. 4, a composition entitled *Lo Souches Martche*. It would be interesting to ascertain if this piece has any relation to the piece by Farnaby.

eight times in the piece, either as conclusion of the sub-episode *a* of A, or as the conclusion of the episode B. This piece, of unequal value, has some charming passages, the result above all of the thoroughly personal manner in which Farnaby conceives the figuration of the melody.

We possess in addition three other *Maskes* by Farnaby (*Fitzw. V. B.*, ii., pp. 264, 265, and 273). All three have the grave and severe feeling of the pavan, and their tonality, in which the minor predominates, has a touch of the legendary and dramatic in it. The first, the plan of which— A B C D E F—is that of a *Medley*, is the most interesting. Virtuosity finds no place in these three little compositions, and the style of variation lends them only the greatest sobriety and refinement.[205, 206]

A few words as to the *Medley*. Thus far we have not met with this term in the *Fitzw. V. B.*; but it has happened to us, on several occasions, to come across pieces the plan of which corresponds with that of the compositions called *Medley* in the celebrated manuscript. Let us recall, under this category, the *Passamezzo pavana* and the *Galiarda passamezzo*, by Philips (see p. 279), *The King's Morisco*, by an anonymous composer (p. 308 ff) and the *Maske*, by Farnaby, of which we have just spoken.

[205] Dr. Naylor (*An Eliz. V. B.*, p. 7) is of opinion that these three pieces really formed part of the music of a Masque. The third (*Fitzw. V.B.*, ii., p. 273) is entitled *Cupararee*—that is to say "by Coperario" (John Cooper)— in the MS. 10444 Plut. of the British Museum. It seems to have belonged to the *Maske of Flowers*, 1613; it bears also in the same MS. the name of *Graysin* (Grays Inn). Dr. Naylor propounds the hypothesis that the seven anonymous allemandes, courantes, and *Daunce*, which in the *Fitzw. V. B.* (ii., p. 266 to 268) immediately follow after the two *Masks* by Farnaby, possibly also formed part of a dramatic "Masque."

[206] The music of the English "Masques" found its way as far as Holland, since a *Mascarade englesa* occurs in the Lute Book of Thysius (Land, *op. cit.*, No. 446, p. 393).

The *Fitzw. V. B.* contains only two compositions specifically qualified as *Medleys*: *A Medley*, by Byrd (ii., p. 220), and *Johnson's Medley*, by Edward Johnson (ii., p. 366).

As we have already said, *Medley* means "mixture"; in fact the compositions by Byrd, and by E. Johnson, which bear this title are kinds of "potpourri" composed of a succession of various episodes. But contrary to that which we noticed in the pieces which we likened to the *Medley* as regards form, we notice in the pieces by Byrd and by Johnson that each episode is followed by a variation, constructed on the melodico-harmonic type.

A Medley, by Byrd, is one of the most exquisite pieces in the *Fitzw. V. B.*; exquisite for the melodic charm that breathes from it, and for its rustic atmosphere, which is not without a reminiscence of the old *Hornepype* of Ashton; exquisite for its vague and poetic cadences, its simple and graceful figuration, its homophonic passages, so clear and so harmonious, its ravishing effects of echo; exquisite for the delightful rhythmic contrast between the last four episodes (5 in $\frac{6}{2}$, 6, 7, 8 in $\frac{6}{4}$) and the first five (in ₵).

The seven episodes which form the *Medley* by Johnson offer scarcely less charm. We notice in addition melodic and formal elements which remind us forcibly of those of the *Medley* by Byrd: sober figuration, homophony, rhythmic contrasts. The fifth episode has very nearly the same bass as the second; and there are the same relations between No. 6 and No. 4. We notice, again, a certain melodic relationship between some of the episodes; but it is not sufficiently close to be prejudicial to their mutual independence. Each of the first six episodes is followed by a variation. The seventh is not varied; it is completed by a short *coda* in the free prelude style. The last four are the most delightful; their courante rhythm, with soft undulations, their melody, full of languor, and their smooth harmonies unite in giving them a colouring which suggests at once the great romanticist of the 17th century, Monteverde, and that of the 19th, Chopin.[207]

IX.—Descriptive Music.

We are not proposing to enter here into the countless controversies as to the true definition of descriptive or programme music, neither shall we discuss the question as to whether or no it holds a position more or less inferior in the realm of æsthetics. We shall content ourselves with drawing attention to a certain number of virginalistic pieces which are allied, either expressly or by inference, to the idea of a programme.

In the course of our previous investigations we have often met with compositions in which the intervention of certain expressive elements might legitimately make us suppose a descriptive intention on the part of the author, although this intention may not have been explicitly put forward by a precise title. The most frequent case is that where the musician has

[207] *Johnson's Medley* is also found in the Lute Book of Thysius under the title of *Le Medly* (Land, *op. cit.*, No. 447, p. 394). Dr. Naylor (*An Eliz. V. B.*, p. 206) regards the *Medley* by Johnson as a pavan followed by a galliard. This opinion may be maintained; we should then have to do with a pavan-galliard constructed almost according to the normal plan, A A¹ B B¹ C C¹.

evoked, consciously or unconsciously, a pastoral atmosphere, by means of melodies of a rustic nature and of harmonies based on the principle of a persistent drone; from the more or less varied combination of these elements there results the feeling of pastoral landscapes, enveloped in that blue mist which makes the English country so poetic.

Already so primitive a work as the *Hornepype* of Hughe Ashton produces this feeling by the turn of its melodies and its persistent basses borrowed from the rustic bagpipes. William Byrd is of all the virginalists the one who most frequently evokes these impressions of nature. Let us recall, in this connection, the following pieces of which he is the author: *Fantasia* (see p. 187); *The Wood's so wild* (p. 212); *Treg. Ground* (p. 230); *Sellinger's Round* (p. 233); *Malt's come downe* (p. 230); *Callino Casturame* (p. 239); *Gipseis Round* (p. 234); *A Medley* (p. 332); *The Hunt's up* (p. 227).

But in addition to these pieces in which the descriptive intention is implicit, the virginalists have left us a certain number the titles of which indicate in a clear and obvious fashion that they have intended to depict some precise object.

This intention is sometimes purely picturesque, at others psychological, in its nature. In the first case, the musician has meant to suggest a spectacle of nature, peals of bells, the movement of a hunt, or the clash of war; in the second, some particular state of mind.

In the class of picturesque ideas, Munday and Peerson will serve to show us how they depict certain natural phenomena. Munday attempts, in a *Fantasia* (*Fitzw. V. B.*, i., p. 23) to describe fine weather, thunder and lightning, as is indicated by the descriptions placed here and there in the piece: *Faire Wether, Lightning, Thunder; Calme Wether, Lightning, Thunder; Faire Wether, Lightning, Thunder; Faire Wether, Lightning, Thunder*; and, to wind up, *A cleare Day*. We recognise at once the simplicity of mind of the musician who amuses himself by depicting an interrupted succession of clear days and tempests on a small scale. Yet its realisation is of living interest from its truth of expression and its perfect adaptability to the resources of the keyboard. To be sure, programme music is infinitely more ancient than the virginalists,[208] and they are very far from being the inventors of it; but it is nevertheless worthy of notice that the *Fantasia* of Munday is the first composition known in which alternations of fine and bad weather have been described. The descriptive means of Munday are extremely simple; but simple as they are, they are none the less remarkable, for they scarcely differ in their essential features from those which in the course of time became the classical methods in use for representing the same phenomena. There is not therefore so great a distance as might at first sight be supposed between the work of Munday and the *Storm* of the *Pastoral Symphony* of Beethoven.

Fine weather is depicted by means of calm and soothing melodies, the charm of which is enhanced by delightful counterpoints which avoid all roughness of rhythm. On the other hand it is the rhythm which describes by its incisive contours the

---

[208] See in *Musique et Musiciens de la vieille France*, by Michel Brenet (Paris, Alcan, 1911), the essay devoted to *Les origines de la musique descriptive*.

brightness and suddenness of the lightning; for
example :—

As for the thunder, it is rendered by the rollings
of the bass :—

However logical these proceedings may be in
principle, they have in application a rather puerile,
mechanical side, which prevents us from taking the
thunders and lightnings quite seriously. Moreover,
by their completely objective character they exclude
the psychological impression of anguish resulting
from a storm. We cannot say so much as regards
the expression of calm weather; here the *Fantasia*
of Munday exhibits a serenity which is in truth an
echo of the satisfaction given to the mind by the
radiant clearness of a fine day.[209] This agrees,
moreover, perfectly with the psychology of the

[209] Certain passages recall the pastoral part of the *Orfeo* of Monteverde.

musicians of the Renaissance, who possessed the power of expressing in the most striking manner the feelings of joy and sorrow in their " static " form, but who had not as yet discovered the secret of exhibiting them under their " dynamic " or " dramatic " aspects.

Of Martin Peerson we have two little pieces, contrasted in character, which suggest the one the joy of the opening spring, the other the sadness of the autumn days. The first, *The Primerose*, (*Fitzw. V. B.*, ii., p. 422), is composed of two episodes, A and B, each treated in a variation A¹ and B¹. Melody and variation are alike graceful and suggestive of joy and spring. The second piece (*Fitzw. V. B.*, ii., p. 423) is called *The Fall of the Leafe*, and is contrasted with *The Primerose*, which is in C major, by its melancholy and sombre colouring, obtained by a pure D minor. We have already had occasion to dwell on certain forms of figuration met with in this piece, which appear to have a definite expressive intention.[210] The delicate impressionism of these two little pieces is to be remarked, as well as the relation—absolutely modern in character—between the *Stimmung* and the keys chosen.

The most interesting descriptive piece which we meet afterwards is *The Bells*, by Byrd (*Fitzw. V. B.*, i., p. 274). The musician has desired in this charming composition to suggest the sound of a peal of bells and the poetic atmosphere, joyous or melancholy, called forth by the shrill and feeble sonority of the small bells, the calm and serene tone of those of moderate size, and the dark and deep drone of the large bells.

[210] See p. 104.

We have previously met with two figured plain-songs, an *In nomine* by Bull (see p. 171) and an *In nomine* by Parsons (see p. 176), certain passages in which sound like a peal of bells. But in these cases it was a question only of isolated fragments, and in addition a conjectural rather than a probable interpretation.

In *The Bells* we are face to face with a work essentially descriptive. The musician has not attempted to give the sound of bells as they really reach us, that is to say with the elements of dissonance which result from the fact that no decided chord has been realised between the various bells which sound simultaneously in a space in which they are near enough together to be heard at the same time. Nor did he intend to give the impression of a peal of bells previously tuned (carillon). What he gives us is a sort of approximation of an impressionist character, in which the reality is at the same time systematized and made poetical. The piece is divided into nine episodes, in which we have no difficulty in recognising an application of the variation style. Variation supposes a subject to vary; in its nature the latter consists of two notes subjected to an obstinate rhythm, the incessant repetition of which forms the " melopœia " of the large bells :—

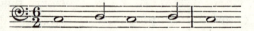

This *leitmotif* occupies the bass in each of the episodes. Generally it is not subjected to any figuration; but when this occurs (var. 2, 3, 6 and 8) the figurations are intentionally monotonous. The variations are thus truly harmonic; in fact, upon this bass, always or almost always identical, are built free counterpoints which change from variation to variation, and aim at suggesting, as much by their individual inflexions as by their inner combinations, the sound of moderate-sized bells and of those highest in pitch. The effect obtained is surprising, in spite of the large allowance of convention which forms its starting point. As we have already said, dissonance has no place in this piece. Still more, we do not find a single modification, and the key of C major reigns without restriction from one end to the other. This fact is the more worthy of attention, since in our days when it is attempted to imitate the sound of bells, the method adopted consists precisely in the use of greatly accentuated dissonances,[211] or sudden modulations with regular alternations.[212]

After these exhibitions of natural phenomena and of bells, the virginalists next provide us with hunting scenes. Bull and Farnaby each give us, in that department, a *King's Hunt.*

We have already alluded to Bull's *King's Hunt* (*Fitzw. V. B.*, ii., p. 115), when we were occupied with the study of the jig. In this curious piece everything helps to suggest in a lively and vivid way the movement of the chase, the deep interest of the hunters, and the breathlessness of the hunt: the melody, rhythmical as a galop; the figuration, which comprises shakes, syncopations, and repeated notes; the tempo, which ought to be taken very quickly.

[211] See, for example, *Les Cloches* by Jean Marnold, in the *Mercure Musical* of January 15, 1906 (p. 55).

[212] See, for example, the scene of the Coronation of the Tzar in Moussorgsky's *Boris Godounow.*

The *King's Hunt* by Farnaby (*Fitzw. V. B.*, i., p. 196) presents the same peculiarities. The plan of the two pieces is different; while Bull varies the two episodes A and B a great many times, Farnaby conforms to the usual scheme of pavans and galliards: A A¹ B B¹ C C¹. The methods of figuration used by the two masters are absolutely identical, and this is also the case as to the degree of virtuosity demanded on the part of the performers. Farnaby has a few daring technical points, the equivalent for which one would seek in vain in Bull.[213]

After the chase, war. Here we light on a piece by Byrd, on which we have previously had a few words to say, on account of its dance plan: *The Earle of Oxfords Marche* (*Fitzw. V. B.*, ii., p. 402) (see p. 308). This piece is also found in *Nevell's Book*, in which it is No. 3, and has for title *The Marche before the Battell*. It there serves as prelude to a collection of pieces, a copy of which exists in the library of Christ Church, Oxford, known under the title of *Mr. Byrd's Battle*.[214] The different episodes of this battle are:—

The souldiers sommons: The Marche of Footemen.
The Marche of Horsmen.
Now foloweth the trumpetts.
The Irishe Marche.
The bagpipe.
And the drone.

---

[213] There exists, in *Forster's Book*, under No. 70, a *King's Hunt* by Bull differing from that of the *Fitzw. V. B.* According to Sir Hubert Parry (*Oxf. Hist. of Mus.*, vol. iii., p. 89), it is remarkable for the extreme modernity of its instrumental style.

[214] The Addl. MS. 10337 of the Brit. Mus. (*The Virginal Book of Elizabeth Rogers*, 1656) contains also (as No. 27) Byrd's *Battle*, but with a different ending from that in *Nevell's Book*: the galliard of victory is replaced by *The Buryng of the dead*. (See *Catalogue of the MS. Mus. in the Brit. Mus.*, vol. iii., p. 107).

The flute and the Droome (drum).[215]
The Marche to the Fighte.
The retreat. Now foloweth a Galliard for the Victorie.
The galliarde.[216]

In the piece entitled *The Marche to the Fighte* at one point there is the inscription : *Tantara, tantara, the battels be joyned.*

It is to be regretted that the *Fitzw. V. B.* contains only the prelude of this suite, which occupies an important place in the history of battles in music.[217] However that may be, *The Earle of Oxfords Marche* allows us to form an idea to a certain extent of the way in which Byrd looked on this warlike music. It is obvious that his intention was to suggest, by means of resources native to the virginal, a fanfare of trumpets in the rhythm of a march. The form chosen is that of a somewhat free variation following the exceptional plan A B A¹ B¹. The application of the principle of the variation serves for the intervention of little figural designs in quavers and semiquavers, which have nothing in common with the technique of the trumpet, and are found here with a purely ornamental object. They do not, however, damage the general impression, which remains that of the fanfare of a march. This impression is produced by means of a strongly

[215] Sir Hubert Parry reproduces an extract from this piece in vol. iii. of the *Oxford History of Music*, p. 95.

[216] Very probably the galliard published by Mme. Farrenc with the title of *Victoria* in vol. ii. of the *Trésor des Pianistes*.

[217] On this subject valuable information will be found in the work of M. Michel Brenet quoted above, and in an article by E. Bienenfeld on *Battles in Music,* which appeared in the *Zeitschrift* of the I.M.G., VIII. v., p. 163.

Z

rhythmed bass, which imitates the beating of a drum on the tonic G or its dominant D, with from time to time passing or interpolated notes, too few to interfere with the harmony or the rhythm; subsequently, by rudimentary melodic figures analogous to those obtained on the trumpet by the use of its natural scale. Let us add to this, frequent open fifths, successions of heavy and solid chords, and combinations of little fanfares answering successively to the various parts (in B♭), and we shall have a notion of that curious warlike music of the end of the 16th century which Shakespeare so frequently introduces in his historical plays.

On this head it is interesting to know that at the period in which *Nevell's Book* was compiled (1591) the trumpet was an instrument held in great honour at the English Court. It appears from the royal accounts referring to 1589, 1590, and 1591,[218] that the King had at that time in his service sixteen trumpets, under the command of a *Sergeant Trumpeter.*[219]

We now come to the descriptive music which claims a psychological origin. "Psychological" is no doubt a very big word to give to the little unpretentious pieces by Munday and Giles Farnaby, the titles of which show an intention of depicting a state of mind, or even a simple impression.

Of Munday (died in 1630) we have a short piece entitled *Munday's Joy* (*Fitzw. V. B.*, ii., p. 449).

[218] See the lists of the *King's Musicians*, in the *Musical Antiquary*, October, 1910, pp. 53 and 54.

[219] We have already met with one or two compositions in which certain melodic phrases seem to attempt to imitate fanfares. *Cosyn's Book* has, under No. 39, a pavan by Bull to which the index gives the title of *The Trumpet Pavin* : presumably imitations of fanfares are to be found in it.

This piece adopts the plan of varied dances, and is constructed after the scheme A A¹ B B¹. It is a fine and delicate work which expresses rather inward content than an outward manifestation of joy. The figuration is graceful and the modulations bold. We find a D sharp,—a somewhat rare modification for the time.

Farnaby gives us a succession of little pieces, the titles of which show that he was trying to depict different states of feeling through which he had himself passed. In the first place there is *Giles Farnaby's Dreame* (*Fitzw. V. B.*, ii., p. 260), in which he describes with sweetness a delightful dream which he had had.[220] Next it is *His rest* (ii., p. 361), which takes the form of a graceful little galliard of which we have already had occasion to speak (see p. 288), in itself a jewel of grace and freedom.[220] Lastly he aims at giving us some idea of his character, *His humour*[221] (*Fitzw. V. B.*, ii., p. 262), and introduces us to its various phases in four episodes, A B C D, the succession of which calls to mind the *Medley*. From A we imagine him capable of serenity and good humour. B, which is fundamentally chromatic—we find in it a chromatic hexachord (from F sharp to D)—shows us that he is not always cheerful, and that his soul is susceptible of grief. But the little sequential rhythmical passages in C soon warn us that he has returned to more joyous feelings, and that his heart dances in his breast. The final episode D is a sort of plainsong in long notes, the melody of

[220] Plan A B C.

[221] Dr. Naylor (*An Eliz. V. B.*, p. 99) believes that *Humour* ought to be interpreted here in its Shakespearean sense, that is to say, " a ' wayward ' fancy."

which is simply the diatonic hexachord *Ut, re, mi, fa, sol, la,* up and down, which we have seen developed in scholastic fashion by Bull and Byrd. The first counterpoints applied to it remind us by their *hoketus* character of the accompaniment figures employed by Philips in his pavan of 1580 (see above, p. 262). Can Farnaby have intended by this double parody to put in relief the mocking side of his character ?

The little programmatic suite reminds us somewhat of a suite in Book III. of the clavecin pieces of Couperin le Grand (1722), in which the master describes, under the general title of *Les folies françaises ou les dominos,* certain aspects of the human character, such as ardour, faithfulness, coquetry, &c. But, in this respect completely French, he attempts to depict only abstract qualities and failings, while Farnaby, more subjective, depicts himself.

Finally, Farnaby has left us quite a little piece, *Farnaby's Conceit* (plan A B), in which he expresses one of his thoughts in a delightfully simple form (*Fitzw. V. B.,* ii., p. 424).[222]

* * * * * *

We have thus grouped and analysed, in mass and in detail, all the pieces in the *Fitzw. V. B.,* in *Parthenia,* and in the other collections, or fragments

[222] Let us notice here in speaking of programme music that No. 50 in *Cosyn's Book,* a pavan by Bull, is qualified in the index under the significant title of *Mallincholy Pavin.*

The fashion of programme music continued well into the 17th century in English keyboard music. Thus in the *Virginal Book* of Elizabeth Rogers (Addl. MS. 10337 of the Brit. Mus.), dated 1656, we find in addition to the *Battle* by Byrd an anonymous piece called *The Nightingale,* to which our attention has been called by Mme. Wanda Landowska, who occasionally includes it in her concert programmes.

of collections, of which we have been able to make the acquaintance.

It only remains for us to cast a glance on a short piece by Farnaby (*Fitzw. V. B.*, i., p. 202) entitled *For two virginals*, which is interesting on account of its exceptionality. It is, in fact, the only piece for two keyboards with which we are acquainted in the whole repertory of virginal music. We find in Italy, in the *Concerti* of 1587 by A. and G. Gabrieli, a pendant to this piece, in a ricercare composed for two keyboard instruments.[223]

The structure of the piece by Farnaby is very simple; it comprises two episodes, A and B. The first virginalist plays the simple version of it, the second the varied version A' and B', *at the same time* as the first is playing A and B. But each of the two might just as well play his part separately, for it is quite complete in itself.[224, 225]

[223] See Seiffert, *Gesch. der Klavierm.*, p. 36.

[224] One may liken this way of playing in duet to the manner of singing of which Dechevrens speaks à propos of Gregorian song (*Des ornements du chant gregorien*) (*Sammelbände* of the I. M. G., XIV., iii., p. 303), which consists in the most skilful singers singing the melody with all its coloratura, whilst the others, less skilful, sing only the "melos" without any ornament whatever.

We find in the *Hortus Musarum* of 1552-53 pieces for two lutes (transcriptions of motets and songs) arranged in the same way as the *For two virginals* of Farnaby. One of the two lutes plays the piece with diminutions, the other without diminutions (see Quittard, *Hortus Musarum*, &c., in the *Sammelbände* of the I. M. G., VIII., ii., p. 263). Quittard remarks that this way of playing was much appreciated and often employed at that time.

[225] Let us add that the virginalists also practised composition for the clavier for four hands. The Addl. MS. 29996 of the Brit. Mus., dating from the opening of the 17th century, contains two pieces for four hands: 1. *A verse for two to play on one virginall or organ, in score*, by Nicholas Carleton; 2. *A fancy* by Tho. Tomkins. (See *Catalogue of the MS. Music in the Brit. Mus.*, vol. iii., p. 151.)

Lastly, the *Fitzw. V. B.* contains a certain number of pieces by Sweelinck.[226] Of these we say nothing here, since they belong strictly to the history of the origins of clavier music in the Netherlands.

[226] They are four : *Fantasia* (ii., p. 297) ; *Praeludium Toccata* (i., p. 378) ; *Psalme* (ii., p. 151) ; *Ut, re, mi, fa, sol, la, à 4* (ii., p. 26).

CONCLUSION.

If, after having studied the remote sources of keyboard music in England, having made an inventory of the new technical material used by the virginalists, and having attempted to group and analyse the different forms and the various *genres* which they cultivated; if, after having done all this, we cast a rapid glance backward, in an attempt to ascertain what it is that musical history owes to that *Pléiade* of artists, we shall notice that in the main the great innovation for which we are indebted to them consisted in the art of *instrumental variation.*

As far back as the 14th century we find the English organists bent on the discovery of an instrumental style, and attaining their end by means of little figurations which constitute the primitive rudiments of that which was to become later the variation.

At the opening of the 16th century Hughe Ashton already shows the art of variation arrived at a degree of development of which the Continent offers no example. Later, in 1562 and 1564, Tallis appears with his two figured plainsongs, *Felix namque,* in which the superabundance of new instrumental figures astonishes us, and gives us a singularly favourable idea of the advanced condition of virginalistic technique at a period when, in Italy, in France, and even in Spain, the art of instrumental figuration was still in its infancy.

Starting with the second half of the 16th century, the evolutionary process of the virginalistic variation may be characterized on broad lines in the following manner :—

At first, a given *cantus firmus*, most commonly taken from the liturgical repertory, was surrounded with counterpoints which were distinguished from the counterpoints of vocal music by their appropriately instrumental character. A crowd of little figures surrounded the *cantus firmus* with a tissue of ornaments the importance of which continued to increase till it came actually to occupy a preponderating place. The English learned by this practice to vary in an unlimited way their methods of figuration. But there exists in this richness, in this very superabundance, a monotony the reasons of which we have already explained. This monotony disappeared in great measure as soon as the virginalists ceased to choose long religious melodies as subjects for variational development, and made use of the shorter popular songs, which, thanks to their better defined rhythm, were more plastic and more amenable to the instrumental style.

At first these new melodies occurred indifferently in the *superius*, the alto, the tenor, or the bass in the successive variations to which they were subjected. Thus we get the polyphonic variation, with its feeling for the past, in that it still conforms to the principle of the expressional equality of the different voices of vocal polyphony.

But the imperfection of the instrument, which is incapable of making a particular part prominent if it is placed neither in the *superius* nor in the bass, soon led the virginalists to make use of the principle of this preponderance of the *superius* or of the bass. From this at once came into existence the *harmonic variation* in which the melody occupies the bass, and the *purely melodic variation* in which it is placed in the *superius*. We have, in fact, seen that not only did the virginalists cultivate these last two forms of variation to only a slight extent, but that they never, or almost never, made use of the principle without certain restrictions; the forms have all the character of a transitional system.

In order that the variation of secular song should develop in its full splendour, it was necessary to go a stage further. This stage was accomplished on the day in which they adopted the new principle of the melodico-harmonic variation. From that time the *superius* and the bass acquired a common importance in opposition to the accessory character of the other parts: the bass served as harmonic support, and the *superius* became the natural vehicle of expressive melody. It is needless to say that this evolution is in no respect a phenomenon exclusively shown in virginalistic art; it is parallel to that which happened, exactly at the same period, in the domain of vocal music, and that led in time to the idea of accompanied monody.

The conditions of perfection became completely united when the virginalists adopted, as themes subject to variation, dance motives of instrumental or vocal-instrumental origin, and applied to them, almost without exception, the melodico-harmonic system of variation. All connection with vocal music was now broken; an instrumental style was created, and the possibility was attained of composing works in which everything—plan, rhythm, build of the melody and of the bass,— avoided any such reproach of monotony and want of proportion as might be made not only against the old figured plainsong, but even against more than one of the numerous series of variations of the secular song which the virginalists have left us.

We' have had occasion to remark that the English of the second half of the 16th and the first quarter of the 17th centuries did not, so to speak, cultivate strict forms. The reason ought mainly to be looked for in the delight which they experienced in juggling with the rich figural material which they had invented. We see them also introducing the latter even into the severer forms, thus depriving these of much of their stiffness. Let us recall, in fact, what the English *Fantasia* was : beginning as a *ricercare*, it was impossible for it to continue on this path to the end; there always came, sooner or later, a moment when the figural fever took the upper hand, and broke the fine regularity of the imitative edifice by embroideries of all sorts, rhythmical designs and sequences.

If we set aside the scholastic pieces, we are in most instances surprised and charmed by the expression which is found in the music of the virginalists, in spite of their innumerable strainings after effect. It suffices to give oneself up to this music, leaving analysis alone, to recognise that it almost always possesses a well-defined *Stimmung*. Apart from the cases of frankly descriptive music, it generally expresses itself in abstract states of

mind which adapt themselves perfectly to our
receptive feelings : joy, sorrow, serenity, love,
aspiration, disquietude, a feeling for nature, appear
in it in turn, under their countless aspects, the
excessive alone excepted.[1] That is to say, this
music is rarely dramatic, rarely pathetic, rarely
overdone; its charm consists above everything in
its general character of intimacy and half-tint.
Superficial or uncultivated intellects may consider
that this continually veiled lyricism results in
monotony. This is to take a point of view too
exclusively modern, and to judge the music of
the time of Shakespeare with a mind too much
taken up with the art of to-day. Let us not
forget that the great English dramatist was
profoundly moved by the music of his own time,
and that it is not for nothing that he makes
Lorenzo say, in an often quoted Scene in
The Merchant of Venice (Act 5, Scene 1) :—

> " The man that hath no music in himself,
>   Nor is not mov'd with concord of sweet sounds,
>   Is fit for treasons, stratagems and spoils ;
>   The motions of his spirit are dull as night,
>   And his affections dark as Erebus ;
>   Let no such man be trusted."

In truth the music which is spoken of in this
passage is more especially vocal music, expressive
beyond everything, which in England, at the time
of Shakespeare, had arrived at a degree of
perfection and charm of which it is difficult to
form an idea unless one has heard sung by one

---

[1] Nothing is more convincing, in forming a judgment on the shades of
expression arrived at in virginalistic pieces, than a preparatory study of the
actual performance of some of them, as for example, the *Walsingham* of
Byrd or that of Bull ; the movement, the phrasing and the *Stimmung*
appropriate to each variation reveal themselves without the least difficulty,
by means of an entirely natural sympathy between our own feeling and the
expressional content of each of them.

or other of the Madrigal Societies[2] which exist and prosper in the United Kingdom such pure gems as the madrigals by Byrd, Gibbons, Morley, Dowland, Bateson, Wilbye, Weelkes, &c. They form a complete repertory which expresses, in a musical language of admirable spontaneity, grace and freshness, the open soul of " Merry England."

By the side of these highest achievements of British music the productions of the virginalists take a comparatively lower position from the fact that they represent an art that had not, like the madrigal, reached its apogee and was unhampered by technical difficulties, but on the contrary an art which was feeling its way, experimenting, and often showing signs of effort. From this resulted undue length, want of skill and decision, so that it happens that we seldom meet with pieces the feeling of which is completely satisfactory from the point of view of balance of proportions. Beauty is found more frequently in the details than in the complete work, and it is only at rare intervals that we distinguish, in the enormous mass of this production, a piece which in its entirety unites the conditions of that perfect harmony which is rightfully looked for in a masterpiece.[3]

However this may be, it is none the less true that it would be difficult to find in the whole history of keyboard music a period more original and more fruitful than that of the virginalists. The exceptional character of their work, and the

[2] The most ancient is *The Madrigal Society*, founded in 1741.

[3] Dr. Walker (*A Hist. of Mus. in Engl.*) lays special weight on the unequal value of English vocal and instrumental music at the time of the virginalists ; but his comparison possibly has an excessive tendency to run down the latter at the expense of the former.

claim it may put forward of having inaugurated a truly instrumental style, give it in the mass the quality of a magnificent "group" or "school." At the time when on the Continent keyboard music was in general only a pale reflection of vocal music, a distant and distorted echo, in England it flew with its own wings, created its own domain, and discovered the means of finding a suitable expression,—independent of vocal expression.

Thus far we have endeavoured only to place in relief the general and abstract expressive feeling of virginalist music, as though the English musicians of the second half of the 16th and the opening of the 17th centuries had lived under the rule of that impersonal feeling which is one of the characteristics of religious music in the Middle Ages. But we must not lose sight of the fact that our virginalists are men of the Renaissance, and that to say "Renaissance" is to say "subjectivity" and "personality." In the course of the analysis which we have made of the principal available documents on which we have founded our observations, we have had on more than one occasion to remark that such or such a piece, composed by such or such a master, presented certain very well-defined personal characteristics. Let us revert for a moment to those individual peculiarities, but on this occasion under the form of a general view intended to bring into relief one of the most striking aspects of the work of the virginalists.

The masters who incontestably occupy the place of honour in virginalistic production are: William Byrd, Peter Philips, John Bull, Giles Farnaby, and Orlando Gibbons. No one of them is a genius of the first order, comparable with Palestrina, Orlando di Lassus, G. Gabrieli, or Monteverde. But they have, each of them, well marked personal features that differentiate them one from the other, and that are capable of definition.

Byrd, the most ancient of the three, is a pastoral poet who loves misty distances, graduated tints, softly undulating landscapes. He has an altogether special affection for tender and suave harmonies, for simple and dreamy melodies. Virtuosity was always more or less foreign to him, and the embroideries with which he ornaments his subjects are rarely meant to make them more brilliant; on the contrary they seem rather intended to intensify the blue mist which surrounds them. Byrd is a rustic, whose rural lyricism decks itself in the most exquisite graces that an artistic temperament at once simple and refined can imagine. He is profoundly English, even where he seems to have been influenced by the Italianism of the madrigal. He carries on the purely British tradition of Hughe Ashton.

Peter Philips is less independent. Italy dazzled him by its brilliant arabesques and its elegant virtuosity. But none the less he maintains at bottom a severity and austerity that remind us of Cabezon; his life, which was a sad one, is unfolded in more than one of his works, in which a grave and profound melancholy is to be noticed. Unfortunately we possess too small a number of his entirely original works to define more precisely the features of his art.

John Bull is, with Giles Farnaby, the most remarkable of the virginalists as regards the

technique of the instrument. These two masters
—whose instrumental production is, moreover, of
more importance than their vocal work—are those
who made the greatest advance in virginalistic
figuration.

Bull was the more universal of the two. We
have discovered him occupied in his scholastic
pieces in finding out new methods, whether of
virtuosity or of figuration, or of the art of harmonic
modulation; we have seen him cultivate all forms
and all varieties with equal diversity and equal
power; we have seen him, finally, practising at
one time a serious art devoid of all superfluous
ornaments, at another the art of the virtuoso who
does not recoil before any difficulty. Under all
circumstances and on every occasion he strikes us
by his vigour, his wish to go straight at his aim
without any fear of opposition, his magistral
knowledge, the breadth of his imagination. He
is a strong man, a musical power with whom we
have to reckon, a mind but little inclined to the
feminine tenderness of a Byrd, a poet of manly
and at times somewhat dry inspiration.

Giles Farnaby forms a complete contrast to
him. He is one of the most graceful musicians
possible. He is also one of the most spontaneous,
even in his audacities; and of these he has as
many as Bull, whether in the realm of harmony
or in that of figural virtuosity. He is an improviser
of melody of an abundant and easy fancy like
Schubert, whose qualities and defects he shares.
He is so great a lover of melody that when he
adorns it with figurations it is often to create new
melodies more delightful and more characteristic
than the one that formed his starting-point. He

is fanciful even to singularity. He is simple, sportive, popular, witty, mocking, even " clownish." He loves piquant detail, and at times carries it even to preciosity. He is the most original of all the virginalists, and at the same time the one who best represents the spirit of " Merry England." Like Byrd, he is profoundly English; but while the elder master embodies the dreamy side of the British character, Farnaby expresses rather the humorous side of it.[4]

Of Orlando Gibbons we have been enabled to examine too limited a number of his works to be able to form any but a superficial judgment of him. The little which we know of him suffices, however, to decide that we are dealing with a true man of genius, of profound and searching inspirations.[4] A humorist, bold even to extravagance, he at times attained to a *Stimmung* the concentrated and pathetic lyricism of which has the quality of that romantic feeling—as yet unborn—which is so often found among the great artists of the Renaissance.

[4] To this it has been objected (see article by Mrs. L. Liebich in the *Musical Standard* of May 31, 1913) that Farnaby was of Cornish and therefore Celtic origin, and the expression " profoundly English " which we apply to him is the less suitable since the characteristics which we recognise in him are those which distinguish the Celtic race, as opposed to the Anglo-Saxon. We have evidently here a wide field for discussion of a very interesting nature, but one in which we are unable to engage in this place as we do not possess a sufficient personal acquaintance with the shades of temperament which possibly exist between the English Celts and the English properly so-called. We must be content to remark that we use the words " English " and " British " in the widest possible sense when speaking of Byrd and of Farnaby, and that we find no essential contradiction between the mind of Farnaby, as revealed in his virginal pieces, and the idea which has been formed on the Continent of the humorous spirit of the English from the masterpieces of their literature.

[5] This opinion rests partly on the vocal works of Gibbons, which are of the first order.

By the side of these five great masters, there are others of a more secondary rank who are represented by a less considerable number of works in the *Fitzw. V. B.* and elsewhere, but of whom these few pieces suffice, if not to determine precisely their æsthetic individuality, at least to give a passing notion of what this may have been.

Thomas Morley, the exquisite madrigalist, is a virginalist of a refined elegance that derives from Italian sources. Ferdinando Richardson is an admirably equipped dilettante, of a subtle imagination, rich in happy, unexpected strokes. Warrock seems, from his two pieces in the *Fitzw. V. B.*, to have been a fanciful and original musician. John Munday delights by his transparency and his feeling for nature ; this same feeling is found, delicately expressed, in Martin Peerson. Thomas Tomkins resembles Bull and Richardson in his love of virtuosity, and surprises us by the charming effects —as of jeweller's work—that he derives from it. Lastly, Tisdall, a musician completely unknown, deserves not to be overlooked if only on account of the expressive richness of the four or five varied dances of his in the *Fitzw. V. B.*

We see, therefore, that side by side with the great masters of the virginal there is a series of "little masters" whose work, fragmentarily as it has come down to us, is not to be disdained, but contributes largely to enrich the virginalistic patrimony of England.

After the great period of efflorescence at the beginning of the 17th century, it seems that the virginalistic tradition was rapidly lost in England. We find in the keyboard music of the second half of the 17th century practically none of those

2 A

features which characterized the art of the Byrds, the Bulls, and the Farnabys. However admirable may be the keyboard works of Locke, of Blow, and of Purcell, they have not that freshness, that spontaneity, and especially that independence which we admire in the masters belonging to the preceding generations. Continental influences— mostly French—found their way into the British Isles, and subjected these later men to forms more strict, more detailed, and less propitious to freedom of inspiration.

APPENDIX.

NOTES ON THE COMPASS OF THE KEYBOARD, THE SHORT OCTAVE, AND TEMPERAMENT.[1]

About 1510 Hughe Ashton,—so one gathers from his *Hornepype*—made use of a keyboard with the following compass :—

That is as near as may be the usual compass of the keyboards of the period. The clavichord and the virginal of which Virdung speaks in his *Musica Getutscht* (1511) have one tone less than this in the upper part;[2] on the other hand the Spanish keyboards generally went down a fourth lower.

It is necessary to go as far back as 1590 to discover English pieces going down as low as the

---

[1] See, on these various questions, the work of Otto Kinkeldey, already cited—*Orgel und Klavier*, &c. The author is more especially interested in Continental keyboard instruments.

Dr. Naylor devotes part of Chap. xiii. of *An Eliz. V. B.* to the compass of the keyboard of the virginal and to the short octave.

[2] The pieces by the younger Schlick (1512) call for a keyboard of precisely the same compass as described by Virdung (see his pieces in the 1st year of the *Monatsh. für Musikg.*).

C of the Spanish keyboard. The first dated piece in which we find this note is *The Wood's so wild* of Byrd (*Fitzw. V. B.*, i., p. 263). We also find it in the *In nomine* of Blitheman, belonging at the latest to 1591, the year of the death of that master. Byrd never subsequently exceeded the following compass :—

The first dated evidence on which it can be stated that the keyboard was extended towards the bass is *Parthenia* (1611): there we find in fact two pieces by Gibbons (*Fantazia of foure parts*, No. xvii., and *The Lord of Salisbury his Pavin*, No. xviii.) which go as low as :—

This note occurs again in eleven pieces of the *Fitzw. V. B.* (four by Bull, one by Farnaby, four by Tomkins, and two anonymous), which are not dated, but which in any case are earlier than 1619-20, the time at which the compilation of this celebrated manuscript was probably completed. The most interesting of these pieces is a pavan by Tomkins (*Fitzw. V. B.*, ii., p. 51), in which this A appears, not standing alone, but in combination with its immediate neighbours B and C.

As to the extent of the keyboard upwards, above A, this is what we have been able to find on the subject : In *Fece da voi* by Philips (*Fitzw. V. B.*, i., p. 286) we notice the B flat; in *A Maske* by Farnaby (ii., p. 265), in the *Piper's Pavan* by Peerson (ii., p. 238), and in *A Grounde* by Tomkins (ii., p. 87), we find B natural. The *Lachrymae pavan* by Farnaby (ii., p. 472) and the *Toccata* by the Italian Pichi (i., p. 373) alone reach to :—

The upshot of all this is that the keyboard of the virginal, which at the opening of the 16th century consisted of three octaves and a major third, was probably maintained within those limits until about 1580-90, at which time it became extended a fourth towards the bottom. In the course of the period which immediately preceded *Parthenia* (roughly, between 1600 and 1611) a minor third was again added at the bottom, so that the keyboard then consisted of four octaves.

The years which followed saw this compass extended by a minor third upward, so that about 1620 the keyboard of the virginal comprised four octaves and a minor third :—

[3] The gradual extension of compass upward is possibly due to a Continental influence. In general the keyboards on the Continent dating from the first third of the 17th century which have not subsequently had the keyboard modified by additional notes, extend less towards the bass and more towards the upper part than the English keyboards. See especially the ordinary harpsichords of the Netherlands in the *Catalogue de la collection Snoeck*, Ghent, 1894 (Nos. 225, 227, and 230).

[4] The virginals of the end of the 16th and of the beginning of the 17th centuries seem more frequently to have had but a single row of keys. The Rev. F. W. Galpin (*An old English positive organ; Musical Antiq.*, Oct., 1912, p. 24) announces the discovery of a *clavicymbal* or *harpsichord* with two keyboards, dated 1590.

* * * * * *

During the 16th century the short octave was often used in the construction of keyboards, that is to say, an arrangement which consisted in contracting the lower octave so that it took less room than the octaves above it. The arrangement most frequently met with, especially in Spain[5] and in England[6] is the following :—

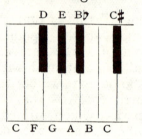

D E B♭ C♯

C F G A B C

As can be seen, the black keys, which on our present keyboard represent F sharp (G flat) and G sharp (A flat), correspond here with the D and E that come between the C and the F. This procedure, the object of which is to economise space, involves the absence of all the chromatic notes—with the exception of B flat—in the space of the octave in question. All the succeeding octaves, on the contrary, have a complete chromatic scale.

In fact, up to a certain time the virginalists dispensed with the chromatic notes which were missing in the short octave. Philips gives us no example of them in any of his works in the *Fitzw. V. B.*, even the latest, *Margott Laborez* (i., p. 332), dated 1605. One of his pieces, the *Pavana-Galiarda dolorosa* of 1593 (i., p. 321),

[5] See Kinkeldey, *op. cit.*, p. 16.
[6] See *Introduction* to the modern edition of the *Fitzw. V. B.*, p. xviii.

contains evident proof that he used at that time a keyboard with a short octave; there occur in it, in fact, various passages which it would have been impossible to play on an instrument provided with a lower octave of the usual dimensions. Thus, for instance, the final cadence of the pavan :—

In fact, the C of the bass occupied in the short octave the place of E on our present keyboard :—

which makes the execution possible without the least difficulty.[7]

But the use of the short octave became more and more unusual during the last years of the 16th century.

Thus two pieces dating at the latest from 1591, the *In nomine* of Blitheman (died in 1591) (*Fitzw. V. B.*, i., p. 181), and the *Walsingham* of Byrd (a piece forming part of *Nevell's Booke* of 1591) (*Fitzw. V. B.*, i., p. 267) contain the F sharp of the bottom octave.

[7] Dr. Naylor (*An Eliz. V. B.*, p. 156) remarks that the *Pavana dolorosa* is the only one of the pieces by Philips containing (i., p. 322) a G sharp situated in the compass of the short octave. How was it possible to play this supposing that the key which takes the place of our G sharp actually produced E? Dr. Naylor very ingeniously supposes that the keyboard used by Philips possessed a supplementary key answering to G sharp, obtained by the division of the one intended for E.

For the use of G sharp, we find no piece with a date either actual or inferential. Those of Bull, G. Farnaby, Tisdall, Tomkins, and an anonymous composer, in which we find it, are manifestly later than 1591, possibly even than 1600.

Tomkins gives us a particularly interesting example (*Pavan, Fitzw. V. B.*, ii., p. 51) which consists of the following chromatic passage :—

The first *Ut, re, mi, fa, sol, la* of Bull (*Fitzw. V. B.*, i., p. 183) contains :—

From the above we may conclude that towards the end of the 16th century a certain number of English claviers had a bottom octave comprising the following succession of notes, C, D, E, F, F sharp, G, G sharp, A, B flat, B natural, C.

The A flat of Bull could be played on the key representing G sharp, but on the condition that the instrument had been previously tuned according to something approaching equal temperament.

A certain number of pieces in the *Fitzw. V. B.*, dating probably between 1610 and 1620, include chromatic notes comprised between the C and the F of the bottom octave. For instance, in an anonymous *Alman (Fitzw. V. B.*, ii., p. 312) we find a D sharp; in a pavan by Farnaby (i., p. 141) and in a pavan by Warrock (i., p. 384) we notice an E flat; lastly a *Praeludium* by Bull (ii., p. 22) has a C sharp.

It follows from these last circumstances, and from the fact that from the time of *Parthenia* (1611) the low A a minor third below the C of the bottom octave was used, that some of the English keyboards of the period between 1610 and 1620 must have had a complete chromatic scale extending from :—

We have found no example of a B flat immediately following the low A, but it may be presumed that this note, which is not essentially chromatic, since it forms part of the diatonic Gregorian system, was not absent from the keyboards which went down as low as A; or if it was absent, it must have been in company with B natural, the keyboard thus being specially arranged with a view to the performance of pieces written in the Æolian mode of A, which was in particularly common use in the virginalistic repertory.[8]

*   *   *   *   *   *

A few words, in conclusion, as to temperament. We have seen previously (p. 328) that the performance of the first *Ut, re, mi, fa, sol, la* of Bull was inconceivable without applying to the clavier a sort of equal temperament. It is certain that this necessity extended to other virginalistic pieces than this scholastic work of Bull, and that composers found themselves in this respect in an

[8] Let us notice, however, that Tomkins's keyboard included, as we have seen above, the B natural.

entirely different situation from that of about the middle of the 16th century, when the Spaniard Bermudo placed a crowd of restrictions on the most innocent transpositions, on account of the unpleasant dissonances which resulted under the sway of unequal temperament.[9]

We saw above that the virginalistic repertory contains examples of E flat and D sharp, sounds very distant from each other in the scale of fifths. The D sharp is not very uncommon with the virginalists of the first thirty years of the 17th century; the E flat is very common, and we meet with even A sharp in certain pieces.[10] As it is obvious that they did not tune the instrument with a special view to a particular piece written in a particular tonality, it must be admitted that they applied a unified system of tuning, thanks to which the black key representing B flat could be used as A sharp, without any dissonance occurring. Now this was only possible by means of the use of equal temperament, or of something very like it.

[9] See Kinkeldey, *op. cit.*, pp. 17 and 18.
[10] Example: *Pavana Chromatica* of Tisdall, *Fitzw. V. B.*, ii., p. 278.

INDEX

2A